The Professor's Guide to Taming Technology

Leveraging Digital Media, Web 2.0, and More for Learning

Edited by

Kathleen P. King
University of South Florida

Thomas D. Cox
University of Houston–Victoria

INFORMATION AGE PUBLISHING, INC.
Charlotte, NC • www.infoagepub.com

Library of Congress Cataloging-in-Publication Data

The professor's guide to taming technology : leveraging digital media, Web 2.0, and more for learning / edited by Kathleen P. King, Thomas D. Cox.
   p. cm. – (Innovative perspectives of higher education: research, theory and practice)
 Includes bibliographical references.
 ISBN 978-1-61735-333-8 (pbk.) – ISBN 978-1-61735-334-5 (hardcover) – ISBN 978-1-61735-335-2 (e-book)
 1. Education, Higher–Computer-assisted instruction. 2. Educational technology. 3. Digital media. 4. Web 2.0. I. King, Kathleen P., 1958- II. Cox, Thomas D.
 LB2395.7.P76 2011
 378.1'7344678–dc22

                                                          2010049814

—

DEDICATION

We dedicate this book foremost to the devoted faculty of higher education who are lifelong learners, invested in continually growing for themselves, their disciplines, and their students. May your good will and effort be returned back to you many times over in rewards of the heart and professional success. We believe it will.

From Kathy: I also dedicate this book to my loving partner, muse, and best friend, Sharon.

From Thomas: I dedicate this book to my parents, James and Melba Cox, who gave all they could give regardless of their circumstances. I would also like to dedicate this book to Dr. Dan Lattimore, Dr. Patricia Murrell, Dr. Jim Preston, and Dr. Ellene McCrimon, who have supported and encouraged me at every turn in my growth and development.

CONTENTS

Preface: Bridging the Gap of Change..............................xi
Kathleen P. King

Acknowledgments..xxi

PART I

VISION AND FOUNDATIONS

1 Using Digital Media in Higher Education: An Adult Learning
Perspective 3
Thomas D. Cox and Kathleen P. King

2 Voice, Empowerment, and Impact: Using Digital Technologies
in the Classroom... 15
Kathleen P. King

PART II

DIGITAL MEDIA

3 Podcasting: Learning on Demand and Content Creation.............. 33
Kathleen P. King

4 Using Online Asynchronous Audio Communication in Higher
Education 51
Jody Oomen-Early, Mary Bold, and Tara Gallien

5 Video Development and Instructional Use: Simple and
Powerful Options.. 67
Kathleen P. King and Thomas D. Cox

6 Blogging as Reflective Practice in the Graduate Classroom............ 89
Teresa J. Carter

7 Narrated Digital Presentations: An Educator's Journey and
Strategies for Integrating and Enhancing Education 105
Brian W. Donavant

8 The Use of Wikis for Collaboration in Higher Education 121
Pooneh Lari

9 Virtual Office Hours 135
Thomas D. Cox and April Williams

10 Skype and Other Virtual Conferencing Tools 151
Ellen Manning

11 Facebook Goes on "Prac": Using Social Networking Tools
to Support Students Undertaking Teaching Practicum................. 165
Jennifer Howell and Rebecca English

PART III

SPECIAL TOPICS

12 Revelations of Adaptive Technology Hiding in Your
Operating System 183
Kathleen P. King

13 Accessible Technology for Online and Face-to-Face Teaching
and Learning 201
Sheryl Burgstahler, Alice Anderson, and Mike Litzkow

14 Incorporating 3D Virtual Laboratory Specimens to Enhance
Online Science: Examples from Paleontology and Biology........... 219
Kevin F. Downing and Jennifer K. Holtz

15 A Guide to Using Technology in the History Classroom 239
Keith Sisson and Kathleen P. King

PART IV

THINKING AHEAD

16 Action Steps for Continued Faculty Success in Taming
Technology.. 261
Kathleen P. King and Thomas D. Cox

The Authors and Contributors 271

PREFACE

Bridging the Gap of Change

Kathleen P. King

"Professor, I never expected to use technology in my future classes. After this class with you, I plan to have student-created blogs and podcasts in order to share the research and understanding they gain from their studies. Creating and publishing content is the most empowering experience of my university life. Thank you for providing a new model of teaching and learning with Web 2.0 tools."

"Not many people can make learning technology seem exciting and possible for professors. But you understand our situations and the many demands. The way you describe podcasting has changed my ideas about classroom preparation and teaching. Thank you for making it possible."

I remember the first time I read such comments in faculty reviews and teacher education journals. I was humbled to think the students had waited that long to see new educational opportunities using the many digital media tools surrounding us. However, the fact is that most faculty who are not technology specialists are too overwhelmed with faculty responsibilities and student demands to learn the barrage of new media tools and technology applications. They are invested in research and academics and are not always in the mainstream of popular culture. However, once they see that there are powerful learning benefits, inexpensive tools, and efficient ways to incorporate these technologies, educators with whom I have worked are ready (and often eager!) to figure out where to begin to learn, adapt, and adopt the new opportunities.

The Professor's Guide to Taming Technology, pages xi–xx
Copyright © 2011 by Information Age Publishing
All rights of reproduction in any form reserved.

Help is here. This book is provided as a guide, encouragement, and handbook for faculty to introduce digital media in language you can understand and provide strategies and activities you can quickly assimilate into your teaching. We are excited that more people will be able to benefit from the powerful help and guidance contained in this book. We are even more exhilarated as we anticipate how each of you will discover applications and new directions we would never anticipate. We look forward to your innovations as you use the material you discover here. But I am running ahead of myself. Let us review for a moment before we proceed.

THE TRANSFORMATION AGE

Just recently, I was at a research lecture series entitled Globalization Models: Insights from Interdisciplinary Research. I was surprised to discover that some of the models that have emerged from interdisciplinary research and thinking across biology, political science, economics, and history bear the same conclusion I have spoken about for the last two years.

> We are certainly no longer in the Industrial age, but neither are we truly in the Technology Age or even the Information Age. Instead, I believe what characterizes the time we are living through is the Transformation Age.

In the midst of vast shifts of government structures, economics, international relations, politics, environment, industry, and more, the paradigm of higher education is shifting drastically as well. As we recall, across the last decade, many of the changes described above with the euphemism "shifts" were actually cataclysmic revolutions and dramatic downswings or upswings. These are not slow, gradual, barely perceptible shifts. We are experiencing a time of dramatic transformations from the customary order of the day to new rules and perspectives.

UNPREDICTABLE CHANGES IN TECHNOLOGY ADOPTION

At this point in time, we know that change will be constant, and rapid, and take strange twists and turns. We know that change will defy previously unchallenged models of economics, politics, and human behavior. In the world of technology, it is customary for change to be dramatic compared to that of our mainstream social and economic systems in the United States. Technology has continued to follow Moore's Law by doubling computer power every 2 years (Lafferty & Walch, 2006). Similarly, from our personal experiences, if we look back at how we did our work, communicated with relatives, and even called friends 20–30 years ago, it was vastly different than it is now.

Consider with me just a few of the major themes within which we are immersed today and that have meaning for us as academics and teachers.

- Communications are nearly instantaneous, entirely inexpensive, and our society has adopted technology by integrating it into entertainment, relationships, work, and education activities.
- The most successful technology solutions are scalable—able to be extended or connected to each other to reach small and large numbers.
- The technologies of today and tomorrow are expected to be so user friendly that they are intuitive.

These few examples demonstrate the pattern of technology that is flexible, accessible, and constantly changing. All of us are looking ahead at a landscape of rapid technological change touching every facet of our daily lives—private and personal matters, work, education, travel, relationships, and more—and it behooves us to be prepared.

Digital and Social Media Set the Trends

One only needs to consider the explosion of the technologies that are the focus of this book—digital media—in the last 5 years to understand the trends of changing technologies with which our society, educators, and organizations must cope. Think about how YouTube, Facebook, Twitter, and LinkedIn have changed the dynamics of work and relationships. Yet colleges and universities seem to be the final stronghold. Have we truly leveraged these forces in teaching and learning?

YouTube emerged in February, 2005 and has been a dominant force in bringing on-demand video to the forefront of entertainment and marketing. Rather than positioning the user as only watching professional videos, YouTube opened the door to user-created content on what was to be an expansive scope and high level. Although other video sharing platforms existed, YouTube's social sharing tools, ease of use, and large community were not only energizing but also able to keep pace and be scaled up to meet the demand as it mushroomed.

In 2010, Facebook celebrated its 5th-year anniversary. Consider the early days of social communities, when we struggled with youngsters being in MySpace and college students in Facebook. The huge decision was whether or not to let them participate in these online social networks. In 2009 and 2010, data demonstrate that the tables have turned and, in fact, baby boomers (those reluctant parents) are now dominating Facebook and Twitter.

What has caused this turnaround? Social adoption, comfort with digital and social media, and the race to share content and information have outrun the pull of traditional practices.

Another profound trend emerged when Twitter seriously began to dominate social and business markets in March, 2006. In 2010, social media is front and center as the leading item increased in marketing and publicity spending for small and big business (eConsultancy, 2010).

Why has such a broad-based appeal for marketing in Twitter developed? Because people of all walks of life engage in Twitter for personal and professional purposes. Likewise, users find that Twitter creates and escalates their information networks far beyond those they would traditionally encounter in terrestrial space.

Consider life before using Twitter... How often did you read about political, economic, and scientific changes

- from other countries,
- from non-reporters,
- on a regular basis?

And without social media networks, how would you have quickly discovered people's continuing

- dialogue and opinions
- about specific topics
- across a global span?

Added to this trend of broader interconnection and dialogue is society's need for instant gratification. The material and convenience aspects of instant gratification are fueled by constant access to content and news choices of on-demand radio shows, newscasts, video, TV shows, movies, podcasts, seminars, classes, and more. In 1995, iTunes popularized a growing trend of on-demand digital audio by including podcasts in its online music library platform (Lafferty & Walch, 2006). iTunes had taken families and organizations by surprise with the introduction of the iPod, a portable media player that could be "filled" with virtually endless content via the Web-based music store (iTunes), one song at a time. When podcasts were added to iTunes, teachers and students gained significant opportunities for teaching and learning through user-created and on-demand digital media.

OPPORTUNITIES FOR TEACHING AND LEARNING

I expect that you have vivid memories of the many changes you have experienced over the past ten years that parallel those I have described. Perhaps you are even thinking about all the online resources, cloud computing, and indispensible devices you use throughout your day. Higher education organizations and classrooms cannot ignore this tsunami of constant technology change. That is the point of this book: The paradigm of transformation has become our way of life, an expectation; join us as we capture the possibilities!

As we embark, consider these questions regarding higher education institutions as a whole.

- How well do higher education institutions fit in with the paradigm of transformation?
- How quickly do higher education institutions adapt to the changes around them?
- How easy is it to plan, develop, approve, and launch new programs in response to workplace or economic needs within higher education institutions?

Your answers are not great news for higher education institutions, are they? Higher education institutions generally move slowly in responding to these changes, and because they are bureaucratic structures, change, even when approved, will be adopted slowly.

While there are inherent reasons for higher education's organizational designs, proclivities, and processes, in a transformation era our community, society, and students are demanding more.

I have seen the best answer for this need for change. In my experience researching, designing, and conducting faculty development in institutions I serve worldwide, I see that the opportunity to address this need for change is in faculty expertise and initiative (Brown, 2003; King, 2003; King & Griggs, 2007; King & Gura, 2009). Obviously, we need a few other items to support this change for the long haul: resources, support and tenure, and merit and promotion incentives for instructional technology innovation. However, one thing is certain and imperative to remember: Faculty is the front line of interaction with students.

Consider that, as faculty members, you have the final decision about what and how the classroom and learning experience will be and feel. Faculty have the ability to create a classroom that embraces co-learning, questioning, change, and life-long inspiration (Brookfield, 1995; Cranton, 2001; King, 2005; Palmer, 2005; Palmer, Zajonc, Nepo, & Scribner, 2010). We have the capability to build a climate of trust and respect in order to grow together as a learning community (even in a one-semester class) (Palmer, 2005; Palmer et al., 2010). We can provide learning experiences that incorporate transformation, change, and technology, even while higher education institutions are still trying to figure out the options available to them (Brown, 2003; King, 2003; King & Griggs, 2007; King & Gura, 2009).

PURPOSE OF THE BOOK

We have written this book about innovative technology applications and how faculty are using and can use digital media in teaching in higher education because faculty make the quickest changes and learn how to do it best. This book responds to the needs of our changing world and students. It is a valuable resource for faculty from faculty because it allows the sharing of successful teaching experiences with digital media with our worldwide colleagues so that they may modify, extend, and improve them.

Moreover, in our work with faculty across all disciplines, we also find that many struggle to devise ways in which they can incorporate technology meaningfully into their teaching. While we might be experts in our discipline (chemistry, philosophy, music, etc.) due to the curriculum of terminal degrees, we might not have strong preparation in instructional design.

This book is written by faculty for faculty and has brought together faculty experts across different disciplines to speak about how and why to use digital media in higher education settings. We realize that we are asking you to think about new ideas and strategies for your teaching; therefore, we try to illustrate them with clear examples. These different approaches include clear descriptions of what these activities look like, why to develop and implement them, and how to do so for your specific needs.

WHAT YOU WILL FIND IN THIS BOOK

The book is divided into three main sections: Vision and Foundation, Digital Media, and Special Topics. The chapters in the first section provide an introduction to our collaborative understanding of using digital media and delve into critical areas that bridge all disciplines in higher education. These chapters are:

1. Using Digital Media in Higher Education: An Adult Learning Perspective
2. Critical Learning With Digital Media: Voice, Empowerment, and Impact

To provide consistency across this volume of rich and varied technology applications, the editors and contributors have used a uniform chapter outline. The chapters each provide an introduction to the topic, overview of related research, and orientation to different uses for teaching. Each chapter also includes examples of classroom applications of digital media, activities for faculty to walk through or use with their learners. Moreover, there are many digital media resource suggestions for further learning on each topic and access to related resources (software, add-ons, equipment, etc.). The book provides varied examples throughout different teaching contexts: on-site classes, hybrid, and distance learning.

The chapters in the second section are:

1. Podcasting: Global Learning on Demand
2. Online Asynchronous Audio Communication in Higher Education
3. Video: Simple and Powerful: Options for Development and Instructional Use
4. Blogging as Reflective Practice in the Graduate Classroom
5. Narrated PowerPoint: Giving Life to Mundane Presentations
6. Wikis for New Dimensions of Collaboration
7. Virtual Office Hours: Reaching Students in Context
8. Skype: Remote Meetings
9. Facebook Goes on Prac: Using Social Networking Tools to Support Students Undertaking Teaching Practicum

The final section of the book covers several critical topics that are not frequently discussed in instructional technology practice books. We will therefore describe them in more detail in this preface. From assistive technology to subject-specific examples, our special topics section is no less than a treasure trove for professors:

1. Adaptive Technology Solutions Hidden in Your Operating System
2. Advanced Adaptive Technology for Disabilities
3. Using 3D Virtual Laboratory Specimens to Advance Online Learning: Examples from Paleontology and Biology
4. Teaching History Using Technology

No one can deny that Baby Boomers are aging, and they will comprise the largest older generation the U.S. has known. However, few people are aware that diminishing eyesight, hearing, and dexterity are mild disabilities that can be accommodated with their current computers. This section reveals not only operating system-based assistive technology, but also advanced applications. In 1975, the Individuals with Disabilities Education Act (IDEA) unlocked education for people with disabilities (U.S. Department of Education, 1975). In 1991, the Americans with Disabilities Act (ADA) legislation (U.S. Department of Justice, 1991) was followed by regulations to provide access for disabled Americans to many more aspects of life considered usual for everyone else: access to employment, public transportation, and public places and accommodations, for instance. Digital media and instructional technology tools provide powerful access in today's world. If faculty are aware of assistive technology solutions and design their instruction to include such opportunities, barriers to new knowledge and life opportunities can be knocked down successfully.

Moreover, the sections include a seldom-discussed but emerging practice of using 3D specimens in science laboratory instruction on computers and online. In addition, the book has a chapter dedicated to teaching history with digital media and other technologies. With these examples and many illustrations from foreign languages, English, education, math, and technology throughout the book, we expect that every faculty member will find themselves and their discipline focus represented in the pages.

The concluding chapter of the book, "Action Steps for Continued Faculty Success in Taming Technology," brings together recommendations and a vision from across the volume to encourage readers to take the next steps needed for implementing what they have learned. In addition, this chapter describes the need for developing the proven, effective campus and global professional learning communities (Brown, 2003) for faculty learning support and sharing.

WHO WILL BENEFIT FROM READING THIS BOOK?

We know that this book will be a valuable guide and professional development book for faculty across disciplines, and it will be helpful for instructional designers, instructional technologists, distance learning support staff, and higher education administration in understanding faculty needs for the application of technology in instruction. This book will also be useful as an introductory to intermediate book for learning to incorporate digital media in college teaching, whether online or face-to-face, and as a supplemental textbook in curriculum development and designing courses.

In many cases, teaching has shifted from a brick and mortar, "chalk and talk" teaching environment to one that is geared toward providing more asynchronous, on-demand teaching and learning. Increasing numbers of learners of all ages are choosing to continue their education online, studying from the convenience of their homes and still meeting the pressing demands of family, jobs, and personal interests (Allens & Seamans, 2009). This book is important because it gives faculty seeking to improve their digital media skills tools to use in adapting their current teaching to meet the needs of a changing world, society, and technologies. In addition, it provides the basis for visualizing and creating new courses with a perspective of integrating digital media for teaching and learning in meaningful ways.

Help is here! This book is written for instructors; teachers; and assistant, associate, and full professors who are seeking to take their student engagement and learning to a new level.

INVITATION

With this preface, we invite you to join us in the discovery of how to respond to our changing world and changing student populations. We have tremendous opportunities through the widely available, inexpensive, and user-friendly technologies that surround us. What is needed is faculty with vision to say, "I see the opportunity, I will step out and try some of these activities with my students and see how they make a difference." This book will guide faculty through opportunities to make choices about which courses and classes to design digital media for and how to design and implement them. We hope it will be an exciting experience, even reinvigorating, as you unleash new ways of thinking about and engaging your students in your content area. Join us by reading the book and choosing what to put into action. And then let us hear from you so that we can include your story in a future volume.

REFERENCES

Allens, I. E., & Seamans, J. (2009). *Learning on demand: Online education in the United States, 2009.* Babson Park, MA: Babson Survey Research Group. Retrieved from http://www.sloan-c.org/publications/survey/pdf/learningondemand.pdf

Americans with Disabilities Act (ADA) of 1990, Pub. L. No. 101-336, § 2, 104 Stat. 327 (1991).

Brookfield, S. B. (1995). *Becoming a critically reflective teacher.* San Francisco: Jossey-Bass.

Brown, D. (2003). *Developing faculty to use technology.* New York: John-Wiley & Sons.

Cranton, P. (2001). *Becoming an authentic teacher in higher education.* Malabar, FL: Krieger.

eConsultancy. (2010, Feb.) *The marketing budgets 2010: Effectiveness, measurement and allocation.* New York: Author. Retrieved from http://econsultancy.com/reports/marketing-budgets-2010

Individuals with Disabilities Education Act (IDEA) of 1975, P.L. 94-142, §§ 12101 et seq. (1975).

King, K. P. (2003). *Keeping pace with technology: Educational technology that transforms. Vol. II. Higher education faculty development.* Cresskill, NJ: Hampton Press.

King, K. P. (2005). *Bringing transformative learning to life.* Malabar, FL: Krieger.

King, K. P., & Griggs, J. K. (Eds.). (2007). *Harnessing innovative technologies in higher education: Access, equity, policy and instruction.* Madison, WI: Atwood Publishing.

King, K. P., & Gura, M. (2009). *Podcasting for teachers: Using a new technology to revolutionize teaching and learning* (2nd ed.). Charlotte, NC: Information Age Publishing, Inc.

Lafferty, M., & Walch, R. (2006). *Tricks of the podcasting masters.* New York: Que.

Palmer, P. (2005). *The courage to teach.* New York: John-Wiley & Sons.

Palmer, P., Zajonc, A., Nepo, M., & Scribner, M. (2010). *The heart of higher education: A call to renewal.* New York: John-Wiley & Sons.

ACKNOWLEDGMENTS

By original design and intent, The Academy was supposed to be the sharing of and creation of knowledge. Perhaps today one of the ways we experience this most is in a truly collaborative team co-authoring a book. In the development of this edited volume, all the contributors become essential elements of its life and final form. Thank you to each for the many hours of good-natured discussions and revisions.

We also appreciate that many of you stepped out to share your own learning experience among your peers. Thank you each for being willing examples of reflective practice and transparency. Your model does us all good to show that we are works in progress even though experts in our fields.

A special thank you to Dakoda Davis for the custom-designed artwork for the book's cover and section plates. We appreciate your great abilities and generosity in sharing them with us and our readers.

Finally, thank you, Seamus King, for your steadfastness and keen eye in copyediting; George Johnson for supporting the publication of this book; and TextBook and Academic Authors professional association for a grant for the editing of the volume.

PART I

VISION AND FOUNDATIONS

CHAPTER 1

USING DIGITAL MEDIA IN HIGHER EDUCATION

An Adult Learning Perspective

Thomas D. Cox
University of Houston–Victoria

Kathleen P. King
University of South Florida

PRELUDE TO THOMAS' TEACHING JOURNEY

When I was first asked to teach an online course, back in 2003, I found myself in the midst of a teaching crisis. I was given a textbook, the log-on instructions for the course management system, and was told to "have at it." I was already teaching in the traditional classroom, and I would like to say that I was already using technology and various forms of media in my traditional courses, but I was not—not even a single PowerPoint presentation! I was strictly teaching using the "chalk and talk" method I had learned from my professors. I quickly learned that online teaching was very different, and in order for me to move this form of learning beyond being simply an email correspondence course, I had a lot of work to do.

The Professor's Guide to Taming Technology, pages 3–XXX
Copyright © 2011 by Information Age Publishing
All rights of reproduction in any form reserved.

Confronting my need to use technology through online teaching was a pivotal point in my growth as an educator.

INTRODUCTION

We share Thomas's journey of learning to teach online because this was the avenue through which he learned to better use digital media in all his classes. And we are sure that various readers will identify with different aspects of it, and we hope that you all will find something that resonates with your technology learning journey. We intend for those who read and use this book to develop a paradigm of the use of digital media in its various forms as a tool that enhances online teaching and learning, more traditional brick and mortar environments, and every combination thereof!

Teaching and learning with digital media have come a long way since 2003, and honestly so has Thomas. Yet this chapter orients readers to the volume by offering both faculty- and learner-centered perspectives through the application of adult learning theories. (Join us in broadening our concept of adult learners to include faculty.) The chapter concludes with a discussion of implications of these approaches in digital media that inform practice.

Our hope is that in the first part of this chapter, faculty readers will identify with aspects of Thomas's experience as he began learning about teaching with digital media in his online and face-to-face classes. The purpose of this section of the chapter is to allow professors to reflect on

- digital media in teaching,
- learning, from an adult learning perspective, and
- the developmental benefits of embracing these efforts.

The second part of this chapter explores how faculty can use adult learning theories and perspectives as an underpinning philosophy for teaching with digital media that focuses on the student. The last part of the chapter discusses the timelessness of digital media and the use of digital media with adult learners.

THE PROFESSOR

There are many possible theoretical frameworks with which to understand how professors can develop skills and expertise in using digital media in their teaching. Although intended as a set of assumptions about how adults learn, we apply Knowles, Holton, and Swanson's (2005) six assumptions of andragogy (*Need to Know, Self-concept, Experience, Readiness to Learn, Orientation to*

Learning, and *Motivation*) as a means of describing what can also be called *faculty development* in the area of digital media (Lawler & King, 2000).

Thomas' Teaching Journey: Facing the Challenges

The Need to Know

For me, the task of becoming an effective teacher with technology was compulsory. I was thrown into the arena of incorporating digital media in my teaching. I did not know what or how to go about doing that. Harasim, Hiltz, Teles, and Turoff (1996) state, "The real question is...what is the best media mix to achieve the goals of the course. More fundamentally, how should the media be used? What approaches to teaching and learning are most effective in a computer networking environment?" (p. 24). In trying to answer these questions for myself, I became acutely aware that I needed to develop my knowledge and skills so that I could enhance my teaching. So, before I even began to develop my technological skills, I was faced with a very strong "need to know." This was just the beginning. The real issue was that I did not know what I needed to know, especially in terms of current teaching technologies—hardware and software—and if or how they would enhance my teaching and my students' learning; but I was up to the challenge.

Self-Concept

I also previously mentioned that my first experience with online teaching was being given the textbook and sign-in instructions. What happened next was totally up to me. As with most of you who will read this, through completing several levels of education, and many life experiences, I already had a self-concept of being responsible for how this experience played out. I knew I had to leave the city of chalk-and-talk comfort and go boldly into the wilderness of technology. I did not expect the institution or the department to nurture me through this—although such an expectation may be legitimate. In order to be successful, I was not going to depend on others to help me with this process.

The literature on self-directed learning suggests that self-directed learners demonstrate a greater awareness of their responsibility in making learning meaningful and monitoring themselves (Garrison, 1997). I also find that when I am able to guide my own learning that I approach the endeavor with an almost childlike curiosity and look at the task as a challenge and not a problem, and I therefore enjoy the learning process. Another advantage of being a self-directed teacher is, as Knowles et al. (2005) state, adults "need to be seen by others and treated by others as being capable of self-direction" (p. 65). I wanted my colleagues to see me as capable of teaching with technology.

Experience

I had a great deal of experience with the use of certain types of technology. For example, email, word-processing, and Internet use were all familiar. However, applying these to teaching and adding to this toolbox was not something with which I had experience. The experience I brought to learning about technology was a base of knowing who I was and knowing that I could learn and improve.

Readiness to Learn

As a "young" academic, there was really no question as to whether I was ready to learn what I needed to know to be a successful teacher. Learning various teaching technologies that would enhance student learning was a "no-brainer." However, this can be problematic for some faculty who are, perhaps, from another generation or a school of thought that does not embrace technology use in the academy. For them, this lack of readiness can be what Jack Mezirow (1990) terms the *disorienting dilemma*, in which the learner (in this case, faculty) may feel distortions in the nature and use of knowledge as they are faced with new or unfamiliar kinds of power, authority, or reality. What happens is that teaching using technology and teaching online are new venues in which participants (faculty) interact differently with their profession (King, 2003). Thus, it is "fertile territory for transformative learning" (Palloff & Pratt, 2007, p. 187). It is not within the scope of this book to explore ways of solving all *disorienting dilemmas*. However, it should be mentioned that whatever forces drive the use of technology and distance learning in higher education, faculty must find a way to respond positively to the changing world. *The Professor's Guide to Taming Technology* is meant to provide direction in this area.

Orientation to Learning

"Adults are motivated to learn to the extent that they perceive that learning will help them perform tasks or deal with problems they confront in their life situations" (Knowles et al., 2005, p. 67). When the application of new knowledge or skills are necessary to perform satisfactorily as a teacher, one's orientation to learning shifts from that of an expert to that of seeking out available resources that will help one become a better teacher. Sometimes, especially as new faculty, we need to assess our orientation or position in the universe. We need to let go of notions that we are the experts and allow ourselves to develop and improve through discovery, curiosity, and a drive to succeed (Fink, 2003).

Motivation

What motivates faculty is difficult to determine. "Adults are responsive to some external motivators (better jobs, promotions, higher salaries, and the like), but the most potent motivators are internal pressures (th[e de]sire for increased job satisfaction, self-esteem, quality of life, and the l[ike]) (Knowles et al., 2005, p. 68). For me, the motivation to succeed at i[ncor]porating technology into my teaching was both internal and external[. Job] satisfaction and self-esteem were increased as I became more fluent in [tech]nology. However, moving from being a graduate student living with [a mea]ger income and resources also motivated me to want to gain the nece[ssary] skills to put me in charge of my career and earning potential. Ultimate[ly I] achieved all of those results.

Merriam and Brockett (2007) refer to Houle's (1988; originally [pub]lished in 1961) classic study in participation by stating that "the mot[ives] underlying adult learning can vary considerably" (p. 132). The result[s of] Houle's research on active participation in adult learning indicated th[ree] orientations to participation that work very well to describe how faculty p[ur]sue learning about and using technology in their teaching. Consider wh[ich] of the following types of learner, or combination thereof, you are using (Figure 1.1).

Framing the "adventure" of learning to use technology in teaching environments in ways that allow faculty members to reflect upon their own learning assumptions and motives can be helpful. As applied here, Knowles et al. (2005) offer a set of assumptions about ourselves as faculty members who are also adult learners upon which we can reflect as we begin a new learning opportunity. At the same time, we need never feel constrained by these

1. **Goal-oriented learners.** These faculty participate because they are invested in a specific objective. For example, some simply need to learn to use technology in order to get a job teaching online courses, or to make a presentation at a faculty meeting, to create a financial spreadsheet, take a picture, or simply record an audio conference.

2. **Activity-oriented learners.** These faculty may decide to learn about and use technology only because it injects more active participation in teaching. However, in teaching, the technology should be considered appropriate to enhance learning. When instructors ground their choice of technology tools in individual course goals, personal teaching philosophy, and disciplinary values, technology tools are capable of enhancing teaching and learning (Svinicki & McKeachie, 2011).

3. **Learning-oriented learners.** These faculty simply seek knowledge for its own sake. This orientation is particularly relevant because here the faculty may simply be willing to learn technology and go where it leads them in terms of using it to enhance their teaching.

Figure 1.1 Three orientations to participation in adult learning (developed from Houle, 1988).

principles because Houle's (1988) work clearly identified a broad diversity of motivation in pursuing adult learning (Merriam & Brockett, 2007, p. 132).

THE LEARNER

We, the editors and the authors of this book, stress the idea that technology use in the learning environment is not just about operating gadgets or software. This book describes the technology and ways to use it, but more importantly, it shares insights and strategies for structuring teaching in ways that incorporate technology while becoming student-centered and enhancing learning.

As with the many possible theories that apply to the faculty member as an adult approaching a learning opportunity, there are likewise many theories of learning that focus on the student. In fact, most learning research and theories focus on the student. With that in mind, we apply Knowles, Holton, and Swanson's (2005) six assumptions of adult learning to the student learner. In essence, this is a parallel approach, applying the same six assumptions that guide our *learning*, as faculty, to our *teaching* with technology-based instruction.

Six Assumptions of Adult Learning Applied to the Student Learner

Need to Know

Many of us realize that adult learners have a need to know. It is rarely a meaningful experience for adults when they do not see why they need to know the material or what is being taught. Since adults need to know why they should learn something, it is incumbent on the facilitator, teacher, or professor sometimes to make the learner aware of why they need to learn. Upon examining the chapter in this book by Williams and Cox about virtual office hours, it is clear that there are many technology tools for and ways to communicate and be available for learners who may need help in realizing their "need to know."

For those learners who need to know why, what, and how, using technology in various ways can aid the professor in providing the learners with what they need. While engaging in virtual conferencing, live video, and audio, the professor can enhance the course or adjust the learning goals based on student feedback, questions, and conversations.

Self-Concept

Adult learners are self-directed. Knowles et al. (2005) state, "The minute adults walk into an activity labeled 'education,' 'training,' or anything synonymous, they hark back to their conditioning in their previous school experience, put on their dunce hats of dependency, fold their arms, sit back, and say 'teach me'" (p. 65). Knowles et al. suggest that at this point we lose the adult learner because he or she lacks a self-concept of needing to be responsible for and guide his or her own learning.

To illustrate this point, Thomas shares an example from when he was a beginning professor and tried to help a student develop from being dependent to self-directed.

> I was teaching a graduate course in Educational Leadership. One evening, while teaching an overview of theories in leadership, a student raised her hand and asked, "Dr. Cox, what is the point of this?"
>
> I was stunned, as most new professors might be. Not knowing quite how to respond, I quickly thought, "Good question."
>
> But what actually "came out" was, "There is not a point. But if there is a point, I want you to make it."
>
> I am not sure if the student "got" what I was trying to say. I wanted to move the student from depending on me for the "point" to a place where she constructed the "point" in ways that were meaningful to her.
>
> Therefore, just as we sometimes have to make the learner aware of the need to know, we also realize that their self-concept is not always intact, and we must try to help them develop it.

In terms of technology use and/or online learning in the forms of discussion boards, wikis, blogs, and the like, the facilitator gives up much of the control of the course and allows the learners to guide and direct the content. This type of environment requires learners to establish their own learning goals and activities (Hanna, Glowacki-Dudka, & Conceicao-Runlee, 2000). Conrad and Donaldson (2004) suggest that the facilitator of the course interact first as an equal and respected person, and secondly as the expert. Thus, the facilitator takes a back seat in the process and uses technology to allow students to guide their own learning.

Experience

How many of us continue to have to explain to our research students that any information of a self-report nature (e.g., surveys, questionnaires, or interviews) is influenced by the circumstances or experiences of the participant at the time the information is gathered? There is no better a place to parallel this idea than when considering the use of technology in a learning environment. Knowles et al. (2005) value the experience that learners bring to the learning opportunity. We tend to think of adults, as Knowles et al. suggest, as having more life experience simply by virtue of having lived longer. However, when it comes to technology, there may be a confounding "digital divide." Adult learners from different generations or socio-economic backgrounds may have very little experience using technology, while others may have been using it efficiently for years. It is necessary for faculty to consider this when deciding which technology to use and how.

Also, sometimes a wealth of experience is *not* an advantage and may alter a person's perception of the use of technology. Consider when learners' recent experiences included their computer crashing and "losing" all of their documents that they had spent hours creating. Reasonably, they may not welcome technology use because their opinions have recently shifted. On the other hand, a person with little experience with technology use may find striving to surpass technological challenges appeals to their orientation to learning—that is, learning for the sake of learning (learning-oriented learner).

Still, there is another, more important aspect of experience to consider: Knowles' (1984) original concept that teachers can draw on the positive experiences of learners and help them to be open-minded toward the experiences of others. The use of technology in teaching and learning can contribute to the possibilities in this area. For instance, group discussions, group live conferences, and online collaborative spaces where learners share course related personal experiences and knowledge enhance learning for adults (Palloff & Pratt, 2007).

Readiness to Learn

Knowles (1984) based his assumption about learner readiness on the idea that forced changes in life often spur the need for new knowledge. He explained, "They experience a need to learn in order to cope more satisfyingly with real-life tasks or problems" (Knowles, 1980, p. 44). Just recently, while developing a completely online master's degree in adult education, I was contacted by a student who was pursuing the degree because he needed it for promotion and to be a greater change agent at his job, but was concerned because he had never taken an online course. While this situation may not be the kind of "life-change" that Knowles suggested, it does provide an example of how a learner will embark on new endeavors in order to adapt to a life situation.

It is important to mention that a person's readiness would not stop at endeavoring to pursue an online degree. Facilitators of adult learning can, through technology use, make the learning concrete and relative to students' needs and goals. Live role plays, audio-video simulations and movies, live interviews, problem-based discussion, and so on can prepare learners to meet their pre-determined needs.

Orientation to Learning

Adults are life-centered in their orientation to learning. The technology-based learning environment will be more effective if it incorporates real-life examples or situations that adult learners may encounter in their lives or on the job. From the beginning of online courses, and even now through the use of Web-based media such as wikis and blogs, the discussion strategy has been employed. However, the focus of the discussions should be geared toward a life-centered orientation to learning, and not just toward the content or subject matter. Real-life examples can be used powerfully as the prompt for discussions, and vignettes can be used for synchronous audio-video role play where the task is to come to a solution of a problem. In general, through the use of technology, a facilitator might assign learners to devise and plan a way of applying a theory to a current or past situation. Furthermore, through simulations, the conditions for such a situation could be dynamic, thereby mirroring real-world or archetype situations. This is powerful and meaningful learning.

Motivation to Learning

The same analysis can be used here as was used earlier regarding professors. The most compelling motivators for adult learners are internal. Self-esteem and quality of life are crucial in giving adults a reason to learn. One of the tools I have come to value in the online environment is a checklist. Students can check off the items they have completed; this gives them a sense of accomplishment and motivates them to keep moving forward. Another value of the discussion board or other software that I have learned is that when I respond directly to students by name and comment on their particular comments, they become validated and feel respected as an important part of the learning endeavor. "Acknowledging learner contributions will serve to further motivate learners to succeed" (Blondy, 2007, p. 126). The online discussion board scales the breadth and depth of classroom dialogue far beyond classroom walls. Faculty quickly discover that engaging questions will elicit substantial and frequent responses from learners. The feedback from the facilitator (private or public) becomes an important element in such exchanges.

DISCUSSION

Andragogy and Technology

Reviewing these ideas on applying andragogy to technology based instruction, we can summarize our findings regarding whether technology-based instruction satisfies the assumptions of adult learning (see Table 1.1).

TABLE 1.1   Andragogy and Technology Checklist

Can technology address a learner's need to know?	☐
Can technology facilitate self-direction?	☐
Can technology draw on the learner's prior experience?	☐
Can technology accommodate readiness to learn?	☐
Can technology address the orientation to learn?	☐
Can technology motivate learners?	☐

When instructors ground their choices of technology tools in individual course goals, personal teaching philosophy, and disciplinary values, technology tools are capable of enhancing teaching and learning (Svinicki & McKeachie, 2011). So, to consider the assumptions of adult learning when using technology in teaching, we must use technology to our and our students' advantage, constantly asking the questions above. Further, technology-based learning must be interactive, learner-centered, and must facilitate self-direction in learners to incorporate these qualities.

REFERENCES

Blondy, L. C. (2007). Evaluation and application of andragogical assumptions to the adult online learning environment. *Journal of Interactive Online Learning, 6*(2), 126.

Conrad, R. M., & Donaldson, J. A. (2004). *Engaging the online learner: Activities and resources for online for creative instruction.* San Francisco: Jossey-Bass.

Fink, L. D. (2003). *Creating significant learning experiences.* San Francisco: Jossey-Bass.

Garrison, D. R. (1997). Self-directed learning: Toward a comprehensive model. *Adult Education Quarterly, 48*(1), 16–18.

Hanna, D. E., Glowacki-Dudka, M., & Conceicao-Runlee, S. (2000). *147 practical tips for teaching online groups: Essentials of web-based education.* Madison, WI: Atwood Publishing.

Harasim, L., Hiltz, S. R., Teles, L., & Turoff, M. (1996). *Learning networks.* Cambridge, MA: MIT Press.

Houle, C. (1988). *The inquiring mind.* Norman, OK: Oklahoma Research Center for Continuing Professional and Higher Education, University of Oklahoma. (Original work published in 1961.)

King, K. P. (2003). *Keeping pace with technology: Educational technology that transforms.* Cresskill, NJ: Hampton Press.

Knowles, M. S. (1984). *Andragogy in action.* San-Francisco: Jossey-Bass.

Knowles, M. S., Holton, E., & Swanson, R. A. (2005). *The adult learner (6ᵗʰ ed.).* New York: Butterworth-Heinemann.

Lawler, P. A., & King, K. P. (2000). *Planning for effective faculty development: Using adult learning strategies.* Malabar, FL: Krieger.

Merriam, S., & Brockett, R. (2007). *The profession and practice of adult education: An introduction.* San Francisco: Jossey-Bass.

Mezirow, J. (1990). *Fostering critical reflection in adulthood: A guide to transformative and emancipatory learning.* San Francisco: Jossey-Bass.

Palloff, R. M., & Pratt, K. (2007). *Building online learning communities: Effective strategies for the virtual classroom.* San Francisco: Jossey Bass.

Svinicki, M., & KcKeachie, W. (2011). *McKeachie's teaching tips: Strategies, research, and theory for college and university teachers* (13th ed.) Belmont, CA: Wadsworth.

CHAPTER 2

VOICE, EMPOWERMENT, AND IMPACT

Using Digital Technologies in the Classroom

Kathleen P. King
University of South Florida

THE CLASSROOM REALITY SHOW: "BEAT THE CLOCK," RETURN TO YOUR CAMPUS EVERY CLASS SESSION?

The students are sharing their interpretations, posing new perspectives, and raising new questions at breakneck speed. I never knew they were such great facilitators! They are drawing one another out and gently asking each other to explain their ideas in more detail while supporting positive approaches.

A conversation gets heated, but leave it to Lauren; she stepped in as peacemaker and provided a way to consider the conflicting views. I wish this dialogue could continue for another hour.

What? We only have 5 minutes of class time left? I thought we had 45 minutes! They must have been in this conversation for 25 minutes *already*.

The Professor's Guide to Taming Technology, pages 15–30
Copyright © 2011 by Information Age Publishing
15

Darn, they have midterm next week and we have yet to do the review. I hate playing Beat the Clock. The students want to engage, and they are so capable. I wish I could find more time and space to do the deeper learning rather than fighting the clock all the time.

I am so sorry we have to stop this great discussion. . . . The midterm is next week and I have to remind you of a few more things. . . .

GETTING DEEP INTO LEARNING:
STUDENT-LED DYNAMIC DIALOGUE

I had posted a question about the meaning of the specific philosophy we were studying for everyday application in students' work settings and had given specific instructions about supporting their responses from the reading, tying it to concrete illustrations, and responding to at least one classmate. So, Saturday morning, I sat down with my cup of coffee to review the discussion board and provide feedback and grading for the students in my hybrid class (combination face-to-face and online).

There are 145 responses! Ok, I must have read that wrong; is something wrong with the system?

Click into it. Be calm; yes there are 145 responses to this posting! What is going on? Usually I see about 80–100, from a class of 20 students; what happened here?

Fantastic, they are really digging into peer learning. For example,

- Manny posted his response and then,
- Ellie asked more questions about the specific examples,
- Manny responded, and
- Ravi shared some references which also amplify the point, then
- Shari shared a similar example, and
- Ellie built on it.

And this happened with almost every post and is still continuing!

It is interesting how the students use both the assigned reading and find additional resources to feed this discussion. Could that really happen in a face-to-face class? We do not usually have those extra resources at hand; it might not be possible. But in an asynchronous online setting, now that they have multiple opportunities to participate, students are taking time to respond and really think about the questions.

In these situations, I am intrigued at how some of the students who are not very participatory in class shine in the online boards. In several cases, I even see how their online participation leads to greater in-class participation over the course of a few weeks (King, 2009b). Written and verbal empowerment, exploring content more fully, engaging in critical thinking, and peer learning: these are strengths of using online discussion boards well (Conrad & Donaldson, 2004; Palloff & Pratt, 2007). Moreover, today, the students have advanced much further in taking advantage of higher order thinking and peer dialogue through online discussion than they did even five years ago (King, 2001, 2009b). No doubt many factors come into play here, but it is evidence that, as instructors, we need to keep utilizing new formats of engagement in order to maximize learning opportunities.

FACULTY DEBRIEFING: MAKING SENSE OF IT ALL

In the "Beat the Clock" scenario, we saw the traditional classroom dilemma of having to shut down student dialogue in order to cover content and stay on schedule. In contrast, the basic example from the online class illustrated how students could participate as much as they wanted to, time allowing. Few of us will debate the power of engagement and dialogue in higher education. When learners interact with one another and/or the instructor about content by expressing their ideas, expanding their answers, and thinking critically, they are much more deeply engaged in internalizing and understanding it.

Yet, much like the '70s television show, *Beat the Clock*, professors fight the tyranny of time in every class session. Can we spend four hours discussing the impact of Zen Buddhism on world culture, art, mindfulness, modern health practice, and world religions in a world history course that lasts only one semester? We would likely be hard pressed to do so, because it is not specifically a religion course. But like many other religious and cultural trends, it has had a significant impact shaping our world cultures and history today, and the connections would be worthy of critical exploration and discussion.

Another example is the extensive history of China: Between military development and campaigns, politics, economics, art, music, agriculture, engineering, cultures, expansion, and religion, it would take the entire year if studied in depth as it needs to be, and yet it is only a fraction of our world. How can we meet this challenge in a global history course? How do we provide both breadth and depth? This is one of the painful challenges we experience as experts in our disciplines and professors of college students.

This chapter offers some solutions to this dilemma, but it comes at a cost. The solutions provided are grounded in professors taking a new orientation towards their classrooms. Doubtlessly, some of you already work with your students from this stance; others have tried, but find it difficult. Still others have vowed it would never happen. *The professor as expert facilitator* is the means to provide a foundational educational experience wherein learners of all ages can engage in in-depth exploration and understanding of content (Herman & Mandell, 2004; King 2009a). With an expert by their side, learners have the opportunity to see the subject area come alive for them through their own experiences and life lenses. The method is *facilitation*; the outcome is voice and empowerment (Brookfield, 2009).

Rather than students being limited to essays and exams, what if we engage them in creating original content that demonstrates their research and understanding of more complex topics in the subject area? A win-win situation, this approach lights fires of motivation and ownership for students and achieves the deeper understanding we strive to cultivate. However, in order for this to happen, we have to let go of the authoritarian control of class time and focus. Moreover, we have to allow students to interact with us more as facilitators For example: students asking questions and exploring ideas; faculty serving as mentor and coach, walking alongside students as they grow in understanding and appreciation of the content. These images should be the norm, not the exception (Brookfield, 2009; Daloz, 1999; Knowles, Holton, & Swanson, 2005).

Are you excited to try new ways to help students learn content better and excite young scholars to enter your field? Are you willing to try some simple new approaches for classroom dynamics that foster dialogue? Will you try some new digital technology that will enable students to express their research and understanding? This chapter explores the cultivation of student voice and empowerment through digital technology in learning situations.

NEW FOCUS

In order to accomplish student voice and empowerment, as professors we need to experience a paradigm shift involving the focus of course content and class time. In prior decades, we were able to discuss the extent of information for many content areas, but since circa 2000, information and new knowledge has been expanding at such rapid rates that this goal is no longer feasible (Enriquez, 2001). Yet few of us have revised our approach to teaching our content areas. The fundamental question we may start from is,

- How do we best prepare learners today to understand and navigate the body of knowledge in this content area?

Additionally, we might also want to consider,

- How do we best prepare them to use this content knowledge in the contexts which are most relevant?

To be sure, these questions are not plucked from thin air: They proceed from an extended body of research and practice called 21st Century Learning (King & Sanquist, 2009; Partnership for 21st Century Learning, 2002, 2008). This model needs to be explained because the economic, political, global, and societal contexts of this century are so vastly different than those of the period in which most of us professors were raised and academically prepared that we have to consciously reconsider the manner in which we teach and prepare the next generations. The old adage of "We teach how we were taught" will no longer suffice because our students come from a different cultural and historical experience and are preparing for a new marketplace and global society (Fink, 2003). "The way we were taught" is an irrelevant cultural artifact for them. We need to connect our content and delivery to be successful in their world instead.

21ST CENTURY LEARNING: HIGHLIGHTS

A guiding framework for developing voice and empowerment among learners, this brief section provides an overview of relevant characteristics and practices of 21st Century Learning. Identified and studied extensively by groups such as the Partnership for 21st Century Schools (2002, 2008) and the U.S. Department of Labor (2008; US DOL/ETA, 2009), this body of skills not only indicates what is needed in the workplace, but how people need to be able to deftly research and apply content in the professions.

For instance, in addition to the rapid changes in information and political systems, there has been a shift from valuing individualism and solo performance in all areas to valuing greater collaboration and cooperation. In addition, employers are no longer only looking for people who will deliver "the" right answer, because multiple contexts and situations can mean that many answers can fit. Our complex society, marketplace, and knowledge demand creativity and problem solving to address situations not solved previously and which might need multiple solutions (Baker, 2006; Gardner, 2006; Hempel, 2007). On the educational psychology front, these are also called *higher order thinking skills* and, as indicated by Bloom (1956), are made up of learners' ability to critically evaluate, analyze, synthesize, and apply content (also see Gardner, 2006).

Self-Directed and Self-Disciplined Learners

While the traditionally valued self-starter characteristic is still important to the 21st Century Learning paradigm, its new form has an important difference that we need to notice. In order to succeed amidst the rapid change of information and world order, we need to help our learners apprehend and internalize skills of self-directed and self-disciplined learning. These traits are tied together with the concept of the lifelong learner (Merriam, Caffarella, & Baumgartner, 2006; Oregon Education Network, n.d.; Wlodkowski, 1998).

Simply stated, while in the 1960s we might have thought that we were finished with our education when we earned our B.A. or even our Ph.D., in 2010 we know full well that if we do not continue to learn, persistently, we will become obsolete and devalued in our field. Lifelong learning is inherent to the character and orientation of the professional in the 21st century. And there is no better place for students to begin this practice than in their academic study of the content of the profession. A valuable benefit in this lifelong learning approach is that they see it modeled by the professional experts as it guides *their* development.

Collaboration

At the same time as this self-sufficiency is valued, the adept ability to collaborate well in diverse settings is absolutely necessary. Consider how the U.S. workplace has been characterized for the last 100 years as silos of independence. And yet, in the book *Wikinomics* (Tapscott & Williams, 2006), it is revealed how the digital practices of collaboration have shifted and drifted quickly from online purchases, entertainment, and social media into other areas of life. The authors also reveal how this mass collaboration is tremendously empowering for individuals and businesses alike.

Our classrooms will serve students, nations, and our disciplines well by providing extensive experience in how to successfully work with colleagues of varied characteristics on projects (Enriquez, 2001; Garner, 2006; Tapscott & Williams, 2006). Moreover, these course projects need to be complex, like real life: research-focused, content-centered, and time-sensitive. Indeed, the lifelines of professionals are often their co-workers and professional associations; yet our classrooms are too often void of collaborative strategies. Why do we keep this solution hidden for so long from the students? Why not instead start the synergy in our classes, so that the content is more deeply explored and internalized while the strategies for success are being developed?

Research Skills

Next in the flow of skills that are essential for academic learning and professional success are information literacy and research skills (American Library Association [ALA], 2006). Since information and knowledge is expanding so rapidly, students are best served by developing strong frameworks, approaches, and skills for literary and empirical research. From marketing research to stock trading, journalism to legal briefs and the social and health service professions, everyone needs to be attuned to the strategies and rigors of researching emergent information and validating information.

Thankfully, the tools for doing such research are immensely more convenient than they were even 20 years ago, but the price we pay is that the expectations are much greater. Since the information is more accessible, it is expected, even assumed, that every person has critically reviewed and analyzed the information prior to delivering a report. Moreover, the professional, academic or student who fails to exercise due diligence in research skills will be quickly labeled as below par in qualifications and potential.

Critical Thinking

Although there are several other critical characteristics of 21st Century Learning, for this discussion chapter, the final one that will be considered is critical thinking. Indeed, by discussing critical thinking we also have the opportunity to weave in problem solving and creativity. The reasoning for this is that the prime application of critical thinking is problem solving and that the best problem solvers are able to be flexible and creative, able to truly explore outside the assumed solutions and ordinary conclusions to discover new perspectives and possibilities (Enriquez, 2001). Therefore, the flexibility and creativity of an astute problem solver is a prime demonstration of critical thinking in action (Gardner, 2006).

As for the primacy in the world society today, rapidly changing conditions result in an endless need for new processes, policies, and procedures. Therefore, the 21st century is accelerating the need for problem solving as a daily strategy for doing the work of the day. No longer relegated to contrived word problems, problem solving is employed in creating the "firsts" and "bests": the *first* time determining the stress and sheer force of materials newly created, the *best* way to ship products to areas without public transit, and the *best* prospects and negotiations to assemble global partnerships with newly birthed nations, for instance.

I SENT MY FINAL PROJECT TO ALL MY FAMILY AND FRIENDS

When was the last time you heard your students say that about their class assignments? No, not for proofing their work, but to share their great research and creativity! You may think I teach videography, but in fact this example is from a class entitled Foundations of American Education. It is one of the least popular courses in teacher education because, traditionally, it gets bogged down in philosophy and history of education. I volunteered for the class because I saw an opportunity to use digital media and create a dynamic experience of research, investigation, and critical thinking. The students far exceeded my expectations.

The approach I used for the class was for us, as a class, to brainstorm hot topics in education and then have students select which ones they wanted to pursue in their reflective assignments. I would also use the list to make sure I incorporated the other ones as examples in the class sessions. Having to examine current critical issues from the field, I was facilitating their thinking about the nexus of theory, history, and practice—not reifying separate silos, but instead, from the first day, seeing vibrant connections. I also stood back and let them heat up the discussion with suggestions and pursue varied directions of topics.

The part that made them a bit anxious the first day was when I explained the formats of the research and reflection essays. Instead of writing a paper that only the eyes of the professor would ever see, we were changing the paradigm in three major ways: (1) the whole class would be able to see and read their work; (2) we would have sessions where their classmates would also ask additional questions of them and follow up on their research; and (3) they needed to choose at least two different forms of media for their three assignments: text/blog post, audio, or video.

As the first group of eager students ventured forth, they had some questions about technical matters. However, with just a little assistance, they figured out how to record audio on a laptop and proceeded from there by creating a script and recording their debate on their research topic. Once their work was posted on the Web, the rest of the class rose to the challenge and were not about to be outdone. Even the quietest students came forward requesting handheld recorders and creating dynamic audio products, which they emailed and posted to their friends. Not only were the students proud of having created the digital media, but it was clear from a review of their work and our conversations that they had spent much more than the bare minimum time researching and preparing these assignments. As a result, they knew their topics completely. Why? The stakes were high: They had their reputations on the line, as they were going public with the course assignments! (King, 2009b)

INSTRUCTOR AS FACILITATOR

As illustrated in the example above, the instructor has to relinquish the role of absolute power and focus mentioned at the beginning of this chapter.

However, the benefits are well worth considering: students who are more invested in course content; engaged in in-depth research and developing content understanding; dialoguing with one another about variations, details, and possibilities for their research and projects; internalizing learning as their own; and developing 21st Century Learning skills simultaneously. For many expert professionals, seeing our students reach these goals is well worth stepping off the pedestal and serving as an empowering facilitator.

One of the images I have of the facilitator is that of someone who accompanies others on a journey, speaking along the way, as we travel the path, and providing some direction about resources and perspective when requested. Eventually the two people follow separate paths, and it is at that point that we can revel in successfully launching another professional on her or his own journey of independent learning and, hopefully, facilitating others along the path of lifelong learning (King, 2003).

This image is one of generosity, selfless giving, and dedication to the development of others. Much like the image of the ideal academic mentor, one can see it is a vital role for a professor because as we invest in these individuals, we invest in the future of our field (Daloz, 1999; King, 2009b; Zachary, 2005). Hopefully some of our mentees will far outlast us in the field, by virtue of years alone. But also I expect that some of mine may surpass me in their insight, development, and application of the content to unique venues they are attuned to and I am not. This scalability multiplies, expands, and reaches much farther through the empowerment of others than I could ever hope to by keeping the knowledge and growth to myself.

In much the same way, the 21st century is an age of facilitation. Again, no one can know all things because information and knowledge itself is just too expansive. Instead, we need to have the freedom and confidence to draw alongside students, the emergent professionals, we trust, collaborate, share information, trade ideas, push the limits of current understandings, and create new perspectives. It is an age of not only collaboration, but also interdisciplinary thinking, development, and marketplaces (Enriquez, 2006; Garner, 2006). Our world is global, our marketplace is international, and knowledge spans domains of content from nanotechnology to biomedical robotics and mathematical models of anticipating consumer behavior and political campaigns (Baker, 2006). Figuratively, one might say that the silo has crumbled and is being replaced by an organic metropolis.

Facilitation Model and Strategies

How do professors cope with such radical changes in teaching, instructional expectations, and the professional context? One of the basic challenges is that we might not have experienced a truly facilitative model in our formal academic training. Therefore, how we can emulate or extrapolate it?

The great news is that several basic steps can be followed that will help any professor make the transition to facilitator over a period of time. You should give yourself time to change, remove the pressure of perfection, give yourself the freedom to try new approaches, and work through new processes making them your own (King, 2003). You will develop how to be a facilitator in ways that best meet the needs of your students, your discipline, your teaching style, and your personality. No two styles will be the same, but your facilitation style should be quite different from the style you use when you are lecturing the class or leading discussions.

The steps to higher education instructional facilitation include:

- Setting clear expectations of the instructor as facilitator.
- Providing examples of classroom collaboration.
- Providing facilitating examples for students before they are asked to do likewise.
- Pulling back from absolute control of the class direction.
- Always monitoring peer dialogue for appropriate, respectful, and safe discussion.
- Being quick to act if there are problems among or with learners.
- Reflecting on what works and what needs to be changed.

Most of these steps of facilitation are self explanatory; however, the first, *setting expectations*, deserves special attention in our discussion.

Setting Expectations

Even though learners today need a different educational environment, the truth is they seldom experience it. Therefore, it is imperative that one clearly communicate the form, details, and expectations of a new instructional context. In the case of the professor as facilitator, the role of the professor shifts dramatically. To be sure, the students will rise to the occasion and thrive in the environment, but they will also need to know what to expect and, to a certain extent, they will follow your lead (King, 2009b).

Recommendations that emerge from such settings include greater transparency with the learners to set the tone of facilitation. Many of the researchers and theorists who specialize in how adults learn indicate the same thing about what learners need from their professors as facilitators. Based on Brookfield (2009), Cranton (1994), Fink (2003), and King (2003, 2005), the following list emerges. Instructors need to provide the following to their students:

- Confidence in the role as facilitator.
- A definition of what that facilitation will be like.
- Explanation of why changes are being made.
- Clear expectations of student roles as active participants.
- Responsiveness to their facilitation needs.
- Protection of their safety as they dialogue together.
- Freedom for learners to step into center stage more often than is customary.

As the focus and strategy of instruction shifts to a facilitation paradigm, the question of what activities could be used with this approach remains. The next section of this chapter addresses this question by providing several different digital media projects that can be applied across content areas to foster voice and empowerment.

ACTIVITIES THAT BUILD VOICE AND EMPOWERMENT

While many of the chapters of this book will delve deeply into specific digital media technologies and their uses in classrooms, this section provides many suggestions that fit along the same broad theme. In the context of discovering and cultivating voice and empowerment among higher education learners, the basis of our discussion has been to shift the orientation of the instructor from the focal point at the front of the room to the facilitator. Having discussed this at length, consider the following selected options for use with this facilitation approach to instruction.

In order to provide a rich, but brief overview of digital media activities, the list in Table 2.1 includes the name, description, technologies, and the strengths of learning outcomes for each recommendation. See if you can complete the missing boxes in the table as an activity. Also add more rows to Table 2.1 as you discover more possibilities.

This table can be used to help instructors plan their classes and select a variety of instructional strategies to use across a semester or course. Thus, faculty can gain experience with a variety of tools to discover which best fit the content, the learners, and their needs. Obviously, selections of tools and activities may be driven by several factors, but using varied activities is helpful in covering several skill domains, learning and teaching styles, learning preferences, and cultivating different teacher–student and student–student communication opportunities (Brookfield, 2009; King & Griggs, 2006; King & Gura, 2009; Knowles, Holton, & Swanson, 2005).

TABLE 2.1 Digital Media Activities That Can Facilitate Voice and Empowerment: Faculty Activity and Resource

Digital Media	Description	Technology Options	Outcomes
Scenarios (Text, audio or video-based)	Posting content-related scenarios that require student problem solving in the online discussion board. Solve scenarios in discussion board.	Discussion Board (Blackboard, Angel, Moodle, etc.) Blog Wiki	Research skill development, critical thinking, writing skills, information technology skills, voice (all have to respond). Transfer of voice from online to face-to-face (f2f) class
Student-created FAQ (Text, audio or video-based)	Groups of students collaborate to generate a Frequently Asked Question posting on a specific content area, subtopic, or focus.	Online learning platform (Angel, Blackboard, Moodle, etc.) Blog Wiki	Collaboration skills, information technical skills, research, critical thinking, analysis, writing, empowerment, voice.
Student-created blog of content	Collaborative content resource development: Students create specific content area questions, responses, or reflections, which they post in a public blog.	Learners need Internet access near home or at work to participate fully.	Collaboration skills, writing, information technical skills, research, empowerment, voice.
Student-created multimedia	Students individually or collaboratively create a multimedia project on the content area AND either post it on the class blog, online class site, or present it in class.	Learners need computer access at school or near home to participate fully.	Collaboration skills, writing, presentation skills (if live), information technical skills, research, empowerment, voice.
Student-created audio digital media	Like the scenario above, students research a course-related topic and write a script that they then record to post publicly. Forms of the script could include • Debate • First-person narrative • Historical reenactment • Simulated on-the-scene news report, etc.	Available computer, inexpensive microphone ($10), and free software OR ≈$30 digital audio recorder	Transfer of voice from online to f2f class. Research skill development, critical thinking, writing skills, information technology skills, voice (all have to respond).

Instructor-created audio digital media	Instructor creates digital audio to supplement the course. Suggestions: • 3–4 minute introduction to assignment or unit of study • Explanation of complex material • Recordings of lectures for student review • Specialized tutorials for review • Exam review materials • Expert interviews • First-person narrative • Historical reenactment • Simulated on-the-scene news report • Recordings of prior classroom guests, etc.	Available computer, inexpensive microphone ($10) and free software OR ≈$30 digital audio recorder	Develops greater independence as students have to take initiative to schedule and listen to the materials. Provides greater freedom for them to listen to content. Alternate learning styles addressed (aural rather than visual for text). Information technology skills. Lifelong learning skills (many podcasts now available for continuing professional development). For instructor: maximized class time (some material presented by instructor outside of class), more dialogue in class!
Student-created video digital media	Like the scenario above, students research a course-related topic and write a script that they then record to post publicly. Forms of the script could include • Debate • First-person narrative • Historical reenactment • Simulated on-the-scene news report, etc.	Inexpensive video recorder (≈$100) OR Cell phone (i.e., smart phone) or digital camera with short video clip recording capability OR Borrowed or rented video recorder from university AND Free software	Transfer of voice from online to f2f class. Research skill development, critical thinking, writing skills, information technology skills, voice (all have to respond).
Blended course formats	Consider whether the needs of students and content may be served better with combined online, on-campus course. Split week, split month, or other sequence.	Online learning platform (Angel, Blackboard, Moodle, etc.) Learners need Internet access near home or at work to participate fully.	Hybrids provide a greater opportunity for students to dialogue rather than focus on the professor. More time to collaborate, pursue complex continuing projects, and build community.
Student-created scenarios, classmates solve	Request that each student create a scenario to post online for their classmates to solve.	Online learning platform (Angel, Blackboard, Moodle, etc.) Learners need Internet access near home or at work to participate fully.	Develops complex and integrative subject area knowledge.

(continued)

TABLE 2.1 Digital Media Activities That Can Facilitate Voice and Empowerment: Faculty Activity and Resource

Digital Media	Description	Technology Options	Outcomes
Small group role playing/simulation	Students participate in an extending online simulation where they role play and have to perform a group task (solve a problem, plan a project, develop a report, etc.)	Online learning platform (Angel, Blackboard, Moodle, etc.) Learners need Internet access near home or at work to participate fully.	Builds application of content to real world settings. Reveals complexities of content.
Interactive office hours	Provide personal support and draw students out individually to ask questions when needed.	If not enough time on campus, try Skype (free voice calls and free video conferencing worldwide) or Dimdim, Logmein, or other free worldwide remote computer sharing (demonstrate via computer).	Increases access to instructor support. Overcome travel and work hour barriers for instructional support.
Electronic feedback	Detailed feedback embedded in the document: track changes, insert comments, offer to have follow-up online conference with student if necessary. Detailed feedback that scaffolds skills to build greater research, critical thinking, and independence.	Word processor with track changes or comment feature. Email submission of papers or dropbox or assignment link.	Improve student ownership and progress in courses.
Online documentation of class assignments and responsibilities	Provide abundant direction and description regarding assignments, scheduling, deadlines, and expectations.	Online learning platform, Web site, or blog.	Rather than pigeonhole creativity and the project, it provides freedom, as students do not have to keep guessing and second-guessing. Increase transparency.
Cultivate community	Create class photo of all class members. They email or upload a photo or representative photograph; class member or instructor pastes them into one class photo.	PowerPoint, Prezi Graphics program (GIMP, Paint, etc.)	Build community, demonstrate respect. Increase collaborative opportunities.
Rotate student discussion leader	Assign students to rotate as discussion leader in class and online. Provide sample questions and techniques.	Learners need Internet access near home or at work to participate fully. Online discussion may be in an online learning system such as Blackboard or a blog or wiki.	Validation built upon experience. Demonstrate respect of prior and professional experience.

CONCLUSION

This chapter introduced the need for a facilitator approach to classroom instruction and the means and instructional strategies faculty may use to develop their own approach. The guiding focus has been cultivating voice and empowerment within each learner as a person, a professional, and a discipline expert (depending on the level of study).

As most of us higher education faculty today were not trained this way, the adjustment will be a journey of learning and development. However, with the results being more student investment in our content areas, active student engagement in deep critical research and discussion in our classes, and meaningful professional mentoring of scholars, most faculty would consider it a worthy investment.

Building on the momentum of change in the 21st century, we have a great opportunity to transform our classes into more dynamic learning communities. By using digital media, online discussions, collaborative groups, and student-created Web-based projects we can also move our students' learning from the isolation of the academy to the forefront of public view. If our students are willing to accept greater stakes for their learning, how can we ignore the opportunity to raise them?

REFERENCES

American Library Association (ALA). (2006). *Information literacy competency standards for higher education.* Retrieved July 29, 2010, from http://www.ala.org/acrl/ilcomstan.html

Baker, S. (2006, January 23). Math will rock your world. *Business Week.* Retrieved August 15, 2009 from http://www.businessweek.com/magazine/content/06_04/b3968001.htm

Bloom, B. S. (1956). *Taxonomy of educational objectives.* New York: Longman.

Brookfield, S. B. (2009). *The skillful teacher: On technique, trust and responsiveness in the classroom.* (2nd ed.). San Francisco: Jossey-Bass.

Conrad, R. M., & Donaldson, J. A. (2004). *Engaging the online learner.* San Francisco: Jossey-Bass.

Cranton. P. (1994). *Understanding and promoting transformative learning.* San Francisco: Jossey-Bass.

Daloz, L. A. (1999). *Mentor: Guiding the journey of adult learners.* San Francisco: Jossey-Bass.

Enriquez, J. (2001). *As the future catches you: How genomics and other forces are changing your life, work, health and wealth.* New York: Three Rivers Press.

Fink, L. D. (2003). *Creating significant learning experiences.* San Francisco: Jossey-Bass.

Gardner, H. (2006). *Five minds for the future.* Cambridge, MA: Harvard Business School Press.

Hempel, J. (2007, June 11). Web strategies that cater to customers. *Business Week.* Retrieved September 4, 2009 from http://www.businessweek.com/magazine/content/07_24/b4038403.htm

Herman, L., & Mandell, A. (2004). *From teaching to mentoring.* New York: Routledge/Farmer.

King, K. P. (2009a). Coaching – mentoring: A different perspective. In M. Miller and K. P. King (Eds.), *Empowering women through literacy* (pp. 147–156). Charlotte, NC: Information Age.

King, K. P. (2009b). Empowerment and voice: Digital media. In M. Miller and K. P. King (Eds.), *Empowering women through literacy* (pp. 271–280). Charlotte, NC: Information Age.

King, K. P. (2003). *Keeping pace with technology: Educational technology that transforms.* Cresskill, NJ: Hampton Press.

King, K. P. (2001). Educators revitalize the classroom "bulletin board": A case study of the influence of online dialogue on face-to-face classes from an adult learning perspective. *Journal of Research on Computing in Education, 33*(4), 337–354.

King, K. P., & Griggs, J. K. (Eds). (2006). *Harnessing innovative technology in higher education: Access, equity, policy and instruction.* Madison, WI: Atwood.

King, K. P., & Gura, M. (2009). *Podcasting for teachers: Using a new technology to revolutionize teaching and learning* (Rev. 2nd ed.). Charlotte, NC: Information Age.

King, K. P., & Sanquist, S. (2009). 21st century learning and human performance. In V. Wang & K. P. King (Eds.), *Fundamentals of human performance and training* (pp. 61–88). Charlotte, NC: Information Age.

Knowles, M. S., Holton, E., & Swanson, R. A. (2005). *The adult learner (6th ed.).* New York: Butterworth-Heinemann.

Merriam, S. B., Caffarella, R. S., & Baumgartner, L. (2006). *Learning in adulthood: A comprehensive guide* (3rd ed.). San Francisco: Jossey-Bass.

Oregon Network for Education. (n.d.). *Self assessment for distance learning.* Retrieved August 2, 2010 from http://oregonone.org/DEquiz.htm

Palloff, R. M., & Pratt, K. (2007). *Building online learning communities.* San Francisco: Jossey-Bass.

Partnership for 21st Century Schools. (2008). *Transition brief: Policy recommendations on preparing Americans for the global skills race.* Tucson, AZ: Author. Retrieved from http://www.21stcenturyskills.org/documents/p21_transition_paper_nov_24_2008.pdf

Partnership for 21st Century Schools. (2002). *Learning for the 21st century.* Retrieved February 5, 2010 from http://www.21stcenturyskills.org/index.php?option=com_content&task=view&id=29&Itemid=185

Tapscott, D., & Williams, A. D. (2006). *Wikinomics: How mass collaboration changes everything.* New York: Portfolio.

U.S. Department of Labor (DOL). (2008). *Office of the 21st century workforce.* Retrieved July 15, 2010 from http://www.dol.gov/21cw/

U.S. DOL/Employment and Training Administration (ETA). (2009). *Workforce3 one.* Retrieved August 28, 2009 from http://www.workforce3one.org/

Wlodkowski, R. (1998). *Enhancing adult motivation to learn: A comprehensive guide for teaching all adults* (Rev ed.). San Francisco: Jossey-Bass.

Zachary, L. J. (2005). *Creating a mentoring culture: The organization's guide.* San Francisco: Jossey-Bass.

PART II

DIGITAL MEDIA

CHAPTER 3

PODCASTING

Learning on Demand
and Content Creation

Kathleen P. King
University of South Florida

INTRODUCTION

Professors are looking for ways to engage students. Students are seeking education that is relevant to their lives. Such aspirations define the tensions between faculty and student needs and purposes during times of rapid social change (Enriquez, 2001; Wright & Kelly, 1974). An unexpected solution for higher education has emerged: the MP3 craze of the 2000s. Digital media such as podcasting offer the capability for students to use their popular media and be critical thinkers and creators of knowledge across disciplines rather than sitting in the background as passive spectators to their own education.

Today it is common to encounter advertisements for podcasts on the nightly news, CD covers, radio shows, Web sites, and in print publications. Podcasts include not only audio books, news shows, talk shows, and lectures, but also self-guided museum tours, job training, story telling, historical fic-

The Professor's Guide to Taming Technology, pages 33–50

tion, and dramatic reenactments. This pattern illustrates that podcasts are a technical product that is defined apart from the content and genre.

Technically, podcasts are digital audio files, posted on the Internet and pushed to listeners through XML/RSS feeds (Geoghegan & Klass, 2005). They are usually made available to listeners via Web sites and podcast directories such as iTunes.com, Podcastpickle.com, and Zencast.com. It is surprising that while the roots of podcasting are in the independent music industry (Geoghegan & Klass, 2005; Lafferty & Walch, 2006), since its beginning in 2004 the consistently most popular podcasts have been related to learning. A review of podcast directory statistics across 2005–2009 reveal that the persistent leading 8 out of 10 top podcasts are language learning podcasts (King & Gura, 2009). This trend is critically important for faculty in higher education because it demonstrates that our society has a general readiness for and has adopted technology for learning. Therefore, when we introduce podcast use in our classes, students will be familiar with the technology and accustomed to educational applications.

As faculty, we have a prime opportunity to appropriate an inexpensive, simple technology to enhance teaching and learning in new dimensions for our specific disciplines and classes. It is an exciting time to build upon our academic expertise and use this digital medium to encourage more students to become critical researchers and leaders across disciplines. Yet only professors can make this happen. We have the power to vibrantly connect content and creativity; to build assignments that generate deeper research, analysis, and knowledge construction; and to raise the bar for the next generation of scholars. What's more, this digital medium is portable and globally shared, therefore we are cultivating the means to building and sustaining global scholarship communities through this and other emergent technologies yet to be discovered. Will we rise to the challenge?

This chapter provides several detailed suggestions for how faculty in higher education can use podcasts for teaching purposes. However, the topic is best discussed with a brief technical foundation clarified and established from the beginning.

BRIEF TECHNICAL ORIENTATION

Podcasts are digital audio files that include several components: a digital audio file, a server where the file is posted, and an RSS (Really Simple Syndication) feed file (which pushes new episodes to listeners; see Figure 3.1). The digital audio file is in a file format called MP3 (MPED-1 Audio Layer 3) because it was found to be the most versatile format in terms of compression, programming, and portability (Felix & Stolarz, 2006; Lafferty & Walch, 2006). Usually, podcasts are created by recording on a computer or

Figure 3.1 Anatomy of a podcast. © Kathleen P. King, 2009.

with a portable digital audio recorder, and then the file is edited, posted, and finally linked to the feed script. Users access computers or MP3 players to listen to the podcast files.

As mentioned, there are many options for listening to podcasts. Listeners may use the computer directly or download files from the computer to a portable listening device, secure digital card (SD), or CD. Portable listening devices include not only MP3 players, but also iPods, cell phones, smart phones, iPhones, and more. In contrst to broadcast radio, listeners have the ability to control when and where they listen to the audio file and how much of the content they listen to at any given time.

In more technical detail, the podcast has an XML (eXtensible Markup Language) format associated with it that includes the RSS feed. This file contains a listing of all of the audio "episodes" that are available and the detailed specifications that allow an MP3 player or computer access and play them. Listeners transparently use the XML file to subscribe to the podcast feed through Web sites or specialized programs that not only provide a listing of different podcasts, but also enable the automatic retrieval of new episodes.

Podcasting Power Scenario

For example, if Juarez likes listening to "Physics with Dr. Spike," he can open iTunes on his computer, search for that series by name, and click "subscribe." Then every time Juarez opens iTunes in the future, the program *automatically* checks for new or modified episodes of the series. This helps Juarez greatly because he does not have to go check the "Physics with Dr. Spike" Web site every day to see if a new podcast is available. Instead, by opening iTunes, all 20, 30, or 75 podcast series he likes to listen to will be automatically updated for him within in a matter of seconds.

A podcast may also be listened to from the Web site without downloading the file; this format is called *online streaming content*. However, streaming audio requires the use of an audio device, be it a next-generation phone or a computer, which maintains a constant connection to the Internet. A more flexible and equally powerful option is for the audio files to be stored on the computer or transferred to any number of different types of portable devices.

Now that the basics of what podcasts are and how they are created and used have been clarified, consider what course-related content you might record and how it could be beneficial for students to have constant access and many options for listening to it.

Faculty Reflection Activity

Please reflect on the following initial questions.

1. Most semesters, do you find that you have a few students who struggle with specific concepts of the course and who need additional assistance?
2. Are there cornerstone concepts and content areas within your courses that need mastery by all students?
3. Do you continue to seek ways to cultivate more critical thinking and creativity among your students within your course content? Do you try to get them deeply involved in the discipline so that they develop their own opinions and points of view and can support them fluidly?
4. Do you have students who work, have family responsibilities, or have other interference in reaching office hours for assistance?

If the answer is yes to any of these questions, podcasting might provide a way for you or them to better address these needs. Before continuing to read, take another moment and note the specifics about the needs, content, or obstacles you currently encounter for the items you labeled "yes."

There are several different applications of podcasting to higher education. Between faculty-created and student-created podcasts, there are scores of possibilities that can be designed based on the specific needs of content, discipline, faculty, and students. The next section of this chapter introduces several examples of podcasting applications to higher education. It is not meant to be an exhaustive guide; it cannot present all possibilities. Instead, it is an opportunity to join us in an instructional think tank laboratory and consider what others are doing, what applies for your setting, and how to take the next steps.

USES OF PODCASTS TO ENHANCE LEARNING: FACULTY-CREATED PODCASTS

The literature reveals that several professors and universities have introduced and are implementing podcasting. To a large degree, this is because one of the benefits of podcasting is the use of audio listening skills that tap different learning styles and modes for content learning than reading does. Moreover a variety of teaching and learning strategies can be incorporated when using student-created podcasts as project development activities. Certainly, the use of recorded audio in education has a long history of effectively impacting student learning (Gould, Langford, & Mott, 1972). However, podcasting affords new unparalleled opportunities for teacher-created and student-created content as well as portability and distribution (Evans, 2006). In the next sections, examples of faculty-created and student-created podcasts will be presented to stimulate thinking about how these digital media can be applied in novel ways to your specific instructional needs.

Lecture Webcasting

iTunes University is filled with examples of lecture podcasts, where professors record their lectures and post them on the podcast feed for public or password-protected use. Students find great benefit in this simple form of podcasting, as they can review difficult parts of the session even while doing other activities and not miss content if they are absent (Evans, 2008). Moreover, English language learners or students with learning needs such as hearing or attention deficits can play back the recording so that they can review sections that might have been difficult for them.

Two major drawbacks to this use of podcasting in higher education arise. First, because there is no redesign of instruction, learners gain very little other than review of the content. Second, in general, higher education has made podcasting synonymous with lecture webcasting. This is most unfortunate because this narrow perspective eliminates the scores of other creative instructional opportunities waiting to be used. Let us dig deeper and explore some of these potential instructional podcasting treasures.

Further Than Lecture Webcasting

A powerful strategy for taking the familiar concept of the lecture to another level begins by recording your class lectures or presentations. However, the strategy here is not to post them in their entirety; instead, only post sections that are especially difficult for many students to understand, summary points, or critical definitions. In this way, professors can take a 50-minute or 2-hour lecture and cut it into pieces that are much more useful for supporting their students and also more useful for student access to critical information. This slicing of lectures into smaller segments is also efficient because faculty are not spending time creating separate content. Instead, record the session intended for delivery and use that content as the basis for your online offerings. Capturing/recording all delivered content is an efficient practice for faculty because therein lies much of the content your students need to review.

Frequently Asked Questions (FAQs)

Question and answer (Q&A) sessions are classic staples of classroom instruction. How about applying the same principle as above? Record the Q&A session, then post it for all the class sections. You might not have to repeat the Q&A session each time in the future. A similar strategy is to have students post their questions in a folder in an online discussion board by week or topic. The faculty member collects the questions and records the questions with the answers and posts the file in print and voice (Bluestein, 2006; Lee & Chan, 2007). Providing auditory responses often opens more opportunity for in-depth explanations and examples than might be submitted just in text, therefore the FAQ podcast has definite merits.

The scalable benefit of this approach is apparent after just one semester, as one sees that students discover that their questions are already answered in the list. Of course, faculty have to gently redirect students to the FAQ podcast when those emails reach your inbox, but students, like everyone else, can learn new habits.

Primary Source Podcasts

Faculty also find that podcasts can be used and created to prepare or to follow up classroom instruction. For example, pre-recorded podcasts that relate to the topic at hand are often overlooked, despite their usefulness. In many cases, primary sources might be accessed easily and included in students' studies through the use of digital audio.

20th-Century American History

The class homework is continuing to explore peripheral experiences of the American Civil Rights Movement and integration through primary sources. Prior to class, in addition to reading chapters 1–10 of Joyce Carol Oates' *We Were the Mulvaneys, Faithless: Tales of Transgression,* Dr. Erinson assigned the students to listen to a 1990 interview with Oates about her book. It was easy to access this interview because Dr. Erinson had added the interview to the podcast feed and the students had listened to it without having to search the Web. The result was an exciting discussion about the classic book and an experience with the voice and character of the author clearly impressed on their minds. In addition, time in class did not have to be spent listening or viewing the interview. It was all class preparation. Now the class time could be spent on deeper discussion, analysis, and debate.

Podcasts as Tutorials

As indicated early in the chapter, professors often notice common trouble spots in the curriculum each time they teach courses. Whether it be verb conjugation, specific scientific laws, math calculations, literary arguments, or theoretical proofs, semester after semester we often see some students stumble across the same difficult concepts and hurdles. Through experience and effort, we also learn how to best explain and guide students through these difficult concepts. How much more effective to take advantage of this experienced instructional vantage point and create tutorial modules that provide additional instructional support for students when they need it. By posting podcasts on the Web site and feed, students need not wait for our email reply or next week's office hours. Instead, they can independently access the needed instructional assistance 24 hours a day, 7 days a week. The fundamental benefits of this efficient and scalable approach are only the beginning, but they include

- providing consistent tutorial assistance;
- providing on-demand, immediate access learning needs; and
- reducing frustration and increasing student retention and success.

However, using podcasts as tutorials also enables the professor to develop more advanced instructional materials, and to provide individualized instructional assistance for special situations. And in the students' case, using tutorial podcasts cultivates engaging in problem solving of their learning needs, taking initiative in pursuing learning resources, and becoming more independent lifelong learners. These benefits are powerful, helping create higher education classrooms that are more capable of producing creative researchers and analytical thinkers.

Podcasting Innovation Ahead

Professors have been creating many innovative applications of podcasting for instructional purposes; we have only provided a few examples to introduce the possibilities. In addition, many faculty include assignments in which students produce and submit their own podcasts to demonstrate content competency. King and Gura (2009) reveal abundant examples of how podcasting has been used effectively across content areas in K–12 education with creative applications as well as offering strategies for developing podcasts in varied disciplines. Higher education has been slower to adopt this most powerful application of podcasting; however, the next section reveals several examples that are already being used. Clearly there is still much room in the realm of instructional podcasting for faculty in higher education to chart new territory.

USES OF PODCASTS TO ENHANCE LEARNING: STUDENT-CREATED PODCASTS

Faculty Reflection Activity

Before we begin the discussion of student-created podcasts, please reflect on the following questions.

1. Do your students need practice in public speaking because they will be presenting at professional conferences in their careers?
2. Do your students create class projects or research projects?
3. Is critique, analysis, original thought, or creativity valued in your discipline?
4. How do you authentically evaluate those achievements currently?

Radical Strategies Ahead

When faculty include content-related podcast creation as course assignments, they break down some traditional instructional barriers. Using podcasts in this manner, faculty invite students to actively engage with the content and demonstrate their competency publicly or privately. Moreover, such assignments communicate confidence that students will rise to the challenge. In universities across the world, learners are exceeding the expectations of their professors in this way. This section of the chapter explores several examples of how faculty might incorporate podcasts into their college and university classes. Again, use these brief overviews as templates or starting points. One of the great opportunities with digital media is the open-ended possibility for deeper thinking, expression, and construction of knowledge.

On-Demand Presentations

In a simple variation of the traditional science lab report, students might be assigned to develop audio podcasts that present the essential elements and findings of their research. In this way, rather than solely completing lab reports, students become involved in evaluating, analyzing, and representing the information to the class audience. This approach bridges learning to much higher learning skills than customary lab reports have in the past.

In addition, instructors can assign provocative questions to extend student lab experiences to real-life situations or further content topics, thus engaging them in thinking beyond the immediate activity. An added benefit to such assignments is that students can then post the podcast inside the private class learning space. In turn, they will see the work and hear the thoughts and analysis of their colleagues. Thus, the conversation extends beyond teacher and student and each classmate can explore multiple perspectives instead of only learning from their own point of view.

Critical Perspectives and Opinions: Position Podcasts

Many academics are familiar with position papers; in the same vein, this assignment might be described as a *Position Podcast*. In this situation, instructors might identify hot topics, pressing issues, current events, or dilemmas that connect to the course and pose them as a list of topics for students to select for debate. They then pair up with another student to research their topics, assign positions, and write their script for their 5–8 minute podcast.

Encouraging students to consider that their podcasts will not only be posted class-wide, but also publicly, raises the stakes even further and includes issues of global responsibility and perceptions that are valuable real-world experiences and complexities. The results can be simply posted on a class blog, and classmates can scaffold ideas and ask questions of the podcasters about their positions.

King (2009) has found that this approach is valuable on several levels. Not only do students discover voice and empowerment through public expression of opinion, but they also invest deeply in research because of their public reputation, and they strive to develop sound arguments for their position. In follow-up focus groups, students remark on the unexpected benefits of peer learning, including varied points of view, pursing the assignment in different ways, and the choices of references. In this way, Position Podcasts can be a form of debate and become an incentive for deeper research and dialogue on targeted issues.

Expert Interviews

The familiar technique for including guest lecturers in the college classroom might be extended to a new level of learning through student-conducted interviews of experts. Faculty teaching historical or political events, or current applications or developments of education, social sciences, math, science, engineering, technology, and more will find many opportunities to assign interview podcasts to students. For example, in a teacher education course, students might interview teachers about their use of specific educational theories; in political science, interviewing housemates or family members about current governmental policies, upcoming elections, or current events; or in technology courses, interviewing computer programmers about the real-life issues in projects, code, and problem solving that they encounter are all powerful means of involving students in developing personal understanding of content. Such situated learning has long been seen successful in engaging students in rich learning that lasts because it can address substantial, complex, and relevant questions and dilemmas (Lave & Wenger, 1991).

Moreover, faculty can plan strategically, and with the permission of the student podcasters, eventually have a rich archive of expert podcast interviews to use in future classes. By rotating the assignment across units of study, each semester students will be creating content that can be used to cultivate deep learning and provide real-life examples and primary sources for future teaching. In a most curious way, significant peer learning can expand across semesters through digital media, exemplifying truly innovative instruction.

First-Person Podcasts: Historical Reenactment

In every field there are famous people who have led the way, changed the status quo, and opened new thinking for us to understand the next level of the discipline. As experts in the field, we often find these historical figures exciting, as they stir our intellectual passion. However, it is rare that our students immediately develop that same thrill. Assigning the development of historical interviews or historical event reenactment podcasts can be just the solution to bring students deeper into the rich history and personal excitement of our disciplines.

Whether you are a faculty member of liberal arts, sciences, math, engineering, or technology, this assignment can be designed to fit your field. For instance, consider how a biology faculty member might list significant events that impacted the development of the field: the discovery of genetics by Mendel, DNA by Watson and Crick, or penicillin by Pauling. Each one of these could be researched for historical context, accurate details of the events, language accents, current events, and more that would be used in the recording. The students might then simulate an interview with the science pioneer or reenact pivotal scenes of the story. The same assignment could be developed focusing on famous authors, military figures, world leaders, explorers, and figures from any field of study.

Of course, the reenactment podcasts are posted for the whole class to enjoy and to learn from about the events and people. However, consider how deeply invested the students can become in the subject of their research. These will be events and figures they will never forget. And again, the depth of learning and peer dialogue can be greatly facilitated in class or online to encourage additional learning. As in the prior example, the astute faculty member will rotate the list of projects and gain permission for continued use from the podcasting students so that over time a full archive will be available to supplement class learning throughout every semester.

Real-Life Application and Involvement

Our final example is taken from the discipline of engineering. In a published paper, professors described how they gave a podcast assignment as a second-year final project. One exciting dimension of this project is situated learning (Lave & Wenger, 1991) as it spans the globe and creates real-world, complex, and meaningful contexts for student problem solving. In this example, 4-member student groups discuss the intricacies of such varied engineering projects as the Hoover Dam, the new Guggenheim museum in Spain, the Three Gorges Dam in China, and sustainable building practices that the LEED standard have promoted (Brevy Cannon, 2006). The final product of student work was a 6-minute podcast that described how these engineering projects impacted or could impact broad dimensions of society, including issues of economics, environment, tourism, and local community quality of life.

Essential outcomes of such assignments include not only the demonstration of competencies in engineering principles, but also problem solving, integration of diverse ideas, collaboration, critical thinking, and discourse, to name a few. All of these are essential skills for engineers to develop throughout their studies, and yet some can be very difficult to cultivate and track. Providing short assignments such as these throughout the course of study can build increased proficiency in perceiving and coping with real-world, complex issues.

These examples of student-created podcasts provide a starting point for faculty to consider how they could incorporate student assignments for deeper learning. Still, we need to explore how to create podcasts and what equipment is needed. The next section of the chapter addresses these needs in a straightforward and non-technical approach to help get every professor started with podcasting.

PODCASTING: HOW-TO AND EQUIPMENT

Producing podcasts can be as simple or complex, inexpensive or expensive as one chooses. This chapter section describes the process of producing podcasts and what is needed.

Figure 3.2 provides a basic diagram to conceptually illustrate the podcasting process. As faculty, podcasting production begins with our content and learner needs (Frydenberg, 2008). Rather than focusing on gadgets and equipment at the beginning, initially we want to make choices according to purposes, content, and needs. Figure 3.2 illustrates that the next major step is production, where the podcast is actually recorded and edited. The final stage is posting it to the Internet and adding the feed so that it is automatically distributed to those who wish to receive it.

Recording Equipment

When considering the recording of digital audio, there are several options: (1) portable and classroom, (2) computer-based, and (3) mixer and computer (Felix & Stolarz, 2006; King, & Gura, 2009). In classroom settings, for interviews and other applications, the portable and classroom option of the handheld digital recorder may be the best solution. These range in price from $40 to $500, but they are very versatile, and the $250 range provides a robust device that can record a classroom without prewiring, computers, or software. Additionally, a specialized microphone or two can be added to a portable device. The small digital voice recorder can

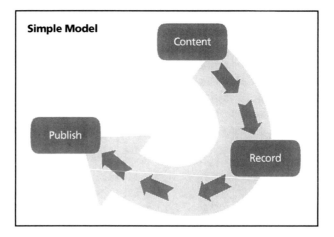

Figure 3.2 Simple model for podcasting development. Created by Kathleen P. King, 2009.

be placed on a podium or table or in an instructor's pocket. In the alternate case, an external microphone can be plugged into the recorder and then attached to the instructor's suit/shirt/dress.

If one uses a computer-based option to record the audio, a microphone is either onboard (usually only in laptops) or plugged in. There are a wide variety of styles and a wide range of price points of microphones to choose from. There are microphones that fit directly into computers: lapel, stand-up, headsets, desktop, and more. Often a microphone of this type in the $50 range will be good quality (Felix, & Stolarz, 2006; King, & Gura, 2009).

The final decision is whether to spend a lot more money and use a mixer. The mixer enables more than one microphone to be connected and controlled. However, for instructional purposes and one- or two-person recording, it is not needed. Mixers are plugged into the computer with either a fire wire or USB plug, and microphones with specialized XLR plugs are connected to it. This setup is much more expensive, as the least expensive mixers cost about $100 and microphones $50; the costs accumulate rapidly.

Software: Recording and Editing

In order to record audio with a computer, software is needed. In addition, usually in academic settings, faculty and students only want high-quality recordings distributed; therefore, using software to edit the audio file is necessary. In fact, the same software can do both: record and edit.

There are several software options available to record and edit digital audio. The free and low-cost software options provide many of the needed recording, editing, and some filtering capabilities. More expensive software provides more capabilities to filter out background noises, combine multiple files, add sound effects, convert formats, change compression rates, et cetera.

Audacity is a popular free program for people to start with, as it provides most features needed for the beginner who is recording and editing podcasts. Audacity is free, open source software that is available in Windows, Mac, and Linux formats. For the Mac, GarageBand is included with the iLife suite of programs. Just like Audacity, one can record and edit audio and even have multiple tracks for additional voices and background music. Other podcasting software applications currently range in price from $60 to $150, include ProfCast, RecordForAll, and Adobe Audition (King, & Gura, 2009; Lafferty & Walch, 2006).

Posting the Podcast

Three small steps remain in the process of creating a podcast: posting the MP3 audio file to the Internet, creating an XML feed, and posting the

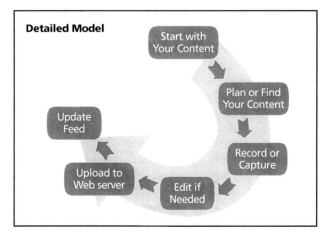

Figure 3.3 Detailed model for podcasting development. Created by Kathleen P. King, 2009.

XML file on the Internet. These steps are represented in the comprehensive figure that reveals the details of producing podcasts, Figure 3.3.

Once an MP3 file is created, faculty need to post the file on an Internet server so that students can access it. It can be posted simply inside an online learning community (e.g., Blackboard, Angel, Desire2Learn) or on a dedicated server (such as university server space, Libsyn.com, Blubrry.com, or iTunes University). If one uses a dedicated podcast service, the system might create and post the XML feed automatically. For instance, Podomatic.com, Libsyn.com, and Bluberry.com perform these functions. However, if instructors post the file separately on a university server, they will have to create the XML file using software or hand coding it. When completed, the feed is uploaded as well (King, & Gura, 2009; Lafferty & Walch, 2006).

Once all the steps are completed, students can subscribe to the RSS feed and receive automatic updates when new podcasts are posted. Alternatively, they can visit the class learning site or Web page where the files are posted and manually check for new content.

COPYRIGHT AND LEGAL ISSUES IN PODCASTING

When it comes to the use of podcasting in education, one area of stark difference that needs to be noticed and addressed is in Fair Use. A common error among educators is to apply the same Fair Use principles for classroom use of media to podcasting. This is not correct. Podcasting is a part of the new field of digital media, which has continued to transform copyright, patent, and intellectual property practices and laws (Lafferty & Walch, 2006; Vogele,

Garlick, & The Berkman Center, 2009). Therefore, it is of utmost importance to have current knowledge of what is allowed. This is not difficult, and a few guidelines will keep you on safe ground. First of all, however, the most current and definitive guide on the topic is *The Legal Guide to Podcasting* (Vogele, Garlick, & The Berkman Center, 2009). This document is continually updated and always available for free in PDF format.

As for basic guidelines, the trickiest areas are permissions. Whether one is including music, voice, or sound effects, the podcaster has to have permission to use that material. Including even 5 seconds of a song from a CD is not permitted unless it is copyright free or Creative Commons share. Therefore, instructional podcasters will do best to become familiar with online resources for free or inexpensive royalty-free and copyright-free sound files that are searchable and available. Caution is advised with most of such databases available online, as they are prime targets for distributing malicious software. Therefore, following is a list of resources that are reputable.

Music
- IodaPromoNet (http://www.iodapromonet.com/)
- Free Sound (http://www.freesound.org/)
- Freeplay Music (http://www.freeplaymusic.com/)

Sound Effects
- Freesounds (http://www.freesound.org/)
- Sound Dogs (http://www.sounddogs.com/)

When having students create podcasts for class assignments, the legal limitations are great examples of information literacy and changing requirements in laws that need to be discussed. Providing a list of resources and agreement to follow legitimate practices will safeguard the instructor's responsibility as well.

HOW TO GET STARTED

Following are several suggested questions to assist professors planning to use podcasts with their classes. By answering these questions, faculty will have a clearer vision of the types of podcasts they could best pursue using, creating, or assigning.

1. Consider the content and discipline you teach:
   a. Where are your students' prominent learning needs?
   b. What course areas could benefit from deeper student inquiry, analysis, and thought?

    c. Consider short-term and long-term benefits of creating your personal instructional archive. For example, if you create one or two podcasts per semester, after 1 year you will have 4, and after 2 years, 8 podcasts to use in those classes forever. For which class does it seem reasonable to develop this approach?

    d. Regarding equipment, start inexpensive and small until you gain sufficient confidence and see the benefits with your classes. This is a wise cost-benefit approach that is less risky and more appealing to faculty and administrators.

2. Your readiness:

    a. Would you like to start with pre-recorded podcasts, such as interviews, original news clips, or recordings from professional conferences?

    b. Do you feel comfortable creating instructional podcasts to assist your students?

    c. Would you like to develop student assignments that incorporate podcast development?

3. Resources:

    a. Do you have a digital recorder available to record in-class content or conduct interviews?

    b. If your laptop does not have a microphone, consider borrowing one from the institution or purchasing an inexpensive integrated headset that provides private listening and recording.

    c. If you will assign podcast production to students, explore
- what audio recording resources are available on campus for student use or loan,
- inexpensive digital recorders you can purchase and have students sign out, and
- student group projects in which groups are self-selected on the basis of one member having an available computer.

4. Design your podcasts: Prioritize the following items for your podcast design projects:

    a. Chunk and subdivide content for instructional podcasts so that they are shorter, critical sections of the course work.

    b. Create tutorial and FAQ materials that will reduce repetitive demands on you and provide immediate assistance through on-demand content for students.

    c. Design instructional assignments that include student-created podcasts. Include clear assignment description, brief instructions for podcast production (found on the Web), and a rubric by which the assignment will be evaluated.

d. Develop a means to evaluate your instructional use of podcasting so that your practice can continually improve. Suggestions include paper or online surveys, class discussions, or reflective essays/journals from students about the benefits and drawbacks of the instructional aids.

Podcasting Resources Online

The *Podcasting Help* page from The Teachers' Podcast (http://teacherspodcast.org/podcasting-help/) includes free tutorials and links to software and resources, including the following:

- Audacity (Mac, Windows, Linux): http://audacity.sourceforge.net/
- ProfCast (Mac, Windows): http://www.profcast.com/
- RecordForAll (PC only): http://www.recordforall.com/
- Adobe Audition (Mac, Windows): http://www.adobe.com/products/audition/

REFERENCES

Bluestein, G. (2006, March 19). *Georgia college pushes for iPod ingenuity.* Retrieved from http://www.msmc.la.edu/include/learning_resources/emerging_technologies/podcasting/georgia_college_ipod.pdf

Brevy Cannon, H. (2006, December 13). *Podcast project inspires engineering students to think big. UVA Today.* Retrieved November 23, 2009, from http://www.virginia.edu/uvatoday/newsRelease.php?id=1202

Enriquez, J. (2001). *As the future catches you: How genomics and other forces are changing your life, work, health and wealth.* New York: Three Rivers Press.

Evans, C. (2008). The effectiveness of m-learning in the form of podcast revision lectures in higher education. *Computers & Education, 50,* 491–498.

Evans, L. (2006). *Using student podcasts in literature classes.* Retrieved November 20, 2009 from http://www.academiccommons.org/ctfl/vignette/using-student-podcasts-in-literature-classes

Felix, L., & Stolarz, D. (2006). *Hands-on guide to video blogging and podcasting.* New York: Elsevier.

Frydenberg, M. (2008). Principles and pedagogy: The two Ps of podcasting in the information technology classroom. *Information Systems Education Journal, 6*(6), 1–11. Retrieved from http://isedj.org/6/6/

Geoghegan, M. W., & Klass, D. (2005). *Podcast solutions: The complete guide to podcasting.* New York: Friends of Fred.

Gould, J. C., Langford, N. G., & Mott, C. J. (1972). Earth science as an audio-tutorial course. *Journal of Geological Education, 20,* 81–83.

King, K. P. (2009). Empowerment and voice: Digital media. In M. Miller & K. P. King (Eds.), *Empowering women through literacy* (pp. 271–280). Charlotte, NC: Information Age Publishing.

King, K. P., & Gura, M. (2009). *Podcasting for teachers: Using a new technology to revolutionize teaching and learning* (Rev. 2nd ed.). Charlotte, NC: Information Age Publishing.

Lafferty, M., & Walch, R. (2006). *Tricks of the podcasting masters.* New York: Que.

Lave, J., & Wenger, E. (1991). *Situated learning.* Cambridge, UK: Cambridge University Press.

Lee, M. J. W., & Chan, A. (2007). Reducing the effects of isolation and promoting inclusivity for distance learners through podcasting. *Turkish Online Journal of Distance Education, 8*(1), 85–103.

Vogele, C., Garlick, M., & The Berkman Center (2009). *The podcasting legal guide.* Retrieved December 1, 2009, from http://wiki.creativecommons.org/Podcasting_Legal_Guide

Wright, J., & Kelly, R. (1974). Cheating: Student/faculty views and responsibility. *Improving College & University Teaching, 22*, 31–34.

CHAPTER 4

USING ONLINE ASYNCHRONOUS AUDIO COMMUNICATION IN HIGHER EDUCATION

Jody Oomen-Early
Walden University

Mary Bold
American College of Education

Tara Gallien
Northwestern State University

INTRODUCTION

Use of technology in teaching and learning has become more than just a trend in higher education—it is now a permanent fixture, especially for institutions that are attempting to meet the needs of global learners and are striving for growth in perilous economic times. The issue now is not whether technologies can be effective; it is how to ensure that the *quality* of education is not compromised. Regardless of the percentage of a course that may be conducted online or through the use of technology, faculty still prefer to teach face-to-face because they perceive that they are more capable of connecting with their students and assessing their understanding of content in

The Professor's Guide to Taming Technology, pages 51–65
Copyright © 2011 by Information Age Publishing
All rights of reproduction in any form reserved.

a traditional setting (Allen & Seaman, 2006; Oomen-Early, Bold, Wiginton, Gallien, & Anderson, 2008; Oomen-Early & Murphy, 2009). Reducing the emotional distance between instructors and students requires an evolving set of teaching skills that embrace Web 2.0 technologies.

The new generation of Web 2.0 technologies includes a number of interactive tools and applications that connect people more effectively online and allow them to share information, ideas, and opinions almost instantaneously, either synchronously (live) or asynchronously (not simultaneous). Some of these tools include discussion boards, instant messaging, text and video blogs, wikis, video casts (vodcasts), Web conferencing, podcasts, social networking, and *asynchronous audio communication* (AAC). This chapter will overview some of the current theoretical and practical applications of AAC as well as highlight best practices and potential uses.

ASYNCHRONOUS AUDIO COMMUNICATION

AAC is the use of delayed (not simultaneous) digital audio technology to deliver verbal communication through a computer. The growing interest in AAC may, in part, be in response to the concern that text-based communication alone is not sufficient to create social presence. In preliminary studies, AAC has been shown to be an effective instructional strategy capable of enhancing teaching presence, fostering collaboration, increasing interactivity, boosting students' sense of community and connectedness, and increasing retention of course material (Ice, Curtis, Wells, & Phillips, 2007; Oomen-Early et al., 2008). Certainly, in a time of deep financial cutbacks and administrative concerns about institutional effectiveness, efforts to improve e-learning are a priority for many universities and colleges because of the ability of e-learning to increase student enrollment and retain students.

As noted above, the use of audio in online instruction is showing great promise. Yet it is not surprising that the majority of instructors continue to primarily utilize text-based, computer-mediated communication in the online components of their courses. By all accounts, this type of communication is easy to develop and does not typically require additional training by faculty. Moreover, it is supported by Learning Management Systems (LMS), such as Blackboard, eCollege, and Angel.

Pedagogical and Theoretical Foundation of AAC

Teaching and learning in an environment separated by space and time require a new set of skills and practices for both instructor and learner. At the center of this paradigm shift is the transition from instructor-centered to student-centered learning strategies. For many faculty, this shift away from oral dialogue and nonverbal cues toward a dependence on written communication poses a challenge for faculty who are not used to teaching online (Oomen-Early & Murphy, 2009; Picciano, 2002).

There are a number of learning theories applicable to Web-based learning, but perhaps the theory best known, most commonly used in online course design, and most applicable to using AAC is Bloom's Taxonomy of Learning Domains. Bloom (1956) introduced this theory in the 1950s and proposed that there were three different types of learning: cognitive, psychomotor, and affective.

Cognitve Domain. The cognitive domain involves knowledge and reasoning. It includes the recall, comprehension, or recognition of specific facts, patterns, and concepts that serve in the development of intellectual abilities and skills. Bloom categorized cognitive abilities into six main categories: *knowledge, comprehension, application, analysis, synthesis,* and *evaluation.* In 2001, Anderson and Krathwohl revised the taxonomy with these terms: *remembering, understanding, applying, analyzing, evaluating,* and *creating.* Both versions can be applied to learners' need to successfully sift, order, and make sense of volumes of information relayed to them within a short amount of time. As shown in Table 4.1, online teaching strategies often used to improve cogni-

---

TABLE 4.1   Application of Bloom's Expanded Learning Domains and Instructional Strategies

Learning Domain	Online Instructional Strategies and Tools
Cognitive	Self-checks; quizzes; exams; drill and practice; case studies; essay; class projects; AAC to provide information and feedback; cognitive mapping; case studies; debates; audio and video clips to inform; slide presentations and productions (e.g., Camtasia, Otomoto); virtual mapping (e.g., Google Earth)
Affective	Audio and video clips; graphics and photos; blogs; personal narratives; pod and vodcasts; digital story telling; guest speakers and interviews; goal-setting; AAC to provide testimonials, personal experiences, and positive reinforcement
Psychomotor	Drill and practice; simulations; virtual worlds (e.g., Second Life); sequencing and ordering activities; AAC to provide directions; video or audio clips showing demonstrations; "how-to" graphics and photos; fieldwork to apply and practice skills and competencies
Interpersonal	Structured team projects with team building and problem solving; audio and video clips; peer review; wikis; instant messaging; text messaging; social bookmarking; discussion boards; AAC to provide individual and group messages; chats and webcasts; blogs and video blogs; social networking (e.g., Ning, Facebook); synchronous and asynchronous debates; digital story telling; virtual worlds (e.g., Second Life)

tive development include graphics to show relationships between ideas, organized class notes, tables providing summary information, quizzes, drill and practice exercises, PowerPoint presentations, and Flash animations.

Psychomotor Domain. The psychomotor domain involves physical movement and motor skills. Development of these abilities require hands-on, tactile experiential strategies. Strategies for e-learning may include drill and practice, self-checks and quizzes, online or face-to-face simulations (for hybrid courses), arranging sequencing of activities in order, video or audio clips showing demonstrations, and fieldwork (Table 4.1).

Affective Domain. The affective domain involves feelings and attitudes. Smith and Ragan (1999) asserted that "any 'cognitive' or 'psychomotor' objective has some affective component to it…" (p. 253). Krathwohl, Bloom, and Masia (1964) proposed that learning, retention, and intrinsic motivation is positively impacted when learners are emotionally engaged. Over the last few years, the literature has underscored the need for humanizing e-learning environments and creating more "affective" online classrooms (Ice et al., 2007; Oomen-Early & Burke, 2007; Oomen-Early et al., 2008; Palloff & Pratt, 1999, 2003; Richardson & Swan, 2003). As shown in Table 4.1, teaching strategies focusing on the affective domain of learning include video, audio, and graphics to enhance concepts and meaning; reflective essay responses; blogs and videoblogs (*vlogs*), which allow learners to express themselves and share their own values and experiences; and guest presentations and interviews to examine diverse worldviews and lived experiences.

Interpersonal Domain. Bloom's (1956) learning domains have been expanded in recent years to include the "social" or "interpersonal" learning domain (Victorian Curriculum & Assessment Authority, 2008). Interpersonal development also encourages learning by allowing individuals to receive feedback from others on their ideas and to debate, analyze, and process course content. The interpersonal domain is not best handled with just text on a screen, but with interactive online tools and strategies. As outlined in Table 4.1, online teaching strategies that employ the interpersonal domain include discussion forums, text messaging, AAC, wikis, blogs and vlogs, digital video hosted by sites such as Youtube and Teachertube, digital photos hosted on sharing services such as Flickr or Photobucket, webcasts, podcasts, instant messaging, social bookmarking, satellite mapping such as Googlemaps, and virtual worlds such as Second Life (just to name a few!).

The theory of *social presence* (i.e., "being there") also supports the need for integrating more interactive tools (Biocca & Harms, 2002; Dettmer, 2006; Richardson & Swan, 2003). The range of interactive Web 2.0 tools differ in their ability to create a sense of social engagement and connect the instructor to the learner and the learners to each other. Therefore, through use and experimentation with AAC, instructors and Web designers can best decide upon the best application of this technology according to the content and scope of the course as well as the needs, abilities, and resources available to the instructor and the students.

Use and Best Practice of AAC

AAC can be used for a variety of purposes, including expounding on course content, providing individualized and collective feedback to students, and transmitting peer feedback and critique. Instructors may use AAC to prepare instructional messages or "lecturettes" to coincide and expand upon course material. Unlike podcasts, which usually involve a live feed and are available to an audience beyond the courseroom, AAC enables the instructor to post individual audio files in asynchronous format within the privacy of the online course or through email. Furthermore, AAC can work with the most basic of internet connections, unlike video casts, which may require high speed or fiber optic connections. AAC files can also be saved, transferred, and retrieved on portable devices such as cell phones or MP3 players. The audio files are best if saved in MP3 format, which is currently the smallest format for audio compression. Usually, AAC messages are short (under five minutes) to ensure that the file size can be saved and uploaded to the online course or delivered through email. Multiple messages can be created if necessary. Figure 4.1 illustrates how these audio files may be used within a LMS such as Blackboard.

Dr. Early's Audio Welcome Message!
Attached Files
<u>audio welcome click here</u> **(1.638 MB)**

Attached is my audio welcome message for you in Mp3 format. You don't need a Mp3 player to hear this message, but you may need to download Quicktime or Realplayer (for free) if you do not have Windows Media Player installed on your computer. Before clicking on the file link, be sure your speakers are working and your volume is up (and not on mute). I will be leaving you AUDIO as well as text based feedback this semester. ☺

Please let me know if you could not hear the message.
*Note: For those that would like a written transcript of this message, please email me.

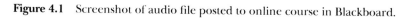

Figure 4.1   Screenshot of audio file posted to online course in Blackboard.

Audio recordings can be created in several different ways. Instructors can create the most basic of audio messages (without editing abilities) using a personal computer and a headset or microphone with common software such as MS Office for PC or Mac. In addition, many cell phones, video cameras, and portable MP3 players and pens (emerging innovation) include audio-recording capabilities.

Directions for creating an audio file using a PC with MS Windows are relayed in Figure 4.2. If instructors want more sophisticated audio recording and editing software, programs such as Audacity (http://www.audacity.com) or Wavepad can be downloaded from the Internet. Most of these programs offer some type of trial use. Software review Web sites such as http://audio-editing-software-review.toptenreviews.com rank some of the most popular audio-editing software available and can be helpful in determining which program to purchase. These files can be transferred or emailed directly from the phone to the computer or email.

Finally, more expensive software programs such as Adobe Acrobat Pro versions 7–9 also have audio capabilities. Audio messages can be created and embedded directly into a document. An icon is embedded to alert students to click on the audio message. The document is sent to the students in PDF format. Students need not purchase the full Adobe software to listen to the message; they can simply open the document in Adobe Acrobat Reader (which is free) and listen to the audio feedback as they click on the designated icons. Figure 4.4 illustrates how this embedded feedback looks, with an icon of a speaker indicating where the student should click.

Even though online learning has existed for decades, only recently have researchers begun to investigate the complex role that instructor feedback plays in online education (Ice et al., 2007; Kim, 2005; Oomen-Early et al., 2008). Recent findings have shown that online learners' levels of satisfac-

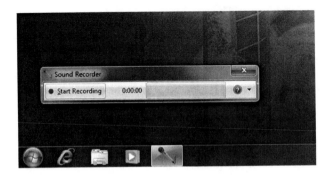

Figure 4.2 Directions for creating an audio message using MS Windows and MS Office.

Steps for Audio and Sound Recording with Microsoft Windows

1. Make sure your headset with microphone or your microphone is plugged into your computer.
2. Check to see that the volume on your headset or microphone is not set to mute or too low. If so, the sound quality will be compromised.
3. Go to the "Start" button on your computer.
4. Go to "All Programs."
5. Scroll up to "Accessories."
6. Click on "Sound Recorder."
7. When chosen, a recording box will appear (see Figure 4.2).
8. Click on the record button.
9. Record your message. Try not to go past 5 minutes or the file may be too large for uploading to your LMS or for sending via email. If you need to compose lengthier feedback, you may need to break up your message into separate files.
10. Press "Stop Recording" and then click "Play" to listen to your message.
11. If you are okay with the message, name and save your file.
12. Your file will be saved in WAV format and can be uploaded onto a course management system (such as Blackboard) or downloaded and transferred onto an MP3 player or other device that plays WAV files. You can also listen to audio files on your computer if you have Windows Media Player or another type of media player compatible with WAV formats.
13. When finished, close Sound Recorder.

Figure 4.3   Steps for digital recording.

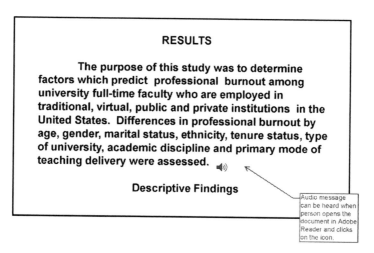

Figure 4.4   Example of embedded audio comment in a PDF document.

tion, performance, and sense of community are related to the interactions they have with their instructors, including the type and frequency of feedback they receive on assignments and course material (Gallien & Oomen-Early, 2008; Woods & Baker, 2004). Until recently, researchers have examined text-based feedback only. The nature of this type of feedback (i.e., lack of verbal and nonverbal information) challenges an important factor related to successful online learning: *social presence.* As mentioned previously, *social presence* refers to the degree to which individuals perceive others to be real and present in the learning environment (Short, Williams, & Christie, 1976; Richardson & Swan, 2003). According to Richardson and Swan (2003), this perception of human presence is essential for students and faculty to develop personal relationships and communities online, which in turn appears to have a positive influence on learner satisfaction and performance (Newberry, 2001; Richardson & Swan, 2003).

In the immediate wake of all of these developments are the big question marks: Could use of this technology (AAC) contribute to more interpersonal online classrooms and enhance connectivity and collaboration between students and instructors? Can integration of AAC impact students' academic performance and motivation? Can use of it reduce course attrition? Emergent research, such as the case studies described below, is leaning toward the affirmative.

The Effectiveness of AAC: Case Studies

Ice et al. (2007) examined the use of AAC versus text-based-only feedback when used in seven asynchronous online classes. The instructors posted AAC in the form of WAV files created by using Audacity software as messages for the class in the discussion area of the classroom, and also sent individual messages containing feedback on assignments to individual students. The instructors sent 50% of feedback for each student in text-only format and the other 50% of feedback in the form of AAC. The researchers found that graduate online learners thought audio was far better than text-based in conveying nuance and helping students retain and apply course content. They also found that audio feedback positively influenced students' perceptions of the instructor as a caring individual. Audio communication also improved students' ability to apply course content to their written assignments as well as within the discussion area of the class. Although audio feedback was perceived to be an effective tool, students still liked text-based feedback as well. A blend of both the audio and the text-based could be ideal.

In another study, Gallien and Oomen-Early (2008) examined student satisfaction and performance through the use of two different forms of feedback—personalized and collective (e.g., entire class)—and determined that students were more satisfied and performed better when they received *personalized* feedback. Although Gallien and Oomen-Early (2008) found that AAC was actually *not* time saving in their study, they did find that it had a positive impact on overall student retention, engagement, and academic outcomes.

Yet another case study by Oomen-Early et al. (2008) examined use of AAC in both graduate and undergraduate online courses and across academic disciplines. MP3 audio files were used by the instructors to provide feedback and instruction within graduate and undergraduate online courses in the areas of reading, health education, and family studies across a 9-month period for 156 students. Instructors sent out both group and individual audio communication, followed by an online survey. Descriptive, inferential, and qualitative data analyses demonstrated that the majority of students and instructors reported that AAC improved online students' perceptions of instructor presence, student engagement, knowledge of course content, and instructor–student interaction.

Though instructors can express themselves and their emotions through text-based communication, 88.5% ($n = 132$) students in this study mentioned that they liked the way they were able to catch the nuances provided in the instructor's audio messages. This study did not find any statistically significant differences in responses according to level of education (undergraduate versus graduate). The great majority, 91% ($n = 142$), of the students found AAC to improve their understanding of course content, and 82.4% ($n = 106$) believed that it improved the instructor–student relationship.

Designing Accessible Online Classrooms

When designing Web-based content and choosing any interactive tool, it is imperative to think about accessibility. A learner who has a hearing impairment or who is completely deaf must be able to access a written transcript for any audio content posted to learning Web sites you require as part of readings and assignments, and must be able to access real-time text captioning for audio, video, and multimedia content you post within the online class. A written transcript can be provided for any audio content posted as long as it does not violate copyright laws; however, Crow (2008) strongly warns that, "it is important to remember . . . that under Section 508 law, a printed version of the text does not substitute for real-time captioning" (p. 52).

Before creating AAC, instructors may choose to type the script, which can then be used with closed caption software. Software such as Dragon Naturally Speaking provides audio transcription for audio content that was not originally typed. However, this software is not 100% accurate, so editing is necessary. It is also important to consider the needs of students whose native language is not English; these students may feel more comfortable reading content rather than relying on audio content. Having a written transcript or audio captions can be helpful for them as well.

More Applications and the Future of AAC

Adoption of ACC is largely dependent on instructor interest and technical proficiency at this point. Primary use has been as instructor feedback to students, either individually or as a class. Some additional uses for AAC may include:

- Audio-based exams for vocabulary and language-building courses such as medical terminology or Spanish
- Practice exercises, assignments, exams, and performances for students enrolled in music courses
- Detailed individualized feedback on students' course papers and projects
- Feedback on graduate students' theses and dissertations, both in specific parts of the manuscript and in overall comments (for an entire chapter, for example)
- Narration for training materials, especially as audio clips embedded alongside screenshots of a computer application
- Narration for assignment guides, including audio clips embedded alongside screenshots of the student's Blackboard course interface
- Narration in electronic portfolios
- Narration of course syllabi
- Student use of AAC as part of a course project, discussion, assignment, or as an oral component of an exam
- Archiving of student discussion groups or field notes

As mentioned in this chapter, the most common methods today for AAC are dedicated audio software (such as Audacity or Wavepad) and recording embedded audio directly in documents (using Adobe Acrobat Pro). The current technologies require the initiative of the instructor to locate software and produce the feedback clips in usable format.

Future adoption by more educators will be a function of the increasing number of embedded tools in learning management systems as well as educators' increasing familiarity with communication technologies. As mentioned earlier, more and more, course management systems such as Blackboard have begun to integrate extra tools such as wikis and blogs in learning management systems. When additions (sometimes called *Building Blocks*) are included in campus systems, they enjoy exposure to faculty members and are usually adopted gradually over time. Other current technologies (for example, the Web-based Voicethread) that are user-friendly and low-cost also spread across a campus or faculty group. Their use for feedback to students is powerful because of the ease of access.

Similarly, a Web-based video can be highly accessible (and free) through interfaces such as YouTube. Either displayed publicly or password-protected, a video clip can be watched online or downloaded. For the instructor and learner who prefer direct transfer of files, that can take place through email or through embedded videos in the more expensive software, Adobe Acrobat.

An enhanced version of AAC is possible through platforms such as Adobe Connect, WebEx, and Elluminate. If the institution does not subscribe to such a platform, individual instructors (and learners) can secure their own free spaces (such as Elluminate vRoom) or low-cost spaces (such as vOffice), although these limit the number of "seats" in the virtual meeting space. These desktop sharing applications permit the recording of audio with document display and document manipulation. An instructor can create a webinar to display a student's manuscript, mark it with text or drawing, and simultaneously speak to it. By saving or archiving the webinar, the instructor's feedback can be preserved for student viewing at any time. A great advantage of the webinar platform is that the recording resides on a server for access any time. (For privacy, access can be set to require a password.) Thus, neither the instructor nor the student is burdened with email or storage restrictions based on file size. If this feedback method enjoys institutional support, the storage also may serve the institution's need by providing an archive of course work and documentation of student works and even documentation of instructional effectiveness.

Vision and Further Development

Further development of AAC is likely to incorporate technology emerging as rich Internet applications (RIAs), social networking environments, and possibly virtual worlds such as Second Life. At least as we understand emerging technologies today, little in the way of communication will fail to be influenced by these developments. Whether predicted as extensions of Web 2.0 or as qualitatively different Web 3.0, new technologies are inevitable.

To propose one possibility for AAC, we can look to Google's 2009 introduction of Wave. The Google engineers asked themselves, "What would email look like if it were invented now, instead of 30 years ago?" Their answer was still Google-like, building on the well-accepted conversation model of Gmail. The evolution of email in Wave took the conversation and put it at the center of correspondents, not as an extension from one emailer sending to another emailer. Translating that model for AAC, we might expect that the audio feedback will be not just "sent" from instructor to student but genuinely shared with the option of response embedded in the audio. This model also matches our expectation for growth in online social networks. Social networks, whether text-based or residing in immersive environments (such as Second Life and other virtual worlds), clearly permit conversation and collaboration.

Resources for Creating AAC

Technology continues to evolve rapidly; therefore, by the time you read this chapter, another wave of widgets, Web sites, tools, and innovations not mentioned here will have emerged. However, some of the most commonly used tools are described in Table 4.2. New versions will be available, and exploring these will lead to more innovations for years to come.

Using AAC: Practice Exercises

These exercises introduce instructors and students to the use of AAC. They are listed in order of complexity, beginning with the simplest application.

1. Create a short audio welcome message to your class (under 3 minutes in length). Upload your audio file (in WAV or MP3 format) to the online courseroom. Be sure to include a written transcript as well. This task may be assigned to everyone in the class as an icebreaker and/or to introduce the use of audio.
2. Create a 250-word (about 1 page double spaced) introduction for one of your online learning modules in MS Word or using another word processing software. Save the file as a PDF file. Open the file in Adobe Acrobat Pro (v. 7 or higher) and use the Record Audio command to begin recording. Read the manuscript page, being careful to match your words with the printed page. Students will be able to open the PDF file using Adobe Acrobat Reader (free download) and listen to the audio recording by clicking on the designated icon.
3. Create an audio clip to accompany your course syllabus, either reading the entire syllabus or just sections about assignments or assessments. In the screen/print version of the syllabus, indicate that an audio version is also available. In the audio version, clearly identify the passage as relating to the syllabus (e.g., "As noted in Section 4 of the syllabus...").
4. Provide individual feedback on a student's work by recording an audio file that details the strengths and areas to improve and sending the student the audio file via email or upload it through your Web-based course space.

TABLE 4.2 Software and Freeware for Creating AAC

Product	Cost	Where to Find	Characteristics/Comments
Adobe Acrobat Pro (v. 7 and higher)	Free to try; $99 to $159 to buy	www.adoble.com and online retailers such as www.academicsuperstore.com; or www. softwaresurplus.com	Creates and transforms documents into PDF format; provides advanced editing features such as embedded audio comments.
MS Office Professional (audio recorder)	Free with purchase of MS Office	Included with MS Windows and MS Office products or by going to http://www.microsoft.com	Simple sound recorder that produces WAV audio files; does not allow for editing.
Audacity	Free; open-source	http://audacity.sourceforge.net	Easy to use, free audio recorder and editor; import and export files; cut, copy, and splice sounds together; and other sophisticated editing functions
Wavepad	Free to try; Older versions free; new, upgrades are $49.40 to buy	http://www.nch.com.au/wavepad/masters.html or http://www.brothersoft.com/wavepad-sound-editor-134629.html	Create and edit audio and music files; designed for easy and intuitive use; other sophisticated editing functions.
Record Pad	Free to try; $38.20 to buy	NCH software Web site at http://www.nch.com.au/recordpad/index.html or other Web sites that offer free beta, older, or trail versions such as http://www.download-cnet.com or http://www.freedownloadcenter.com	Sound recording software that allows you to hear text in natural-sounding voices, record music, or other audio; reads text files; voice activated; allows for sound editing; paste in text from any source; see words highlighted as spoken; simple to use.
Audio MP3 WAV WMA Converter	Free to try; $19.95 to buy	http://www.audio-converter.com	Converts audio files into different formats such as WAV to MP3, WAV to Ogg, and WAV to WMA. Very easy to use and interface is attractive.
AbleReader	Free to try; $49.95 to buy	http://www.ablereader.com	Converts text to audio so a person can listen as they read along. Customize voice tone and style or use ones included.

REFERENCES

Allen, E. I., & Seaman, J. (2006). *Making the grade: Online education in the United States, 2006*. Needham, MA: The Sloan Consortium. Retrieved from http://sloanconsortium.org/sites/default/files/Making_the_Grade.pdf

Anderson, L. W., & Krathwohl, D. R. (Eds.). (2001). *A taxonomy for learning, teaching and assessing: A revision of Bloom's taxonomy of educational objectives.* New York: Longman.

Biocca, F., & Harms, C. (2002). What is social presence? In F. Gouveia & F. Biocca (Eds.), *Presence 2002 Proceedings* (pp. 7–36). Porto, Portugal: University of Fernando Pessoa Press.

Bloom, B. S. (1956). *Taxonomy of educational objectives, the classification of educational goals—Handbook I: The cognitive domain.* New York: David McKay.

Crow, K. L. (Jan/Feb, 2008). Four types of disabilities: Their impact on higher learning. *TechTrends, 52*(1), 51–55.

Dettmer, P. (2006, January 1). New blooms in established fields: Four domains of learning and doing. *The Free Library.* Retrieved from http://www.thefreelibrary.com/New%20blooms%20in%20established%20fields:%20four%20domains%20of%20learning%20and%20doing.-a0141755392

Gallien, T., & Oomen-Early, J. (2008). Personalized versus collective instructor feedback in the online courseroom: Does type of feedback affect student satisfaction, academic performance and perceived connectedness with the instructor? *International Journal of E-Learning, 7, 3.*

Ice, P., Curtis, R., Wells, J., & Phillips, P. (2007). Using asynchronous audio feedback to enhance teaching presence and student sense of community. *Journal of Asynchronous Learning Networks, 11*(2), 3–25.

Kim, E. (2005). The effects of digital audio on social presence, motivation and perceived learning in asynchronous learning networks (doctoral dissertation, New Jersey Institute of Technology). *Dissertations & Theses: Full Text.* Publication No. AAT 3221738.

Krathwohl, D. R., Bloom, B. S., & Masia, B. B. (1964). *Taxonomy of educational objectives, handbook II: Affective domain.* New York: McKay.

Newberry, B. (2001). Raising student social presence in online classes. In W. Fowler & J. Hasebrook (Eds.), *Proceedings of Webnet 2001 World Conference on the WWW and Internet* (pp. 905–910), Orlando, FL. Norfolk, VA: Association for the Advancement of Computing in Education (AACE).

Oomen-Early, J., & Murphy, L. (2009). *Self-actualization and e-learning: A qualitative investigation of university faculty's perceived barriers to effective online instruction.* International Journal on E-Learning, 8(2), 223–240.

Oomen-Early, J., Bold, M., Wiginton, K. L., Gallien, T. L., & Anderson, N. (2008). Using asynchronous audio communication (AAC) in the online classroom: A comparative study. *MERLOT Journal of Online Learning and Teaching, 4*(3), 267–276.

Oomen-Early, J., & Burke, S. (2007). Entering the blogosphere: Blogs as teaching and learning tools in health education. *International Electronic Journal of Health Education, 10,* 186–196.

Palloff, R. M., & Pratt, K. (1999). *Building learning communities in cyberspace: Effective strategies for the online classroom.* San Francisco: Jossey-Bass.

Palloff, R. M., & Pratt, K. (2003). *The virtual student: A profile and guide to working with online learners.* San Francisco: Jossey-Bass.

Picciano, A. (2002). Beyond student perceptions: Issues of interaction, presence, and performance in an online course. *Journal of Asynchronous Learning Networks, 6*(1), 21–40.

Richardson, J., & Swan, K. (2002). Examining social presence in online courses in relation to students' perceived learning and satisfaction. *Journal of Asynchronous Learning Networks, 6*(1), 68–88.

Short, J., Williams, E., & Christie, B. (1976). *The social psychology of telecommunications.* Toronto, ON: Wiley.

Smith, P.L. & Ragan, T. J. (1999). *Instructional design* (2nd ed.). Upper Saddle River, NJ: Merrill.

Victorian Curriculum and Assessment Authority (VCAA). (2008). *Victorian essential learning standards: Interpersonal development: Physical, personal, and social learning strand.* Melbourne, Australia: Author.

Woods, R. H., & Baker, J. D. (2004). Interaction and immediacy in online learning. *The International Review of Research in Open and Distance Learning, 5*(2). Retrieved from http://www.irrodl.org/index.php/irrodl/article/view/186/268

CHAPTER 5

VIDEO DEVELOPMENT AND INSTRUCTIONAL USE

Simple and Powerful Options

Kathleen P. King
University of South Florida

Thomas D. Cox
University of Houston–Victoria

INTRODUCTION

How many of the following YouTube videos have you seen?

Pop Culture Scorecard

- ☐ The wedding where everyone danced down the aisle, including much improvisation and even a handstand (TheKHeinz, 2009).
- ☐ The reunion of the wild lion and owner in Africa (PFW21, 2008).
- ☐ Amateur video being used on the nightly news.
- ☐ YouTube videos being played on a mainstream TV show (talk show, game show, entertainment show, etc.).
- ☐ A cat doing silly things on a YouTube video.

Figure 5.1   Every person as video creator. (Image is from TheKHeinz, 2009).

☐ People singing badly on a YouTube video.
☐ People who became famous through a YouTube video (e.g., Allsopp, 2008; daichibeatboxer, 2009).

In the spring of 2010, YouTube turned 5 years old. It is hard to comprehend how young the site is because of its widespread domination of not only new media, but also the Internet, traditional media, and our daily lives. As illustrated in Figure 5.1, not only has video become a currency of communication and self-expression, but it has become the expected media for communicating the value of business, services, products, and learning.

Today, higher education students of all ages are accustomed to accessing news and entertainment; sharing their opinions, gossip, and memories; and seeking information via video and other instant digital media forms. However, in general, when these same digitally savvy adults enter colleges and universities, they find all-too-often that their classes are void of opportunities to use or create digital video.

Today, as faculty, the opportunities are stacked in our advantage to successfully use digital video in instruction. Why? Because digital video is

• easy and quick to create,
• inexpensive to produce,

- efficient for faculty to incorporate into their usual routines,
- and highly effective as learning media.

The power of digital video as learning media is seen in several traits that have been elusive previously. Today, digital media affords the capability to develop instructional materials that are

- available on demand (24 hours a day, 7 days a week);
- able to be retrieved an infinite number of times;
- able to incorporate visual and audio learning styles;
- able to serve the needs of both teacher-centered and self-directed students;
- able to integrate interdisciplinary study, research, critical thinking; project-based learning, and other 21st Century Learning skills (see Chapter 2) when planned appropriately;
- and able to afford consistent delivery of core content.

This chapter provides an overview of some ways most higher education faculty can begin to use digital video immediately in their classes. It is designed and written with technical novices in mind. No prior knowledge of video applications, terms, and design is expected.

Moreover, this chapter provides a dynamic foundation for leveraging popular media and video to make instructional efforts more effective at engaging students and building greater student responsibility for learning, helping them learn to construct knowledge. By accomplishing these goals, faculty are both teaching content and cultivating learners who will continue to investigate their content area and grow and participate in the ever-changing world of knowledge development.

INSTRUCTIONAL USES OF DIGITAL VIDEO

Let us dive right in and consider how faculty might use digital video in their classrooms. Four major ways to think about them are the following:

- Integrating video into the course delivery.
- Video *as* course delivery.
- Assigning the creating of video presentations as student projects.
- Participating in live video exchange.

Integrated Video

When faculty integrate video into course delivery, they may use a number of different strategies and resources. For instance, this approach includes linking your class Web site or online learning class to digital video posted on the Web, or downloading it and posting it in your online space. Relevant digital videos of every nature may be found in many places on the Web, including YouTube.com, Vimeo.com, Teachertube.com, and Schooltube.com (see Figure 5.2).

It is essential to think beyond traditional contexts and consider that using digital video in our courses can mean that students watch the videos before or after a class session by following a Web site link in the content. Today, we use not just desktop and laptop computers, but also smart phones, iPhones, Blackberrys, netbooks, and iPads to view digital videos. On-demand access to online video therefore enables us to think beyond the walled spaces and assigned sections of traditional classes to flexible, mobile, and "just-in-time" learning and study opportunities. Considering these observations, reflect upon the "Point to Ponder" in Figure 5.3.

Equity and access are important considerations in instructional planning, and with digital video there are no barriers. Even if a student does not have useful Internet access, professors can have videos saved to DVDs or mobile devices. They can also have the audio "stripped" out of the video file and provide students with the audio portion for listening only.

Course Delivery

A very different instructional use of video is course delivery. Even in the 1990s, corporate America was using synchronous (same time) video connections to conduct meetings and delivery training across multiple locations simultaneously (Simonson, Simonson, Albright, & Zvacek, 2008). While, at that point in time, such technology usually required specialized and expensive ISDN lines, today there are many free or inexpensive tools to do the same via a broadband Internet connection.

With minimal effort, faculty can use simultaneous video connection for many powerful instructional purposes. Examples include:

- Including guest speakers in our campus classrooms without travel time or expenses.
- Efficiently facilitating remote group projects.
- Conducting "face-to-face" office hours with students at a distance, including with working or disabled students who cannot easily travel to campus.
- Examining current events, scientific discoveries, and onsite demonstrations of content areas as they occur.
- Hosting virtual field trips to near and remote locations without travel, liability, or additional time costs.

Figure 5.2   Online digital video directory sample: Vimeo.com.

Point to Ponder
Everday and Lifelong Learning

The higher education model which most of us experienced was one of separation, seclusion, silos and irrelevant to everyday life. In contrast, digital video is one example of a technology resource and media which traverses instruction and everyday living. Today we use it to see experts deliver addresses, watch current events as they happen, archive our toddlers and teens precious moments, and collaborate on multi-national projects. Access to vibrant informal and formal learning resources and opportunities is at an exponential growth phase.

Figure 5.3 Points to Ponder: Everyday and lifelong learning.

Yugma.com, Skype.com, and Dimdim.com are just a few of the free online video and learning platforms that I have used with success for instructional synchronous sessions with video (see Figure 5.4). Different online platforms have different features, and it may be that your college or university has a site license for a paid product such as Elluminate.com or WebEx.com available for your selection.

Student Projects

Beyond the capabilities of delivering instruction and dialogue via video, faculty can also leverage the ease of digital video creation by assigning video presentations as student projects. Such projects can be designed as capstone projects that demonstrate not only the students' understanding of the course content, but also its application to real-life situations. Project-based learning and presentation progress provide chances for content review, research, synthesizing learning, transfer of learning, and collaboration if structured in that way.

Many educators struggle with the assessment of group projects and presentations. However the literature reveals that it does not need to be difficult. The key is using a well-designed rubric. There are many benefits to using rubrics. Specifically, well-crafted rubrics afford greater student accountability and ownership through transparency of the grading system (King & Gura, 2009). They communicate the goals, purposes, and requirements of the assignment more completely, which results in better work, and they afford a more objective means to evaluate projects, group work, and creative works (Montgomery, 2002). The good news is that well-designed rubrics can be created simply and then revised for different projects within and across courses.

Figure 5.4   Yugma.com: Free and pro version Web conferencing.

Other Live Connections

The opportunities to connect in live video conferencing are limitless and growing every day as more features and types of technologies continue to be developed and released. Frequent, simple applications of live video for college classrooms include a variation of the traditional guest lecture. Instead of spending money on travel, rearranging your schedule as "host," and not being able to dedicate an entire class to one speaker, video conferencing affords a solution that is convenient, always available, and now easy to use. These expert guests can now conveniently visit, individually or as part of a panel. Your distance guest could also provide a virtual tour of their lab or site for a campus-based classroom. The benefits of students interacting with content area and practicing experts is indisputable. Being able to provide such quality discussions more frequently is a winning strategy.

Faculty can also use video conferencing in a very different way to provide more convenient and accessible office hours, virtually. In this case, professors could log into the private video space (which can include chat as well) to work with students individually or in small groups. Professors find that this format serves well in answering questions, solving problems, providing advising, or facilitating many other instructional and academic support functions. In a unique instructional approach, some faculty connect distant students to local classes with these same video and chat conference tools. Such hybrids of local and distant students in synchronous learning experiences enables all to participate in live presentations, participate in the dynamic verbal exchanges, ask questions, see student reactions, and view teacher and student presentations (Cherrstrom & King, 2010). The same free and paid systems listed above can be used for these purposes.

WINDOWS INTO INSTRUCTIONAL DIGITAL VIDEO

Bringing the Conference Experience to the Students

Dr. Lucy Zhang is presenting a paper in Latin America about the acceleration of cultural change experienced in China over the last 10 years. She knows her students in the International Cultural Transformations classes would have found the conference to be immensely beneficial, but the logistics and costs of conference fees and traveling were prohibitive for these undergraduates from rural communities.

Thankfully, a colleague had lent her a small digital video camera, much like the SONY Flip, for the journey. Lucy had been using the camera to take videos of the stunning beaches and colorful celebrations. However, she had spotted several people recording conference sessions. Her curiosity was piqued, and sure enough, she could buy a small tripod and attach the video camera to it. She asked some of the presenters for their permission to record them for her class use. They were gracious and pleased to support her efforts to "bring" this international experience in the content area into the classroom experience of her students.

Flash-forward 3 weeks. Dr. Zhang's next class will include showing segments of the conference videos. She has listed objectives and discussion questions to accompany the classroom viewing of the video clips. When she displays the videos with the usual LCD projector on the screen, the session is electrified with questions, discussion, and talk of future aspirations. Sharing relevant real-life examples with the classroom has been an invaluable experience in expanding the application of course content, worldview, global awareness, and professional scope of her students.

Technical resources needed: Portable digital video recorder ($45–$300), tripod ($1–$15)

Technical expertise level: Novice

Academic expertise: Varies by faculty criteria

The HullabaBuggy Race-off

The Hillsland College engineering students had to create a prototype 3-wheel rescue buggy that would be "green" (environmentally friendly), economically feasible, and able to endure rugged terrain driving conditions for

72 hours non-stop. They were provided with 2 boxes of raw materials at mid-semester and expected to draw a plan for, construct, and sufficiently test their final product to be able to compete in the HullabaBuggy Race-off.

Mr. Charles always found it challenging to accurately evaluate individual work on these extended group projects, but this year he had stumbled upon a new approach. As expected, the undergraduate students had embraced the opportunity to video record their collective journal entries rather than write them. After all, they also had extensive technical laboratory notebooks they had to turn in weekly.

Surprisingly, the videos chronicled the group process and involvement much more accurately than the journals ever had. When students were missing for multiple group meetings, they were simply missing from the videos—that was obvious. When students were leaders in the project, that could be seen in their interactions as well. Finally, post-project, the students were able to look back across the journey and specifically recall the details, barriers, victories, and emotions more completely. Thus, in its entirety, the digital video afforded valuable information for learning, assessment, and professional portfolios.

Technical resources needed: Video recording device, for example, cell phone, smartphone, digital video recorder ($45–$200)

Technical expertise level: Novice

Academic expertise: Varies by faculty criteria

DEVELOPMENT OF VIDEO FOR INSTRUCTION

In considering the broad topic of developing video for instructional purposes, we have adopted four major criteria:

1. Keeping our suggestions in the free to moderate cost range.
2. Proposing solutions that are suitable for novice to intermediate technology users.
3. Suggesting efficient work flow strategies.
4. Keeping our focus on teaching rather than technology fascination.

These guidelines provide the foundation for the choices and recommendations provided in this section about developing instructional video. Therefore, you will not find all the latest and greatest equipment options and high-end software solutions. The reason for these choices is that, in our experience, most professors do not have access to huge budgets to support their instructional design efforts, nor do they have time to master the use of complicated equipment and software. If you are a media specialist and already have advanced knowledge of the field, this chapter might be basic in terms of equipment and software. However, for most professors of other disciplines, the chapter will fully address your expertise and focus.

Choices: Platforms and Participants

When considering the equipment and software to use for creating instructional video, other factors that need to be considered are the intended audience and use of the final product. Table 5.1 provides an overview of how these factors and more can be framed to help instructors consider options and make decisions. It would be nearly impossible to create an exhaustive matrix to illustrate all the possibilities, but we will describe a few of the ones presented here so that you can consider all of the ones listed and continue to generate new configurations to meet your changing needs and new technologies as they arise.

Software Links for Free Video Editing Programs
- Apple iMovie: http://www.apple.com/ilife/imovie/
- Microsoft Movie Maker: http://www.microsoft.com/windowsxp/downloads/updates/moviemaker2.mspx
- Avid FreeDV (more technical than the others): http://www.avid.com/freedv/
- Avidemux: http://fixounet.free.fr/avidemux/
- LIVES: http://lives.sourceforge.net/
- WAX: http://www.debugmode.com/wax/

For learning the details of these video editing programs, most of them have great online videos tutorials to guide you step by step. There are few books about how to design instructional video for higher education. Fortunately, several good digital video development books exist that can guide most faculty through the relevant aspects of design, composition, sequencing, editing choices, and distribution ideas (Barrett, 2005; Darkin, 2008; Goodman, 2002; Rubin, 2008). In addition, there are many public domain video databases (Youtube, Vimeo, Howto, etc.) where you can find video tutorials on the topic.

Repurposing Existing Content

As illustrated in Table 5.1, one of the strategies we strongly recommend is to develop ways to use your content and teaching efforts in different ways. One example of this principle of repurposing content centers around materials you probably already use in some of your classes. Today, many faculty

TABLE 5.1 Instructional Video Development Matrix: Platforms and Processes

Intended Use of Video	Format Setup	Options for Recording Setups	Equipment Options	Production Software
On-demand course content Introductory content Archival recording for review or absent students	Lecture	Video record during class session with one or two cameras	Video camera ($200–$2000) Portable mini video camera (Flip, Kodak, etc.) ($100–$300) Webcam ($15–$200)	Edit, trim, add titles, compress, and save in formats for different users with software listed in this chapter or more advanced programs. (iMovie, Movie Maker, WAX, Avid FreeDV) Screen shots, photos, images, or slides can be interspersed in video.
Archival recording Reuse of special guest interview	Guest interview	Video record outside of a class session		
Archival recording Reuse of special guest interview as course content	Special event performances			
Archival recording of student work (video or e-portfolio) Performance assessment Reuse student work as sample or content	Student presentations			
On-demand course content Introductory content Special topic content/tutorial Review session	Lecture with slides or screens shots embedded	Video record the lecture/event that includes slides, notes, screen shots, and voice over; combining video of the speaker is optional.	Combine equipment above plus use of multimedia slides, graphs, diagrams, and screen shots to record and illustrate concepts or problem solving dynamically.	Use programs like Camtasia or Jing to capture screen shots while faculty illustrate and narrate software use, problem solving, or concept development. Use video editing program to add more slides or graphics as needed in final development. (Movie Maker, etc.)
Archival recording of student work Performance assessment Student work as sample or content	Student presentations with slides or screens shots embedded			
Primary source resources	Expert Interviews Community interviews Research interviews or reports News reports, media	Video record the interview or download the video of the news report If desired, add slides, notes, screen shots with voice over.	Combine equipment above plus use of multimedia slides, graphs, or diagrams as needed.	Edit the recorded video with listed software. Then use programs like Camtasia or Jing to capture screen shots and narrate graphics, images, or diagrams. Use video editing program to add more slides, or graphics as needed in final development. (iMovie, WAX, etc.)

create multimedia files to accompany some or all of their class sessions or lectures. If you use PowerPoint or other tools, many of these materials can be transformed into robust on-demand formats that serve additional purposes. Consider the possibilities of turning these materials into on-demand resources for 24 hours a day, 7 days a week student learning support.

For instance, if you are teaching a 2-hour class on the topic of XYZ, you might split your presentation slides into 4 different 20-minute segments. Prioritizing your choices, you might choose the section that most students need review of and prepare it to be your first on-demand student learning module. Using a program like PowerPoint, SnapKast, or VoiceThread, you can easily add narration to the presentation slides. Usually, the same programs give you the option to create a stand-alone file that you can post on your class Web site. Then, when students want to review the material or if they have questions, they can click the link and watch the slides while hearing your explanation. What is more, they can listen to it as many times as they wish in privacy. The power of this approach is that you are not starting from scratch. Instead, you are *repurposing* your current materials, simply recording audio to supplement them.

While the list is veritably inexhaustible, other familiar modes that may be used to repurpose content include those listed in Table 5.2.

TABLE 5.2   Repurposing Content: Matrix of Production and Use

Existing Content	Additional Process	Repurposed Content
PowerPoint slides	Audio narration added in PowerPoint.	"Video" or self-playing file—graphics and audio file that can be distributed on-demand within a learning management system (i.e., Moodle or Blackboard), Web site, or blog.
Pre-recorded (existing) video of faculty from a class session or a conference	Splice into segments that fit the content of the course.	Specialized video segments that can be used in different parts of courses as required or optional videos.
Prerecorded webinar a professor conducted on a topic related to your course	Splice into segments which fit the content of the course.	Specialized video segments that can be used in different parts of courses.
A tutorial or example that the professor usually solves in class	Record a screencast of working through an example of this type of problem.	Specialized tutorials that provide differentiated learning opportunities for support on demand.
A procedure, lab project, equipment protocol, software procedure, etc. that the professor, guest expert, technician, or other person usually demonstrates to each course section	Request presenter's permission to video record and use the session for future instructional sessions.	Post a collection of video demonstrations performed by experts for current and future students to learn and review the procedures.

TABLE 5.2   Repurposing Content: Matrix of Production and Use (cont.)

Existing Content	Additional Process	Repurposed Content
Professor presents at a conference	Use a small video digital recorder and tripod to record your session.	Specialized video segments that can be used in different parts of courses as required or optional videos.
Field trip to local museum, physical location, organization, agency, etc. that students are expected to complete on their own	Create a guided tour of the field trip and post in class online space.	Students can review their personal guided tour video before or during their visit.
End-of-course student observations of skill proficiency	Request each student's permission to video record and use the observation session for instructional purposes. Video record and use the observation session for instructional purposes and also use for course improvement.	Use with current student to discuss points of success and improvement. Use with future students to have them identify strengths and weaknesses. Use with future students to have them generate a rubric to score best performance. Start a library of video demonstrations performed by students.
End-of-course student presentations	Request each student's permission to video record and use the observation session for instructional purposes. Video record and use the observation session for instructional purposes.	Use with current student to discuss points of content and presentation success and improvement. Use with future students to help them identify strengths and weaknesses. Use with future students to have them generate a rubric to score best presentations. Start a library of video presentations on the semester focus to be used as on-demand content in future classes: Video created by students for students!

Continue to develop the chart for your specific situation!
What else do you do in your classes which can be leveraged with video?

Existing Content	Additional Process	Repurposed Content

Design Recommendations

In considering creating instructional video, faculty need to recognize design issues as an important part of the development process. This section briefly reviews issues and recommendations related to graphic design tips, learning styles, expertise, and interactivity that will greatly assist faculty in developing their video instructional products.

Graphic Design

Regarding graphic design, two aspects have emerged as especially important: (1) chunking and (2) visual design. We have described the strategy of chunking instructional content several times already in this chapter. For instance, when reviewing a prerecorded video lecture, chunking strategies advise educators to divide a 2-hour segment into six 20-minute segments or 12 segments of 10 minutes. Further triage of the instructional process would encourage the selection of the most essential chunks to preserve and streamline both learning and video production.

It is helpful to consider that not all the things we do in the face-to-face classroom transfer well to a remote audience or to a review session. Therefore, it is important to select the sections that are the most relevant to the target audience and course purposes.

The second part of graphic design to emphasize regards visual design being pleasing, attractive, and professional. Basic elements of design that assist in this otherwise complex attribute may be focused on to achieve good results (Bourne & Bernstein, 2008). Rather than be obsessed by this issue, we focus on these few universal design elements to guide our digital video productions (Bourne & Bernstein, 2008; Burgstahler, 2005; Chisholm & May, 2008).

- Composition: Is the main screen shot of your video/presentation clear? Does it highlight your main subject? White space or blank space (whatever the color of your background is) provides a much needed organizational basis for composition and also relief for the eye.
- Color Balance: Do the colors in the video and graphics complement one another? Have you avoided or minimized clashing colors and themes? Given the complexion of your speakers, which colors best compliment their strengths? Most experts recommend refraining from wearing striped design clothing or having striped backgrounds for video recording, as they create distraction and aberrations in the final product.
- Lighting: Think about the homemade photos and videos you shoot that are too dark or too bright; we are all aware that lighting is an important issue in video and photography. In the context of video,

poor lighting can turn away many viewers and learners. On the other hand, good lighting can retain and *gain* viewers and listeners more often. How do faculty create good lighting without expensive equipment and time consuming setups? There is a simple 3-point rule for lighting with video and photographs. Following it is one of the best things a photographer or videographer can understand, plan for, and use. This simple rule recommends having 3 lights to illuminate your subject when shooting video or still shots. These three lights are named *key light, fill light,* and *back light.* The key light is positioned slightly in the front and to the left or right side pointing toward the subject. The fill light provides opposite or complementary light for the key light. Finally, the back light is positioned behind the head of the subject pointing to the head from an angle and it both softens and brightens the overall lighting to balance and complete the image. This back light is paramount in providing even light distribution, which fills in different aspects of the space and image. The final result is much more 3-dimensional representation.

Learning Styles and Expertise

Any faculty member who has taught for a few years becomes keenly aware that students have different learning styles (Fink, 2003; Lawler & King, 2000). For instance, some students are much more visually oriented, while others are text or activity predispositioned (Galbraith, 2003). Adult learning and instructional design experts recommend using a variety of instructional strategies and methods when designing classes, including digital video (King & Griggs, 2006). Moreover, adult learners come to our classrooms with varied life experiences, some having been experts in different professions and walks of life (Galbraith, 2003; Lawler & King, 2000).

Professors can maximize what they know about learner styles, preferences, and expertise in order to plan instructional videos that vary genres and techniques and use real-life contexts. For example, rather than having a professor merely speaking on camera (what is known as a "talking head"), one can vary the final presentation by strategically inserting text slides, images, graphics, and Web screen shots to illustrate key concepts, principles, organizations, et cetera. Moreover, real-life contexts may be incorporated in digital videos through the use of case studies, practical examples, expert or participant interviews, et cetera. Altogether, this approach to planning the flow of learning and composition of instruction in digital video provides a powerful final product that can be used with good results for many semesters.

Interactivity

In the field of distance learning and digital media, there is one principle that is especially crucial and yet all too often ignored. Interactivity is a "make or break" instructional design principle that is easy to plan for and implement and that reaps great rewards in terms of learning.

Consider how you, as a faculty member, feel when you sit in faculty meetings for 60–90 minutes and are asked to only listen and not interact or engage in discussion or participation. It is very difficult for even those of us who are accustomed to academic discourse to stay focused on the topic at hand and be intellectually involved in the presentation. How much more challenging must it be for people who are more accustomed to frequent changes of topic?

Moreover, the Information Age, Internet Age, and Age of Transformation have created an even greater demand for self-directed learning. Consider that college students and adults who frequently use the Internet and social media expect instant access to content (on-demand) while being able to instantaneously direct their intellectual queries for information of every type. They may be searching for anything from entertainment to travel, news, and financial information to careers—but they expect to be able to discover their own solutions through the Internet and their connected social network.

Faculty can build on this self-directed expectation by not spoon feeding students, but instead designing digital video that is problem-posing, foundational, and thought-provoking. Moreover, great instructional video design will engage the viewers in researching their interests, digging deeper into the issues, and presenting their resulting perspectives in the learning community through dialogue (online discussions, face-to-face class sessions, virtual synchronous sessions, etc.).

Following are just a few of many simple interactive strategies that may be considered for use with instructional video development:

- Shifting our focus from telling to *engaging* the students, we cultivate their interest, ownership, and growing understanding.
- Incorporate the introduction of related short activities into the video. In this format, the viewer stops the video, completes a task, and then resumes the video again.
- Assign the development of viewer journals and viewer reflections. In these brief writings, students watch the faculty-created videos and record a learning summary, critical points, reactions, and next questions for each section. Faculty might further incorporate the sharing of those comments in a host of ways within the course and privately in one-on-one meetings.

Like many readers, you might now have a clearer picture of what you will create for your first or next instructional video; however, a looming question is in the background. Where exactly are faculty to post their videos on the

Web so that students can access them whenever they are needed (on-demand access)? The next section of this chapter answers this critical question by pointing out the different types of video hosts available for free for faculty.

Venues for Video Distribution

There are a many worthwhile and convenient places online one can use to host video free of charge. The obvious choice, of course, is YouTube. com. A giant of free media on the Internet, YouTube may nonetheless be a poor choice. There can often be copyright issues with other videos seen there, possibly exposing faculty to legal liability. Another area of possible liability can develop if any of the students or other subjects in your video decide to have a problem with being posted for all the world to see (King & Gura, 2009). University Web sites can be troublesome also, but for a different reason: If your posted content becomes too popular, the heavy traffic can cause serious trouble for the University bandwidth, slowing it down or even crashing it.

There are several free places that are better choices, however. School-tube.com, Teachertube.com, OurMedia.org, Archive.org—these can all provide free hosting for your video content in a more secure setting than YouTube and without consuming your University's precious bandwidth. Vimeo is also a good resource, but as with many non-education, commercial ventures, they have to balance services and costs and will limit free accounts or increase subscription rates to compensate for it.

There are also times when faculty want to distribute video recordings to a global audience. For instance, they might be distributing conference presentations to association members, research results to journal readers, video to a wide audience, or requests for research participation or collaboration, or students might choose to distribute their work. As illustrated in Figure 5.5, TubeMogul.com is a one-stop shop for meeting that need

Figure 5.5 TubeMogul.com.

because it serves as a meta-video distribution site to deploy video to many different major video hosting services and social media channels in one step. By setting up a free account and configuring TubeMogul with the account information for each of the other databases (Youtube, Facebook, Vimeo, Howcast, Bing, Yahoo, and many more), faculty and students can have a much wider dissemination of their work with a fraction of the effort.

Intellectual Property Issues

Just like in our research and publishing, protecting intellectual property and abiding by copyright rules are key factors in producing video content. As in our other work, faculty need to determine policies of intellectual property (IP) with their universities and follow those guidelines. In the case of video, an important aspect of IP is to include an accurate copyright statement in prominent view (maybe the opening and final screens). Secondly, and just as importantly, make sure not to misuse others' intellectual property. This principle includes having written permission to use copyrighted material (long quotations, images, anything not in the public domain).

Both of these principles are critical for faculty to help students comprehend and internalize for their professional practice of history as well. For instance, copying hit songs off of commercial CDs for a video soundtrack is illegal, just as much as plagiarism. In the digital world, intellectual property and copyright are moving targets as they constantly change to keep up with new technologies and issues. One authoritative source on the topic that is frequently updated is New Media Rights (2010), which provides an excellent legal guide to publishing digital audio and video recordings (http://www.newmediarights.org/guides/legal_guide_video_releases_use_publication_audio_and_video_recordings). Remember: While video content is a fantastic tool, it must be used responsibly, just like anything else.

ACTIVITIES

The following activities guide faculty to explore and develop the video-related instructional strategies discussed in the chapter. Based on needs and preferences, the activities may be completed in any sequence. The focus of the activities is to use video in the faculty member's specific instructional settings and reflect on best ways to (1) select or design video, (2) use video, and (3) facilitate video's use. Therefore, keeping a journal, collecting data, and/or reflecting on each activity will be beneficial for faculty in identifying the things that help them most, discerning patterns, and facilitating sharing with colleagues.

Activity 1: New Perspectives Through Video

Consider a course that you are teaching this or next semester. Identify 3 to 4 topics within the course that are related to historical figures or current popular figures. Search Youtube.com, TeacherTube.com, and Vimeo.com to see if there are primary source interviews with those people that could provide students with a better sense of the perspectives and issues studied. We often find that when learners see and hear the historical person in action, her or his message becomes more meaningful and compelling. Once you find a good choice of a video clip, select the code that provides the link (http://...) or embed code that will allow you to post it inside your course Web site or online learning environment (Blackboard, Moodle, etc.). Setting up the assignment can be basic even the first time around. Ask your students to share their insights about the topic based on having read the course content and viewed the videos. They might share in class, in a short written essay, or in an online space. There are many opportunities for faculty to move such projects ahead at their own pace. Instructional video does not have to be difficult.

Activity 2: The Efficient Professor: On Demand While Sleeping!

As you look at the courses you will be teaching next semester, you might recall that during the first class you often use some similar examples to emphasize the importance of studying the course content and then review the class policies and procedures and major assignments. Did you ever notice that some people always miss the first class and that it seems that students will often ask for the same information to be repeated several times? This activity provides strategies that will make faculty work more efficient and ubiquitous.

Two weeks prior to your first class, notify media services (or related department) to have a tripod and video camera delivered to your classroom. If you are fortunate, a camera person may be available to record your introductory section as well! Video record the first sessions with the usual opening information, syllabus review, and introduction to the primary course assignment. Next, use Format Factory (a free shareware program) to save the file in video formats MP4 and Windows MOV.

Now post both versions of your video on your class Web site or learning management system for all students to be able to review as needed. Students who add the course late or who wonder about details from the first class can retrieve and view the video at any time. Your introductory class will be available on-demand 24/7. In addition, when the same questions come up in class, you can refer students to the video rather than losing more discussion and content time. That is service and efficiency—even while you are sleeping students can be listening to you!

Activity 3: Refresher Learning On Demand

The last project is a beginning step of using video for instruction; however, it has a significant impact on learners' subject area understanding, vision, and growth. As mentioned in the chapter, once you start recording your presentation, interviews, and guest and teaching content, you build an archive that can be drawn upon for many classes in the future.

Examine the current course you are teaching and the questions students usually ask you every time you teach it. Are there particularly difficult concepts that you need to explain several times or with great detail? Do students ask for explanations about certain issues, activities, or concepts? Such areas would be prime candidates for short video tutorials (4–6 minutes) that could be posted on a class Web site or learning space. In the same manner as number two above, these video tutorials can be accessed whenever students need additional assistance, and as many times as they need it! Certainly, when reviewing content or preparing for an exam, it is wonderful to be able to pause or fast forward a video clip.

Steps to Create Special Topic Instructional Videos
- Narrow down topics for the instructional video to 2 or 3.
- Create a bullet point list of the critical issues that need to be communicated.
- Retrieve slides from other lectures/materials and create additional ones that illustrate the points you are considering.
- Sequence the presentation for swift and complete comprehension.
- Either record the video with you presenting the content or use the narrate function in PowerPoint to create this custom instructional video.
- Upload it to your class Web site or learning management system for student use.

CONCLUSION

Digital video is a powerful instructional tool and is easier than ever to create. From custom instructional tutorials and featuring interviews with major figures in your field to student video projects, the opportunities are endless for bringing your content area to life easily with video. Thankfully, the resources needed are few and inexpensive, and free software can do everything you need. Video offers the opportunity to extend your instruction beyond the classroom walls, make your teaching more efficient, and engage students in critical research and content development. Build on your faculty expertise and enjoy the new opportunities with the activities offered in this chapter.

REFERENCES

Allsopp, G. (2008, Jan 2). 10 people made famous by YouTube. Retrieved June 9, 2010, from http://www.pluginhq.com/youtube-celebrities/

Barrett, C. (2005). *Digital video for beginners.* New York: Lark Books.

Bourne, J., & Bernstein, J. (2008). *Web video: Making it great, getting it noticed.* Berkeley, CA: Peachpit Press.

Burgstahler, S. (2005). *Universal design of instruction.* Washington, DC: DO-IT. Retrieved from http://www.smith.edu/deanoffaculty/Burgstahler.pdf

Cherrstrom, C., & King, K. P. (2010). Five powerful Skype hybrid learning strategies to include distance learners in F2F classes. *American Association for Adult and Continuing Education 51st Conference.* Clearwater, FL., October 24–29, 2010.

Chisholm, W., & May, M. (2008). *Universal design for web applications: Web applications that reach everyone.* Sebastopol, CA: O'Reilly.

daichibeatboxer. (2009, April 12). Daichi for Beatbox battle wildcard [video file]. Retrieved from http://www.youtube.com/watch?v=8ZsML4uWoiw&feature=fvw

Darkin, C. (2008). *The really, really, really, easy step-by-step guide to creating and editing digital video using your computer: For absolute beginners of all ages.* Middlesex, UK: New Holland.

Galbraith, M. (Ed). (2003). *Adult learning methods: A guide for effective instruction* (3rd ed.). Malabar, FL: Krieger Publishing.

Goodman, R. M. (2002). *Editing digital video: The complete creative and technical guide.* New York: McGraw-Hill/TAB.

King, K. P. (2003). *Keeping pace with technology: Educational technology that transforms.* Cresskill, NJ: Hampton Press.

King, K. P., & Griggs, J. K. (Eds.). (2007). *Harnessing innovative technologies in higher education: Access, equity, policy and instruction.* Madison, WI: Atwood Publishing.

King, K. P., & Gura, M. (2009). *Podcasting for teachers: Using a new technology to revolutionize teaching and learning* (2nd ed.). Charlotte, NC: Information Age.

Lawler, P. A., & King, K. P. (2000). *Designing effective faculty development: Using adult learning strategies.* Malabar, FL: Krieger Publishing.

Montgomery, K. (2002, Winter). Authentic tasks and rubrics: Going beyond traditional assessments in college teaching. *College Teaching, 50*(1), 34–40. doi: 10.1080/87567550209595870

New Media Rights (2010). *Legal guide to video releases & the use and publication of audio and video recordings.* Retrieved August 3, 2010, from http://www.newmediarights.org/guides/legal_guide_video_releases_use_publication_audio_and_video_recordings

PFW21. (2008, July 8). Christian the lion [video file]. Retrieved from http://www.youtube.com/watch?v=btuxO-C2IzE

Rubin, M. (2008). *The little digital video book* (2nd ed). Berkeley, CA: Peachpit Press.

Simonson, M., Simonson, S. E., Albright, M., & Zvacek, S. (2008). *Teaching and learning at a distance* (4th ed). Upper Saddle River, NJ: Prentice Hall.

TheKHeinz. (2009, July 19). JK wedding entrance dance [video file]. Retrieved from http://www.youtube.com/watch?v=4-94JhLEiN0

CHAPTER 6

BLOGGING AS REFLECTIVE PRACTICE IN THE GRADUATE CLASSROOM

Teresa J. Carter
Virginia Commonwealth University

INTRODUCTION AND BACKGROUND

With the advent of freely available, easy-to-use digital media software and Web-publishing services, a small but significant revolution is underway, one that promises to change the landscape of teaching and learning in both subtle and dramatic ways. The World Wide Web is no longer a place where learners in face-to-face classroom settings, as well as in virtual environments, go to search for content. Instead, the Web has become a site for constructing knowledge (Jenkins, Clinton, Purushotma, Robison, & Weigel, 2006) in which learners become content creators, collaborators, and community builders. One of the most visible contributors to the Web 2.0 world of digital media is the Weblog, or *blog*. This chapter describes the practice of blogging from a faculty perspective and introduces the reader to blogging as reflective practice in the graduate classroom, one of many possible uses in higher education.

A blog is a frequently updated Web site characterized by a reverse chronological listing of entries that can be searched, archived, and categorized according to labels, called *tags*, assigned by the author. Blood (2002) credits John Barger with coining the term *Weblog* in 1997 to describe this emerging genre of Web-writing. In 1999, another Web writer, Peter Merholz, pronounced it "wee blog," which led to the inevitable shortening of the term to *blog* (as cited in Blood, 2002). A unique feature of a blog is its ability to connect to other Web sites by hyperlinks, resulting in an interactive publishing space linking resources as well as authors to permit easy sharing of information. Free Web hosting services, such as Blogger (https://www.blogger.com/start), Edublogs (http://edublogs.org), LiveJournal (http://www.livejournal.com), and others, offer customizable designs and features that allow anyone to publish on the Web.

Another distinctive feature of the blog is the ability for readers to comment on posted entries, which are dated. This sharing of reactions and commentary between blog authors is what creates the collaborative knowledge-building capacity of the blog and differentiates it from a personal Web site or home page comprised of mainly static content (Richardson, 2009). As a medium for sharing knowledge, a blog can lead to an ongoing conversation among a community of readers who are responding to the ideas of the writer and contributing their own, "a genre that engages students and adults in a process of thinking in words, not simply an accounting of the day's events or feelings" (Richardson, 2009, p. 20).

The first blogs began to emerge in the late 1990s as filters of burgeoning content on the Web when a few dedicated surfers sought to make available for others the most interesting sites and information found in perusing the Internet on a daily basis. They shared these as hyperlinks interspersed with pithy comments comprised of their own reactions to current events (Blood, 2002). For the most part, these early Weblogs were the exclusive domain of Web site designers and computer programmers with the technical savvy to write in computer programming code (Blood, 2002). After the events of September 11 in 2001, however, the immediacy of blogs as a source for breaking news and reactions to it catapulted their popularity (Downes, 2004).

Around 2002, the first easy-to-use free blog creation software emerged on the scene, and others, not so technically adept, began to be drawn in from the periphery as blog readers to become blog writers (Herring, Scheidt, Bonus, & Wright, 2004). Linking Web content and responding to others via comments became the coin of the realm in the blogging world: The status of a blog was (and still is, for many) measured by the amount of traffic it generates (Technorati, 2008). Freely available blog hosting services proliferate now, and users have a wide range of choices for publishing in the public domain.

It is hard to underestimate the explosion in popularity of blogs as a mode of expression, although sources differ in their accounts. Technorati (2008) publishes an annual report on the state of the *blogosphere*, a term used to describe the worldwide blogging community. Among the numbers they cite are those recorded by Universal McCann in March 2008 of 184 million Internet users worldwide who have started a blog and 346 million who read blogs, with blog readers representing 77% of all active Internet users. Blogs have evolved beyond personal uses to include corporate and professional blogs, and even blogs whose main function is to generate profit for the owner from hosting advertising.

While some assert that blogs are a writing medium native to the Web (Blood, 2002), others view them as a hybrid genre that has evolved from the intersection of earlier online journals and paper diaries with computer-mediated modes of communication (Herring et al., 2004). Blogs on the Web today clearly include a wide spectrum of formats, styles, and purposes. They contain content composed as text, commentary, and personal narrative with varying degrees of self-disclosure; links to other Web sites; and embedded video, graphics, and still images. Their form, as well as the structural elements they contain, can be as distinctive as each author. Faculty use this new medium as a portal for organizing class content in lieu of a learning management system (LMS), as a personal writing space to reflect on their own teaching practices, as a network to engage with professionals who share similar interests, and as a digital writing space for student assignments or as an e-portfolio of class-based work.

ANDRAGOGICAL FOUNDATIONS FOR BLOGGING

Within the literature on adult learning, Lindemann (1926/1961) was among the first to explore the motivations and interests of adults as learners, but it was not until Knowles (1970, 1980) termed the facilitation of adult learners *andragogy* and contrasted it with pedagogy, the teaching of children, that adult educators had a framework of humanistic principles and practices to guide them as teachers. Knowles asserted that adults have a deeply embedded need to be self-directing through learning that addresses real-life problems or situations encountered at home or on the job. Today, these motivations can become the subject matter for bloggers as they reach out to others as resources, situating their learning in the context of life experiences.

BLOGGING AS SOCIALLY SITUATED LEARNING IN A COMMUNITY OF PRACTICE

During the 1980s and 1990s, a diverse group of researchers, including cognitive anthropologists and psychologists associated with the Institute for Research on Learning in Palo Alto, California and instructional technologists at the Cognition and Technology Group at Vanderbilt University (which later evolved to a successor entity, The Learning Sciences Institute), began exploring the nature of learning as socially situated in context, or "in situ." Through their research and writings, they began to articulate a view of learning that differed radically from traditional cognitive learning theories, asserting that learning was embedded in the social and cultural practices in which it occurred. In this view, learning and work were inseparable (Lave, 1988; Lave, Murtaugh, & de la Rocha, 1984; Lave & Wenger, 1991; Orr, 1990; Scribner, 1984; Wenger, 1998).

Exploring how an individual moves from novice or apprenticeship status to one of full participation in a community of practitioners, the epistemology that emerged from these studies differed considerably from that of learning that takes place within a group, team, or other collective. Instead, members in a community of practice were not only engaged in learning through role modeling and by executing small parts of the task before attempting the whole, they also constructed knowledge and contributed to shared ways of knowing through their actions, learning the unique vocabulary, shared norms, and common meanings specific to the community. Such activity was considered "legitimate" peripheral participation (Lave & Wenger, 1991). When examined through a situated learning lens, the experiences of a novice blogger can be considered legitimately peripheral with participation in the worldwide blogging community. The novice blog writer soon begins to learn the jargon specific to the community (e.g., *tags*, *posts*, *pings*, and *trackbacks*), gaining knowledge of the craft of blog writing with its unique etiquette for commenting and replying to comments received. Expectations for content, quality, and "voice" are specific to the genre.

Bloggers, particularly through exchange of comments with individuals with similar interests, are engaged in a form of social co-participation in a community of learners. Embedded in the process are opportunities for "thinking made visible" (Collins, Brown, & Holum, 1991) and use of a tool, the computer itself. Wenger (1998) identified the tool-dependent nature of practices specific to a community, such as the surgeon with his scalpel, as an identifying attribute of a community of practice. Whether or not a blog is created to serve an intentional learning purpose, the blogger becomes a person who is negotiating meaning and identity through social participation in the virtual community of blog writers.

BLOGGING AS REFLECTIVE PRACTICE

For most adult educators, writing is a mainstay of the graduate education experience, often constructed as an exercise in developing critical thinking skills. One of the uses of the blog in higher education has been as an extension of the online or paper journal in which the author expresses thoughts, feelings, and reactions to lived experiences in an attempt to reflect critically and deliberately on what has been learned (Dippold, 2009; Du & Wagner, 2007). As a reflective journal, the blog has the potential to expand a learner's network of colleagues and professional relationships through the creation of a community of virtual colleagues, mentors, and coaches. When attempting to introduce blogging into the classroom experience, an educator needs to consider how to make this transition as seamless as possible for learners.

USE OF BLOGS IN THE CLASSROOM

Whether blogs are created by students in the virtual classroom or in a face-to-face setting, the essential elements for using a blog remain the same. Students will need to be introduced to at least one of the free blog-hosting Web services to establish their own blog accounts or take advantage of the feature that now exists within many LMSs to create a blog. To support new users, most blog hosting services have developed online tutorials.

Instructors need to decide whether to establish a single course blog accessible by all students as co-authors or whether individual students create their own blogs. Most educators who require blogging as a course expectation have created their own blogs to model the process. Another alternative is to use a single course blog as a portal, with different pages established for a syllabus, list of assignments, roster, and posted documents. An example of this type of blog is one created by instructional technologist and adjunct faculty member Jim Groom at the University of Mary Washington in Virginia, http://bavatuesdays.com. He has demonstrated the versatility of a blog by embedding a wiki (a collaborative authoring space) into the blog with pages that link to presentations and publications, tutorials for various classes, syllabi, and class projects.

It seems obvious that when an instructor asks learners to create blogs she needs to read them on a regular basis, but this task can become daunting if not planned and managed well. Even in the graduate class with its smaller numbers, reading, commenting, and keeping track of student blogs in more than one course requires a commitment of time. This investment can yield insights into how course concepts are being understood, however, allowing an instructor to make adjustments, clarify content, and see the connections learners are making to work and professional experiences. Providing feedback to the writer through the commenting feature of a blog requires care and sensitivity since an educator's relationship to her learners is infused with differences in power and authority (Fenwick, 2001). Dippold (2009) adopted the strategy of acknowledging students' work by incorporating selected quotes from students' entries into her own blog posts. Modeling this cross-sharing of ideas can spur students to read more of their classmates' work and help build a learning community that has the potential to extend around the world as students learn to link to content and connect with others virtually, developing a network of colleagues as they do. One possibility for how blogs can be used in the classroom is to develop habits of reflective practice. The example shared here describes how graduate students who are adult educators and human resource development practitioners adopted blogging for this purpose.

A CASE STUDY IN DEVELOPING REFLECTIVE PRACTITIONERS

Expectations for engaging in reflective practice have long been a part of Virginia Commonwealth University's Adult Learning graduate program. For many years, students kept reflective journals as part of their program requirements in this master's degree in education, first in paper form and then as an electronic journal. In 2008, faculty introduced blogging in hopes that it would deepen students' understanding of course concepts through reflection that was more immediate in nature than the traditional end-of-semester essay. In this new digital medium, we anticipated that they would be able to post short entries frequently to capture learning as it was happening—a moment of insight in the workplace or an "ah-ha" moment during or after class. The goal was also to develop educators who were exposed to Web 2.0 technologies and could appropriate their use well enough to incorporate these tools into their own practices.

The Challenges and Obstacles of Getting Started

During the first three weeks of fall semester, students were introduced to the use of blogs and time was devoted to setting up blog accounts on one of the free Web hosting services in a computer lab. Faculty had already established blogs as models for reflective practice and introduced students to blog features by emphasizing the basics of choosing a design template and posting entries. A list of all student blog Web addresses was shared among class members to enable access to each other's writing. While use of a feed reader (such as Google's Reader or Bloglines) was suggested to aid in the aggregation of blog content, most students did not readily pick up on the concept of feeding content into a single source at this time and chose, instead, to link others to their blogs through a blogroll, a list of hyperlinks posted on the blog.

In spite of the initial set-up time during an early class session and the availability of video tutorials, establishing blog accounts and learning to use them were not intuitive skills for most students. One referred to this initial introductory period as "techno-hell" as he figured out how to customize a header, add a blog title, and establish the domain name with a catchy phrase indicative of the purpose of the blog. We addressed the need for ongoing "how-to" instruction during the first semester of blogging with an occasional 15-minute tutorial during class time to address questions as they came up. By the end of the semester, student comments were extremely positive about the experience of blog-writing, and general agreement existed that this was not only a good learning experience, but one they enjoyed. One student exemplified this initial attitude of both fear and excitement when writing this early post:

> How exciting to be writing my first blog! I feel slightly uncomfortable about the whole thing, but I'm not sure why I have that feeling. Every few years I buy a beautiful journal that I keep next to my bed for recording thoughts. I usually only make it a couple weeks before it finds its way under the bed collecting dust. I have always struggled with writing, formally or informally. It may be painful, but I believe this class will challenge and improve my skills.

Another student, whose blog posts always reflected a very polished public persona, wrote,

> To those of you reading my first blog post, welcome! I am excited about using this new tool to share with classmates and professors my thoughts, works, and reflections as I continue my quest for a Master of Education in Adult Learning. Although I currently feel as though I had a "crash course" in using the blog tool, it amazes me how great minds and technology continually create new tools to enhance the learning process.... I think that using this tool will be an excellent way to link together all of the separate courses involved in this program.

Meeting the requirements for an assignment is always a priority for motivated adult learners and the technical overlay caused a few some angst. In a study of students learning to blog for an advanced German class, Dippold (2009) experienced similar issues in which her students, in spite of having grown up in the digital age, remained inexperienced in the use of classroom technologies. For faculty in higher education, pressured in many institutions to respond to the growing drumbeat to adopt technology in the classroom, this disconnect between students' adept use of technology in their personal lives and their lack of savvy with digital media in the classroom comes as a surprise, a quality that Levin and Arafeh (2002) describe as the "digital disconnect." In reality, many adult learners of all ages have scant exposure to the use of technology for educational purposes; teaching the use of these tools *is* necessary. Ultimately, all of our students mastered the technical aspects of becoming a blog writer and the more technically adept students were able to provide help to others.

Creating Blog Assignments That Built Community

Faculty experimented with a variety of assignment types and formats; some worked better than others. For skill-based classes, students were provided a set of guidelines and a simple rubric to assess the practice of blog writing but not the content, since content was allowed to be the personal expression of the learner. In other classes, students were expected to post at least five to seven blog entries whenever something occurred over the course of the semester that spurred a new insight, idea, or thought that they wanted to explore as they made their thinking visible to others. They were encouraged to exchange comments by reading classmates' blogs; however, without the structure of assigned blogging partners, few initiated this effort on their own.

By far the most successful practice with blogging in the classroom involved three-person teams who committed to read each other's blogs and exchange comments as assigned. Each blog author was considered a "reflector" and asked to create a weekly post related to class readings or a question posed by the instructor. The other two students of the triad were to respond to the reflector with comments on the post, acting as "mirrors" to offer alternative viewpoints or to provide support for ideas expressed. Guidelines for this Reflector–Mirror exercise, along with the rubric used to assess participation, are presented in the Resources section of this chapter.

In a focus group session held at the end of the academic year to gather learner perspectives, students commented that the Reflector–Mirror exercise required them to attend to each other through reading and commenting, enhancing their learning as a result. One student commented on the positive influence that blogging had on her by requiring her to pay more attention in class, since her classmates would be commenting on her writing afterwards:

> During class, I felt like I needed to really stay engaged and keep up with everything because I knew I'd be reflecting later. And I think it was also a great learning tool because when we were mirroring each other, the other person may say something to you that would get another thought going, or it would help me understand better what I had just read. Maybe I was on one point and someone who was mirroring me would say something else, and I could learn more from that.

Reading others' blogs was valuable in allowing classmates to get to know one another on a personal as well as professional level, as reflected in these focus group comments:

It gave me a lot of insight as to what was going on in people's minds. It allowed me to, you know, just to see what intrigued them about the class, or when they shared something about their professional life or their personal life, it gave me a little bit of insight into that person.

For others, the most important aspect of the Reflector–Mirror assignment was the sense of community it created:

It was really the first time that I'd had a chance to get to know folks in a way other than what they said in class. It really did build a sense of community. Where the learning was important, I think, and I like being challenged on what I was saying and having things added [through comments], the community was really powerful.

With the Reflector–Mirror exercise, I believe we came closest in practice to the goal of fostering a true community of learners who were sharing a common meaning system through their shared educational experiences.

BLOG USE FROM A FACULTY PERSPECTIVE

Educators who are considering adopting blogs as part of their teaching practice have a small but growing body of research literature to guide them in adopting digital media in the classroom, and an even larger body of first-hand anecdotal experiences from which to draw lessons of experience within the community of educational blogs now on the Web. Several of these are presented in this chapter as exemplars of educational practice.

Within the existing body of research on learning through blogs, Williams and Jacobs (2004) assert that blogs have the potential to be a transformative technology for teaching and learning because of their reach into the virtual world of learners beyond the confines of the university, providing a forum for academic discourse without parallel. In addition to providing enhanced opportunities for interaction with peers, blogs provide autonomy and opportunities for expression of authentic voice, empowering and encouraging students to become more analytical in their thinking (Oravec, 2002). Wesch (2009) describes this transformative potential of a participatory culture as a social revolution that should empower educators to rethink concepts of what it means to be educated, noting that

[n]etworked digital information is also qualitatively different than information in other forms. It has the potential to be created, managed, read, critiqued, and organized very differently than information on paper and to take forms that we have not yet even imagined. . . . At the base of this "information revolution" are new ways of relating to one another, new forms of discourse, new ways of interacting, new kinds of groups, and new ways of sharing, trading, and collaborating. (para. 2)

For educators who want to employ innovative uses of blogs in classroom practices as part of their own information revolution, Richardson (2009) suggests that blogs can be used to collaborate with subject-specific experts, to archive learning, to share results of experiments, and to collaborate with peers in different sections of the same course through a single blog, extending the network of learners engaged in a common pursuit. Possibilities for cross-disciplinary work are limited only to the instructor's imagination:

> Science experiments can be run concurrently at any number of different sites across the country or around the world with student researchers comparing and reflecting on the results on a Weblog. Language students can create conversations with native speakers, physical education students can log and analyze their workouts or diets, and history students can construct resource sites for their study of ancient civilizations and conflicts. (Richardson, 2009, p. 32)

In a study of university students in German and French foreign language classrooms, Ducate and Lomicka (2008) noted that blogs provided students with a window into the target culture in a way that their textbooks did not when students were asked to read native speaker blogs weekly and collect information about the target language and culture. These researchers described a scaffolding process for learning as students explored the blogosphere, selected a foreign language blogger to follow, took steps to engage with that blogger through their writing, and ultimately established an online identity as a foreign language blogger.

Blogs can also be used to provide blog mentoring to groups of students, such as pre-service teachers (Richardson, 2009); as repositories of student work; or as journals for chronicling a doctoral student's journey from beginning stages to dissertation. As educators begin to embed blogging as an instructional strategy into course designs, experiments in the classroom are likely to inform and direct research as we learn more about the potential of digital media to enhance collaborative learning.

RESOURCES TO INTRODUCE BLOGGING AS REFLECTIVE PRACTICE

For educators who want to engage in blogging as reflective practice, the resources provided here are ones adopted for classroom assignments, but they can easily be used in online learning environments as well. Table 6.1 is an excerpt from a syllabus explaining the Reflector–Mirror exercise, which is loosely based on the idea of a person acting in the role of a projector screen to mirror and reflect back what another says, an exercise presented in Senge, Roberts, Ross, Smith, and Kleiner's (1994) *Fifth Discipline Fieldbook*. We

TABLE 6.1   Instructions and Grading Rubric for the Reflector–Mirror Exercise

This is a major assignment for reflective writing in your blog during the semester. The assignment is very loosely adapted from a projector-screen mirroring exercise described in Peter Senge and colleagues' (1994) *The Fifth Discipline Fieldbook*. Each week following our class session, as a "reflector" you are to write a post to your blog entitled **Reflections for My Mirror**.

You can give this entry a subtitle to differentiate it from similar posts during different weeks of the semester. For example, you might title your first blog post for this course as **Reflections for My Mirror: Entry 1** or you may want to add a catchy subtitle that describes the gist of your reflections.

During the first class session, you will have an opportunity to organize into teams of three by finding two individuals in our class willing to be your "mirror" to reflect on your writing by providing their observations and thoughts. Each person in class will serve as a "mirror" to two others.

The idea is to post a weekly reflection on the meaning you are making from our assigned readings and what you are learning in the course, and to receive comments from two others in class on your reflections. Other class members are welcome to follow your blog and comment on your reflections as well, but mirrors will follow you throughout the whole semester. They are providing you with insight into your thinking through their comments. A blog is a tool for *socially* mediated learning as much as it is reflective practice. You will be graded according to your contribution to our collective learning experience, as follows:

A	As a reflector, you have contributed weekly reflections in a *timely* manner that allowed others (mirrors) to have time to read and comment on your ideas before the following class session. Mirrors have posted timely comments on the blogs of those they are following. Reflective posts and comments were thoughtful entries that reflected your ideas, experiences, and growing awareness and knowledge of course concepts. You used the blog in a way that enhanced your own learning and provided the opportunity for others to learn from you.
B	Blog entries or comments were written as assigned, but, on occasion, posts and/or mirror commentary were missing or incomplete, or a few blog entries were late or of a superficial nature.
C	Many blog entries were late / incomplete or of insufficient thought or reflection to provide useful learning material for others.
D/F	You failed to use the blog in the manner intended, and thus deprived yourself and others from what you have to contribute to our mutual learning.

created these guidelines specifically for learners in a blogging environment and included a simple grading rubric to promote quality blog posts without judging the specific content of a student's reflections. Table 6.2 contains guidelines for constructing blog posts in the two roles, as a reflector and as a mirror to others' reflections. Of all assignments created for courses during the first year in which we used the blog as a tool for reflective practice, students commented on the Reflector–Mirror experience as the one that built community among learners and engaged them the most in developing a reflective habit.

TABLE 6.2 Guidelines for Reflectors and Mirrors

What do reflectors write about in their blogs?	What do mirrors comment on in the blogs they follow in their role as mirrors?
• Reflectors create a blog post that contains their thoughts, feelings, and reactions to what they experienced in class and through reading and dialogue with others. • These should be shared to the extent that you are comfortable expressing your ideas in a public forum. Always remember that your writing is available to others on the Web. • Private reactions, thoughts, and experiences can also be written in a blog post, but be sure to select the option for "private" before publishing.	• Mirrors, first and foremost, adhere to the golden rule: They do unto others as they would have others do unto them. • Mirrors should remember that their comments are also viewable in a public forum.
• Reflectors monitor their own reactions and use them as sources of learning about self, others, and the content of their experiences.	• Mirrors respond to the words and thoughts of others AUTHENTICALLY. They make comments, not simply compliments. • "I agree" is not a comment that will mean anything to the reflector without explanation. Comments should be meaningful, even if they are only a few sentences.
• Reflectors relate what they are learning to their experience in the workplace.	• Mirrors don't have to write a lot, but what they write should be of quality, expressing their own thoughts and reactions to what the reflector has said. If the reflector's thoughts evoke learning on the part of the mirror, then the mirror can comment on the insight provided by the reflector's post.
• Reflectors integrate what they are learning in this class with the whole of what they have learned in this program of study.	• A mirror may have different reactions, ideas, or experiences from those of the reflector, in which case s/he should feel free to respectfully offer another point of view for the reflector's consideration.
• Reflectors post to their blogs on a weekly basis, at a minimum, and more frequently when they have more to say.	• Mirrors should check the blogs of the reflectors before the next class so that they can provide timely comments.
• Reflectors learn from the experience of writing to their blogs and receiving comments from their mirrors.	• Mirrors learn from the experience of reading others' blogs and by providing their own thoughts and reactions to the reflectors.

AN EXERCISE FOR EDUCATORS

An educator contemplating the introduction of blogging as reflective practice in higher education will need to create her own blog to model the process and gain first-hand experience before asking learners to do so. It may be a worthwhile investment of time to explore the blogs of other educators and professionals in the workplace, including these:

- Britt Watwood, Online Learning Specialist, Center for Teaching Excellence, Virginia Commonwealth University, *Learning in a Flat World*, http://bwatwood.edublogs.org/
- Michele Martin, *The Bamboo Project*, http://michelemartin.typepad .com/thebambooprojectblog/
- Gardner Campbell, Director of the Academy for Teaching and Learning, Baylor University, *Gardner Writes*, http://www.gardnercampbell .net/blog1/
- Joanna Dunlap, Associate Professor, School of Education, University of Colorado, Denver, *Thoughts on Teaching*, http://thoughtsonteaching -jdunlap.blogspot.com/
- Alex Reid, Associate Professor of English, SUNY-Cortland, *Digital Digs*, http://alexreid.typepad.com/
- Tricia Stohr-Hunt, Assistant Professor of Elementary Education, University of Richmond, *The Miss Rumphius Effect*, http://missrumphius effect.blogspot.com/
- Readers are also welcome to visit the author's blog of reflections on teaching and learning in the 21st century, *Coming About*, http:// comingabout.edublogs.org/.

After seeing how others are using blogs, these questions may help educators crystallize their ideas for establishing blogs in the classroom or as part of their own professional practice:

1. When exploring others' educational blogs, what underlying themes or messages do you see in how the blog is used? What message do you want your blog to convey to readers?
2. How does the blog-writer's style and manner of expression contribute to the theme or message of the blog?
3. What resources, tools, and faculty support services are available for help in getting started? For instance, does your university have a faculty development center to support use of technology in teaching? Seek out and make the best use of existing resources, including faculty who are already incorporating digital media into their teaching practices.

4. Consider your own content area and determine where blogging might be used to accomplish your goals for the course. How will you construct your blog for the purposes you intend: As a course portal? A single class blog with all students as contributors? A blog as an ongoing site for reflective practice, or for hosting certain assignments?
5. How can your blog be a role model for what you want to see in your learners' blogs?

AUTHOR NOTE

The author wishes to acknowledge the support of colleagues William R. Muth, PhD and Wendy A. Garland, PhD for their assistance during the implementation and study of blogs in the Adult Learning program at Virginia Commonwealth University during 2008–2009, and to express special appreciation to the students who participated in the study of blogging as reflective practice. Special recognition is given to my colleague, Jeffrey S. Nugent, Associate Director of the Center for Teaching Excellence at Virginia Commonwealth University, for his recommendation of blog sites listed in this chapter and for his ongoing support in helping me to learn how to use digital media effectively in the classroom.

REFERENCES

Blood, R. (2002). Weblogs: A history and perspective. In J. Rodzvilla (Ed.), *We've got blog: How weblogs are changing our culture* (pp. 7–16). New York: Basic Books.

Collins, A. S., Brown, J. S., & Holum, A. (1991). Cognitive apprenticeship: Making thinking visible. *American Educator, 15*(3), 6–46.

Dippold, D. (2009). Peer feedback through blogs: Student and teacher perceptions in an advanced German class. *ReCALL, 21*(1), 18–36. Retrieved from ERIC database (EJ827515).

Downes, S. (2004). Educational blogging. *Educause Review, 39*(5), 14–26. Retrieved from http://www.educause.edu/EDUCAUSE+Review/EDUCAUSEReview MagazineVolume39/EducationalBlogging/157920

Du, H. S., & Wagner, C. (2007). Learning with weblogs: Enhancing cognitive and social knowledge construction. *IEEE Transactions on Professional Communication, 50*(1), 1–16.

Ducate, L. C., & Lomicka, L. L. (2008). Adventures in the blogosphere: From blog readers to blog writers. *Computer Assisted Language Learning, 21*(1), 9–28.

Fenwick, T. J. (2001). Responding to journals in a learning process. In S. Imel (Series Ed.) & L. M. English & M. A. Gillen (Vol. Eds.), *New directions for adult and continuing education: No. 90. Promoting journal writing in adult education* (pp. 37–47). San Francisco: Jossey-Bass.

Herring, S. C., Scheidt, L. A., Bonus, S., & Wright, E. (2004). Bridging the gap: A genre analysis of weblogs. *HICSS*, Vol. 4, p. 40101b. *Proceedings of the 37th Annual Hawaii International Conference on System Sciences.* Retrieved from http://doi.ieeecomputersociety.org/10.1109/HICSS.2004.1265271

Jenkins, H., Clinton, K., Purushotma, R., Robison, A. J., & Weigel, M. (2006). *Confronting the challenges of participatory culture: Media education for the 21st century.* Boston: MIT Press (The John D. & Catherine T. MacArthur Foundation Reports on Digital Media). Retrieved from http://digitallearning.macfound.org/atf/cf/%7B7E45C7E0-A3E0-4B89-AC9C-E807E1B0AE4E%7D/JENKINS_WHITE_PAPER.PDF

Knowles, M. S. (1970). *The modern practice of adult education: Andragogy versus pedagogy.* New York: Association Press.

Knowles, M. S. (1980). *The modern practice of adult education: From pedagogy to andragogy.* New York: Cambridge Books.

Lave, J. (1988). *Cognition in practice: Mind, mathematics, and culture in everyday life.* New York: Cambridge University Press.

Lave, J., Murtaugh, M., & de la Rocha, O. (1984). The dialectic of arithmetic in grocery shopping. In B. Rogoff & J. Lave (Eds.), *Everyday cognition: Its development in social context* (pp. 67–94). Cambridge, MA: Harvard University Press.

Lave, J., & Wenger, E. (1991). *Situated learning: Legitimate peripheral participation.* New York: Cambridge University Press.

Levin, D., & Arafeh, S. (2002). *The digital disconnect: The widening gap between Internet-savvy students and their schools.* Washington, DC: PEW Internet and American Life Project. Retrieved from http://www.pewinternet.org/Reports/2002/The-Digital-Disconnect-The-widening-gap-between-Internetsavvy-students-and-their-schools.aspx

Lindemann, E. C. (1961). *The meaning of adult education.* Norman, OK: The University of Oklahoma Printing Services. (Original work published 1926)

Oravec, J. A. (2002). Bookmarking the world: Weblog applications in education. *Journal of Adolescent and Adult Literacy, 45*(7), 616–621. Retrieved from ERIC database (EJ642919).

Orr, J. (1990). Sharing knowledge, celebrating identity: Community memory in a service culture. In D. Middleton and D. Edwards (Eds.), *Collective remembering* (pp. 169–189). Newbury Park, CA: Sage.

Richardson, W. (2009). *Blogs, wikis, and podcasts, and other powerful web tools for classrooms.* (2nd ed.). Thousand Oaks, CA: Corwin Press.

Scribner, S. (1984). Studying working intelligence. In B. Rogoff & J. Lave (Eds.), *Everyday cognition: Its development in social context* (pp. 9–40). Cambridge, MA: Harvard University Press.

Senge, P. M., Roberts, C., Ross, R. B., Smith, B. J., & Kleiner, A. (1994). *The fifth discipline fieldbook: Strategies and tools for building a learning organization.* New York: Doubleday.

Technorati. (2008). *State of the blogosphere annual report.* Retrieved September 18, 2009, from http://technorati.com/blogging/state-of-the-blogosphere/

Wenger, E. (1998). *Communities of practice: Learning, meaning, and identity.* New York: Cambridge University Press.

Wesch, M. (2009, January). *From knowledgeable to knowledge-able: Learning new media environments.* Retrieved October 18, 2009, from http://www.academiccommons.org/commons/essay/knowledgable-knowledge-able

Williams, J. B., & Jacobs, J. (2004). Exploring the use of blogs as learning spaces in the higher education sector. *Australasian Journal of Educational Technology, 20*(2), 232–245. Retrieved from http://www.ascilite.org.au/ajet/ajet20/williams.html

CHAPTER 7

NARRATED DIGITAL PRESENTATIONS

An Educator's Journey and Strategies for Integrating and Enhancing Education

Brian W. Donavant
The University of Tennessee at Martin

INTRODUCTION

Creative and engaging education utilizes not only the expertise of the facilitator, but also the vast resources available to supplement evolving methods of educational delivery. The use of narrated digital presentations is one means of meeting learners "where they live" and providing them with rich material that will bring meaning to their learning experience. This chapter tells the story of one professor's journey into personally discovering the needs, benefits, and details of using narrated PowerPoint presentations. Moreover, it offers practical advice for those educators who may be considering using or are exploring narrated presentations to enhance their online courses, online components of hybrid classes, or archives and tutorials for face-to-face classes.

The Professor's Guide to Taming Technology, pages 105–119
Copyright © 2011 by Information Age Publishing
All rights of reproduction in any form reserved.

The chapter focuses on the emergence of this valuable educational tool, its utility for learners, and how narrated presentations fit within a comprehensive approach to education. Although the chapter sometimes includes references to specific software packages, these should not be construed as an endorsement of any particular product; they are mentioned only because these are some of the more common programs currently in use.

Regardless of the software chosen or the content area or specific setting in which it is used, the concepts and practices presented are universal in their application and are based upon the contemporary state of adult education, research, and praxis. As the field of education and its delivery methods evolve, so too must the approaches of facilitators if they are to maintain their focus on serving the needs of the learners to whom they are ultimately responsible.

As background for this chapter, I explored the literature for information and insights that would provide greater depth in pedagogical applications and instructional design with this specific medium. I read everything I could find on narrated digital presentations, which, admittedly, was not much. There is a lot of peripherally related information available, but this mainly consists of step-by-step instructions for producing presentations with specific software packages or online sites.

There is a gap in the current literature that aims to help faculty understand how best to use narrated presentation tools to deliver educational material. As faculty and teachers strive to provide a comprehensive approach to education in this virtual age, do we really need to explore best specific digital educational practices or, rather, best overall educational practices within the context of today's digital world? The fundamental characteristic that leads one to consider "best overall practices" may be found in one of the major building blocks of this book: Technology is changing rapidly and technology-focused workplaces and collaborations mean that we need to have strategies to keep our professional practices up to date. If we always focus on specifics, we will lose the bigger picture as well as the ability to discriminate among differences, identify similarities, and craft innovative solutions.

THE *WHYs, HOWs,* AND *SO WHATs* OF UNDERSTANDING STUDENT NEEDS IN OUR CHANGING WORLD AND CLASSROOMS

Why should we examine the efficacy of online education or the implications of its inclusion in a comprehensive educational approach? In order to appreciate the current changes in higher education delivery modes, we need to have an understanding of what constitutes effective education and who our learners are. Looking around our classrooms for the past 15 years it is evident that the number of returning adult students and "mature adults" are becoming the norm rather than exception in some post-secondary settings. Consider the reports from the National Center for Educational Statistics (Snyder, 2010) that from 1990 to 2007 there was a 20% increase in attendance of 25-year-old or older undergraduates and the demographics of the classroom also became increasingly female-dominated (from 54% to 57%) (p. 12).

At the same time, with all of adulthood's responsibilities and limitations regarding time and resources, adult learners focus on the immediacy of application regarding educational endeavors. The concept of andragogy (Knowles, 1980, 1990) is admittedly not without its critics, but its assumptions (particularly, the self-directed approach of adults to education and their orientation to education within the context of their social roles) provide a framework within which to consider online educational endeavors and how those endeavors meet the needs of learners. Each of the assumptions has come under unfavorable scrutiny on a variety of fronts, and some skeptics have questioned andragogy's status as a theory at all, arguing that the assumptions were simply "principles of good practice" (Hartree, 1984, p. 205). The most recent criticisms, and perhaps the most universal, have centered on Knowles' isolation of the individual from the sociohistorical context in which learning occurs (Merriam, 2001). But Knowles (1980, 1990) said that adult education should address practical issues of life that learners ascribe to their life situations and that it must consider the real-life experiences of the learner in order to find this application and provide a basis for further learning, a position that indicates an appreciation for the social nature of the educational experience.

While andragogy is not a panacea for adult education practices, its usefulness as a rubric for better understanding the adult learner should not be ignored, and the principles provide an appropriate perspective from which to examine a variety of educational issues, including those within the online environment. The andragogy-like traits of any educational endeavor and, hence, its effectiveness may well depend upon the voluntariness of the experience, a measure often assessed in light of the self-directedness of the learner (i.e., the *willingness* to participate relative to one's life experience and adult role). In short, if education does not meet the needs of learners within the contexts of their lives, they simply will not participate, or their participation and benefit from the endeavor will be minimal. Such considerations are paramount to effective education, whether in the traditional classroom or online. Within the context of education in today's digital world, adult education researchers advise us that new technology and evolving methodologies must be incorporated into educational activities (Bingham, 2002; Donavant, 2009; McCullough & McCullough, 1994; Merriweather & Bell, 1994; Rachal, 1995). Garner (2000) admonished adult educators to pursue the development and implementation of technology into their endeavors, positing that learners require and deserve its inclusion.

Confronting the Challenge: Transitioning to the Online Environment

I have been teaching both in the traditional face-to-face classroom and the online environment for years. The goal of many (most) educational institutions that deliver online courses often seems to be to try to make the online class as good as its traditional counterpart. Indeed, I find that my greatest strength in the traditional classroom is the ability to relate various examples of practical application through the use of dialogue and discussion (i.e., verbally), and I have struggled to find ways to incorporate this component into my online courses. Students can glean only so much from books and slides projected onto a screen. It is the anecdotal information provided by the facilitator, the real-world examples, that bring the material to life. Otherwise, learners might just as well enroll in a self-directed correspondence course.

My earliest forays into the online classroom as a facilitator were mediocre at best and, often, a pratfall. Most were dismal attempts at throwing information out there for students to sift through in hope of achieving some increase in knowledge about a particular subject. This usually amounted to some fairly extensive reading assignments; a synchronous chat once or twice a week about some mundane issue that we seldom examined in depth; the posting of some PowerPoint slides; and, if students were lucky, an occasional video clip. Of course, the PowerPoint presentations were where I could truly shine, as they exemplified my personal touch upon the class: The more impressive I could make my slides, the more effort I had put into "developing" the course and the more "interaction" I believed I had with learners.

But ultimately it was up to the students to apprehend the content; from my current perspective, I do not think they gained much help from me! And often, my only measure of whether I was improving in my delivery of the material was whether my PowerPoint presentations were better than those of my colleagues, as reflected in the personal flair of the slides. Have we not all gone through this also in our traditional classrooms?

As much as I hate to admit it, the reality was that many of us who were teaching online did not really know what to do to transition into the online classroom. Online education is not the same experience as researching a topic, compiling notes, and standing in front of a passive group of students and talking for hours at a time (thank goodness!). In too many instances, excellent classroom facilitators attempt to bundle their material and "stick it online." This leads to frustration for both the facilitator, who does not understand why students are not getting it, and the learner, who is forced to self-educate. Students often come away from these experiences, whether online or face-to-face, exasperated that they had to enroll in a course when they could have learned just as much by simply buying the book and reading it on their own.

Innovation Needed

The virtual classroom has forced us to recognize the opportunity and need for innovative approaches that help learners become engaged in the experience. Yet still today, online education continues to suffer from a lack of imagination and willingness by facilitators to employ new approaches to delivering educational material. I recently read a well-known publisher's instruction manual for developing online courses that said that nearly all communication in the online classroom is written. This assessment included not only the correspondence among participants and facilitators, but the delivery of educational material as well. Although probably accurate, this notion is self-limiting. The manual went on to explain how instructors should incorporate this reality into their courses as they transition to the online environment. In my experience, this "tenet" is wrong!

While most of us could benefit from honing our writing skills, we should not limit ourselves to only one method of communication or educational delivery. We might as well admit that many people simply find writing to be an unpleasant experience. How many of us have memories of writing assignments given us by teachers as punishment for some transgression during our early schooling, or the dreaded term paper that loomed out there all through high school as that horrible thing we would all have to tackle? These early experiences conditioned many of us to resent or try to avoid writing. Why, then, would we base an entire educational delivery system on something that so many people find distasteful? Even those who do not mind writing often find it difficult to accurately convey their thoughts or intended messages. And we wonder why we are having trouble connecting with students!

As I became increasingly aware of this disconnect, I began searching for ways to bridge the gap by finding any way I could to make myself a "person" to my students. I began by posting a picture of myself on the course Web site so that my students could connect a name with a face. Today, this may seem to be a small gesture that many online facilitators recognize as standard practice, but, at the time, it was a monumental step. I also started using voice discussion boards and email rather than the traditional written variety. Now, not only could students see that I was a real person, they could actually hear me. Voice inflection is difficult to convey in written correspondence, but now they could hear points of emphasis. And I could hear inflection from them, allowing me to better gauge areas where they were struggling or in need of additional assistance.

Next, I recorded traditional class sessions and developed podcasts that students could access at their convenience. While my online students were not actually participating in the class discussions that I podcast, they were able to hear my complete lectures, something that previously had been unavailable to them in the online environment. These lectures and class discussions included questions from students regarding various issues.

Discovering Efficiencies

Most of us who have been teaching for any appreciable length of time come to the realization that only students' faces change each semester; the course and subject matter issues, concerns, and topics of discussion are fairly consistent. Students in the same course often raise the same questions regarding any given topic from semester to semester. Online students, in my experience, are no different. Once I began podcasting my face-to-face class discussions, I noticed that questions from students in my online classes decreased dramatically. Points of clarification for which they previously sought me out individually through email or on discussion boards were being answered before they were asked.

There were many benefits embedded in providing this audio content for the students to refer to and review at will. Not only did this greatly reduce the time I had to spend responding to a myriad of emails, but because of the reduction in the time lapse between question and answer, students were better able to apply the concepts to their learning. The evidence was seen in improved test scores and critical assessment in written assignments.

The Next Iteration of Development Needed

The early reactions of students to my incorporation of podcasting were extremely positive and encouraging. Each semester, students would rave that they had never had a professor that had met them where they lived and provided a mechanism for them to access material through technology with which they were so familiar and comfortable. But I soon discovered a problem. As each semester progressed, students accessed the podcasts less and less. They simply were too long and time consuming. In the online environment, where convenience and accessibility within the hectic schedules of many learners is of paramount importance, I had created a situation in which my students needed to spend much more time "in class" than their traditional counterparts in order to access the same material. Students were looking for some middle ground, a way in which they could experience the benefit of my lectures without having to spend the same amount of time as would be required by going to class.

My inquiries and preparation for this chapter provided the answer to this dilemma. With narrated digital presentations, I am able to use the same PowerPoint slides that I use in face-to-face classes and provide detailed explanations to salient points but can reduce an hour-long class session to approximately 20 minutes because I am not entertaining questions or engaging in prolonged discussions. And I have the flexibility of providing links to these presentations on the class Web site, or through emails or podcasts, which offers my students a choice of ways to access the material.

To be clear, I still podcast traditional class sessions; however I now direct students to these as supplemental material. The podcasts can provide more detailed information and clarification of topics in which they may have a particular interest. This purpose is in contrast to being the only mechanism for accessing the subject matter.

An unexpected benefit of this more diverse approach has been that students are accessing the podcasts more now than they did before, and their access does not wane as the semester progresses. In fact, the number of hours that students are accessing the overall course material has increased significantly since I began using the narrated presentations. Student correspondence indicates that they are seeking out the supplemental material in the podcasts for more in-depth exploration and inquiry regarding the information presented in the PowerPoints. Discussion board postings are well-developed and more articulate, and student papers and emails now exhibit more critical analysis of course topics and increasingly reference points made in the presentations and podcasts. What began as an attempt to ease the burden on students by providing a more concise delivery of course material has piqued their curiosity, and their response has been to demonstrate a seemingly insatiable desire to learn as much as possible about the topics and issues presented!

While these materials originated in my online classes, online students are not the only ones who have benefitted from my development of narrated presentations. I also make the presentations available to students enrolled in traditional face-to-face classes. While online students often use the podcasts of my lectures as supplements to the narrated presentations, onsite students do just the opposite and use the presentations as study material to supplement their lecture notes and to review for upcoming exams. What began as a tool specifically designed for my online students has evolved into a valuable resource for all of my classes and demonstrates how this tool is but one component of a comprehensive educational approach.

THE PRACTICE OF PRESENTING WITH NARRATION

Getting Started

There are a number of quality software packages that can be used to create narrated digital presentations, and almost all providers offer free downloads of trial versions. Although some software packages may be better suited for certain types of presentations, for most applications the choice is simply a matter of personal preference. Of the plethora of available software packages and tools, PowerPoint is probably the easiest to master since it is so familiar to both learners and educators, and this is a good place for those new to developing narrated presentations to begin. It is almost certainly the most widely used presentation tool in the face-to-face and online education environments. In addition, you will see that it is arguably the most versatile software in terms of application in a variety of educational settings and topics.

Overview of Popular Software

One of the most readily available and user-friendly software packages for producing narrated PowerPoint presentations is Adobe Presenter, formerly known as Macromedia Breeze Presenter. Camtasia Studio is another popular option that lends itself to more advanced applications, and several of my colleagues have used it quite successfully. Adobe Presenter is designed specifically for creating enhanced and narrated PowerPoint presentations, while PowerPoint is basically the entry-level application for Camtasia Studio, which has the capability of creating many other types of more sophisticated presentations.

The Adobe software, once downloaded, places the Presenter option directly on the PowerPoint toolbar. With this application, the narration is recorded onto the PowerPoint presentation itself. Animations and videos can be incorporated into individual slides for additional impact, just as with any other PowerPoint presentation. The software also allows the presenter to record each slide separately, making it immensely easier to make corrections or add slides later.

Camtasia Studio, on the other hand, provides on-screen video capture, meaning that anything that occurs within the designated area of the computer screen is recorded as part of a video presentation. For PowerPoint presentations, the presenter scrolls through the slides while speaking into the microphone. The Camtasia software combines the visual slide show with the recorded audio into an audiovisual production. But the software can more easily add additional features to the presentation than its Adobe counterpart. For example, the software can incorporate highlighted cursors and pointers in various colors, record keyboard sounds and audio voiceovers, import logos and watermarks, et cetera. These additional features are especially useful when producing presentations other than PowerPoint, such as when highlighting cursor clicks to demonstrate Web-based exercises or making points of illustration within captured video clips.

Most of the available software packages can be purchased individually, but institutions often can obtain licensing agreements at more economical rates. Another benefit of institutional purchase is that many colleges and universities can provide support in addition to that offered by the respective software providers, including technical assistance as well access to server space. Many of the popular online educational platforms such as Blackboard can be overwhelmed by placing large files on individual course sites. A better approach is to place these files on independent servers and provide links to the material through the individual course site or correspondence with students.

Once the appropriate software application is chosen, the facilitator need only have access to a quality microphone in order to produce the presentation. While the factory-installed microphones on most computers will suffice, better quality can be achieved through the use of a microphone-equipped headset, which also is readily available at minimal cost. The ability to move about without having to maintain proximity to a desktop-mounted microphone can help to create a more natural speaking environment for the presenter. Use of a headset and the freedom of movement it provides can enable the speaker to mentally transition to a face-to-face environment and replicate the tone found in the traditional classroom. I am somewhat animated when I speak and tend to "talk with my hands." It is not uncommon for colleagues to observe me through my office window, fully engaged in lecture and walking around waving my arms as I explain some salient point. Because I am able to move about and speak in a manner that is natural for me, I am better able to put myself "in" the classroom.

Pre-Production Activities

Preparation is the key to developing and producing quality presentations. This may not be as easy as it sounds. Developing and delivering an informative and stimulating presentation at anything above an average level of competency is a feat accomplished by all too few educators; considerable time and effort is required, as well as a fair amount of skill. Good preparation does not ensure good delivery, but without it, the chances diminish significantly. And although the preparation for developing lectures given in any format is similar, there are a few tips that may help reduce the anxiety and prevent the pitfalls of producing online presentations. With a little planning, developing and using narrated digital presentations is not as difficult as one might think.

First, the facilitator should outline the lecture. While this is a good idea in any setting, it may be particularly helpful here. Many lecturers draw upon energy from the audience to fuel their delivery. In the online environment, that feedback is absent; the only "audience" is an impersonal machine. This often tends to disorient the speaker, especially in the beginning. The beauty of producing narrated PowerPoint presentations is that the outline is basically the slide show, which is on the screen right in front of the speaker. Additional notes may be helpful, but the bulk of the outline is already prepared once the slide show is developed. Some may prefer to develop an entire write-up of the material. But using an outline may be a better choice because it reduces the chances of reading the lecture, one of the deadliest sins in any educational setting. Remember, some things are meant to be read, and others are meant to be heard; seldom are these one and the same. It is the detailed explanation of central points that only the facilitator can provide that, when combined with the skillful infusion of anecdotal comments, brings presentations to life.

How long should a narrated presentation be? Many of the presentations used in face-to-face settings contain more than 50 slides, and the presentation may cover the span of several class sessions. In traditional classes that meet two or three times a week, this usually is not a problem because the facilitator can begin the next class session by picking up where he or she left off the day before. But for narrated presentations used in the online environment, this is almost certainly too many. McLeish (1976) points out that learner interest typically begins to decline after about 10 minutes, reaches a low point at about 40 minutes, and increases somewhat during the last 10 minutes. Eliminating the "middle sag" leaves facilitators with about 20 minutes of quality time to hold the learner's attention. A 50-slide production leaves only a few seconds for each slide if used in a 20-minute presentation, meaning that the presenter will necessarily omit important information. Worse yet, the presenter will, in essence, resort to reading the presentation because there is simply no time to present any information other than or in addition to what is on the slides. A better approach is to divide the topic into shorter, more manageable presentations that can be covered in sufficient detail within a reasonable amount of time.

We tend to view our carefully prepared longer presentations as needing to remain intact in order to maintain a sense of continuity, and the thought of ending our presentation rather than continuing into the next logical sequence of discussion is uncomfortable and seemingly disruptive to the educational process. This need not be the case. Saying a lot about a little requires a narrowing of the topic to a few essential concepts. Once the most salient points have been identified and explained, the presenter can illustrate each one with pertinent real-life examples, relate these to familiar or previously-covered material, summarize the concept, and then move on. When producing narrated presentations, "moving on" often means ending one presentation and developing the next concept in another. This is not easy to do, especially when there is a great deal of material to cover, but mastery of this skill will help learners to develop relevant, useful applications of the issues and concepts presented. And, once developed, the skill of producing more concise educational segments can help facilitators refine their delivery within all settings, whether online or in the traditional classroom.

There are additional benefits to developing shorter presentations. With shorter productions, users find it much easier to locate and go directly to the segment of material they want. Shorter presentations will be smaller in file size, and easier and faster to download. Once again, the emphasis is on convenience and ease of accessibility for the learner. Shorter productions also assist the facilitator when updating material. What happens when the field of knowledge or information included in a longer presentation changes significantly? If the entire topic appears in one long presentation, there are basically two options: The presenter can either re-record only the necessary segment and splice it into the old presentation, potentially resulting in a somewhat disjointed finished product, or the presenter can re-record the entire presentation for consistency. If the major topic was originally covered through a series of smaller productions, updating is simply a matter of re-recording one short presentation.

The slide show itself should have the same qualities as what would be used in a traditional face-to-face setting: visually appealing, uncluttered, et cetera. With online courses, there is a tendency to create slides that "stand alone" and contain, in written form, all of the available information about a given subject. The result can be an overly wordy presentation that contains a host of valuable information but is visually overwhelming and no more engaging than reading overhead transparencies! This is an understandable reaction based upon good intentions and the fear that important information will be lost because there is no opportunity to explain the topic. Fortunately, it also is precisely the type of educational fodder that producing narrated presentations can help to eliminate.

Recording

Recording narrated presentations is fairly simple but may be a bit intimidating until the presenter becomes familiar with the technique, and it always takes longer than anticipated. The first few attempts will almost certainly require several "takes" to get it right, and the presenter should allocate sufficient time to accommodate this. An experienced user can easily take two or three minutes to record a one-minute presentation; a beginner might need 30 minutes or longer. Developers of narrated presentations should not worry about perfection the first time out. They should, instead, enjoy the accomplishment of getting a finished presentation produced and made available to learners. Imperfections in presentations will be much more apparent to the presenter than to the end user, who will undoubtedly be impressed with the incorporation of this new medium into the educational environment. Besides, the facilitator will probably need to re-record the presentation within a few months to remain current with ever-changing subject matter. There will be plenty of time for revision at that time, and these subsequent iterations will come much easier than earlier attempts since the presenter will be much more comfortable with the techniques.

A quiet, disturbance-free environment is critical to producing quality narrated presentations. There is a learning curve that accompanies the acquisition of any new skill, and the presenter should remember that she or he is venturing into an unfamiliar area. Anything that helps relieve the natural anxiety that accompanies the experience will provide a smoother transition to this new method of educational delivery. Of course, such a location also enhances the quality of the presentation by eliminating background noise that can distract the learner during playback. All telephones, including cell phones, should be turned off or switched to silent. Positioning the microphone correctly can make a big difference in the quality of the finished audio file. Better sound quality is often achieved by placing the microphone above the nose, pointed down toward and positioned slightly to the side of the mouth. This positioning can help to soften the sound of some letters and eliminate those annoying breathing and lip-smacking sounds so often heard in audio tracks. A glass of water, but not soda, kept nearby is quite handy for avoiding dry mouth. Using a conversational tone and infusing colloquial speech and humor into the anecdotal comments used to explain the presentation's major points helps the facilitator make a personal connection with the user, creating a more comfortable learning environment and maximizing the educational potential of the experience. Casual tones are appropriate for certain topics, while others call for a more formal demeanor. In either case, the presenter should always speak naturally and in a manner that is comfortable within the proper context of the presentation.

Production and Publication Action

As with most endeavors, the planning and preparatory work is the most labor-intensive. Once the facilitator has decided upon the appropriate material and tone for the presentation, its production is relatively simple and straightforward. Capturing of the presentation is accomplished by following the instructions for the chosen software application through a few simple steps. After the presentation has been captured, the presenter is able to edit or revise it by cutting, pasting, or re-recording as needed. In

Adobe, this can be done for each slide before moving on to the next or at the end of the presentation with the single click of the mouse. This is a particularly nice feature for beginners, who usually prefer a simpler process while they are becoming familiar with recording tools. With Camtasia, because the presentation is captured as a video file, the presenter generally must wait until the production is completed before editing. Potential users should note that the process can be a little overwhelming and involve some additional steps in comparison to the Adobe software. However, more advanced presenters may find these challenges offset by Camtasia's versatility, especially when recording dynamic introductions to their presentations or adding audio overlays to already-completed productions.

Once the presentation has been captured, the software converts it to the appropriate file format for deployment and storage. These files can take up huge amounts of server space and will almost certainly overwhelm the individual course sites in Blackboard, so it is best to store them on servers that will not hinder retrieval by learners or otherwise compromise other technical services. Presentations created with Adobe Presenter can be stored on the Adobe server, which archives them in individual folders. This file management system can be set up to accommodate separate folders for each course or category of subjects and creates a link for each presentation that can be provided to students. Camtasia files can be stored in their own proprietary format, readable only by Camtasia itself, or exported to common video formats, such as MPEG-2 or MPEG-4, that can be read by most computers even if the Camtasia software is not installed. Both software packages allow users to access presentations via a link that can be posted on the course Web site or provided through email or other means. In order to access the presentation, users simply click on the link provided, and the presentation begins to play. Learners also can easily navigate through the presentation by manually selecting any of the slide titles that appear in the navigation menu and can pause or replay any portion of the presentation to review important points.

Finally, learners often find it helpful to print PowerPoint presentations to use as guides for note taking. This option it not available with narrated presentations created with Adobe or Camtasia, but can be made available by posting a non-narrated version of the presentation (i.e., a "regular" Power-Point presentation) on the course site, which students can then access and print. Some facilitators may not want to do this because allowing students access to the full PowerPoint presentation also allows them to download and copy the presentation in its entirety, including some materials over which the facilitator may wish to maintain control. However, the facilitator can provide usable handouts by posting read-only PDF files that can be printed without granting access to the entire presentation.

CONCLUSION

Narrated PowerPoint presentations and other forms of narrated digital media presentations provide a viable and convenient means of conveying educational material to learners in many settings, but they are particularly useful in the online environment, where facilitators often struggle to present information in rich and meaningful ways. It is hoped that this chapter has provided insight into the practical use and applications of these tools and helped to alleviate some of the anxiety associated with the development or adaptation of new educational techniques. Although it may seem intimidating at first, the development and production of narrated presentations is a skill that is easily mastered. And the accomplishment of successfully tackling such a heretofore daunting task can provide educators with a "can do" attitude and renewed sense of confidence that is an invaluable resource in any educational setting.

As more and more learners embrace digital media and digital media presentations in the workplace, they have expectations, skills, and tools for using them with ease. This situation provides an advantageous opportunity for faculty to use the same tools to create enriching educational experiences. It is the responsibility of educators to bridge the gap between motivated learners and the static methodologies that separate them from truly meaningful education. As learning facilitators, we must be willing to attempt new techniques—to free ourselves from the boundaries of doing the same old thing in the same old way. We must actually transition to the online environment, with all of the resources and opportunities that it has to offer, and be limited only by the boundaries of imagination and innovation within the parameters of sound educational practice.

The use of narrated digital presentations is not a panacea to solving the perceived lack of personal interaction with the facilitator that is so often cited as detrimental to attracting and retaining online learners, or even requisite to creating quality online courses. But, it is one tool within a comprehensive approach to online education that can help to bring the experience to life. Moreover, this powerful tool's energy can be easily harnessed by those of us who are not afraid to admit that we can do better . . . and, are willing to try.

REFERENCES

Bingham, M. J. (2002). *Effects of computer-assisted instruction versus traditional instruction on adult GED student TABE scores.* Unpublished doctoral dissertation, University of Southern Mississippi, Hattiesburg.

Donavant, B. W. (2009). The new modern practice of adult education: Online instruction in a continuing professional education setting. *Adult Education Quarterly, 59,* 227–245.

Garner, B. (2000). Welcome by editor. *Focus on basics: Technology, 4.* Retrieved Dec 19, 2009 from http://ncsall.gse.harvard.edu/fob/2000/wel_dec.html

Hartree, A. (1984). Malcolm Knowles' theory of andragogy: A critique. *International Journal of Lifelong Education, 3,* 203–210.

Knowles, M. S. (1980). *The modern practice of adult education: From pedagogy to andragogy.* Chicago: AP/Follett.

Knowles, M. S. (1990). *The adult learner: A neglected species* (4th ed.). Houston, TX: Gulf.

McLeish, J. (1976). The lecture method. In N. L. Gage (Ed.), *The Psychology of Teaching Methods* (pp. 252–301). Chicago: University of Chicago Press.

McCullough, K., & McCullough, J. S. (1994). The promise of the telecommunications superhighway. *Adult Learning, 6*(2), 28–30.

Merriam, S. B. (2001). Andragogy and self-directed learning: Pillars of adult learning theory. In S. B. Merriam (Ed.), *New update on adult learning theory: New directions for adult and continuing education, 89* (pp. 3–13). San Francisco: Jossey-Bass.

Merriweather, J., & Bell, B. (1994). Don't give us the Grand Canyon to cross. *Adult Learning, 6*(2), 23–25.

Rachal, J. R. (1995). Adult reading achievement comparing computer-assisted instruction and traditional approaches: A comprehensive review of the experimental literature. *Reading, Research, and Instruction, 34,* 239–258.

Snyder, T. D. (2010). *Mini-digest of education statistics, 2009 (NCES 2010-014).* Washington DC: National Center for Educational Statistics, Institute of Education Sciences, US Department of Education.

CHAPTER 8

THE USE OF WIKIS FOR COLLABORATION IN HIGHER EDUCATION

Pooneh Lari
North Carolina State University

INTRODUCTION

What is a wiki and what does it mean? Wikis are the perfect tool for collaboration, as they are easily editable. Anyone who has been provided full access to a wiki can create or modify the pages of the Web site. In addition, other users can search for information within the collaborative space. In a study conducted by Madden and Fox (2006), they found that wikis are increasing in popularity and found that 30% of the Internet users visit Wikipedia to search for terms and meanings.

One of the most well-known open source wikis on the internet is Wikipedia (http://www.wikipedia.org/), a multi-lingual encyclopedia, which anyone can edit. Wikipedia contains more than 2.9 million articles in English and more than 10 million articles in 250 languages. Wikipedia (n.d.) defines a *wiki* as a Web site that "allows visitors to add, remove, edit, and change content" (n.p.n.)

The Professor's Guide to Taming Technology, pages 121–133
Copyright © 2011 by Information Age Publishing
All rights of reproduction in any form reserved.

This chapter will explore the instructional applications of wikis in a holistic but specific manner. Beginning with definitions of terms, the chapter addresses pedagogical concerns and many applications for wikis in teaching and learning, recommendations for their use, resources and guidelines for choosing the right wiki platform, and suggestions for assessing student learning in wikis. The discussion references research and theory but also demonstrates practical application that can be immediately put into practice in all higher education classrooms.

DEFINITIONS

Howard G. "Ward" Cunningham is the American computer programmer who developed the first wiki. He started programming the software Wiki-WikiWeb in 1994 in order to make the exchange of ideas between programmers easier in his company. The term *wiki* comes from the Hawaiian word *Wikiwiki*, which means quick. Even though wikis were developed more than ten years ago, they are still fairly new to higher education (Chao, 2007; Evans 2006). It has only been in recent years that wikis have been put to use in higher education to aid students in experiencing deeper learning by being able to incorporate their own experiences into these new learning opportunities (Chen et al., 2005).

When faculty plan appropriately, wikis allow learners to actively participate in their own knowledge construction and also participate in co-writing with others (Boulos, Maramba1, & Wheeler, 2006). Bonk, Lee, Kim, and Lin (2009) state that wikis are a great example of "writing as thinking," where thoughts can be revisited, reused, and repurposed. They believe that wikis can provide the opportunity for learning transformations in which learners are introduced to new topics and perspectives and also are given the opportunity for critical reflection and examining their own assumptions and meaning-making (Mezirow, 1998). Bonk et al. (2009) noted that learning begins as social process (Vygotsky, 1978, 1986) and that adult learning theorists (Knowles, 1984; Rogers, 1983) and distance learning experts (Moore, 1989; Wedemeyer, 1981) believe that when adults are presented with self-directed learning opportunities, the greater their chances are of learning the information. Bonk et al. (2009) state that wikis provide learners meaningful, interactive, reflective, and collaborative opportunities in which learning takes precedence, requiring immediate application of skills learning and promoting motivation and engagement.

With basic knowledge of technology, wikis can be easily and quickly created, used, and maintained. Kirkpatrick (2006) states that the advantages of using wikis is that they require few technical skills and allow the student to focus on collaboration and information exchange without getting distracted with technical difficulties. If you choose to use a commercial-based wiki, then technical support will be provided to you, whereas open source wikis may require more technical skills.

ADDRESSING WIKI-RELATED CONTENT CONCERNS

Wikis can be very useful in educational settings, but the limitation of this tool is that it can be edited by any individual who may post inappropriate or irrelevant content to the wiki, which in turn may take away from the focus of the wiki. However, as you create your wiki, you may password protect your Web site. As an administrator, another feature you can set up is the "notify" feature, which will inform you of any changes. In this case, you have the ability to remove any irrelevant content. Also, in order to track the postings on your wiki, you can activate the history function of the wiki, which will provide you with the person authoring the postings and the time and date of the additions or deletions.

Wikis are powerful collaborative tools that provide students, faculty, and administration new dynamic opportunities in working together (Richardson, 2006). However, as Boulos and Wheeler (2007) note, the content of wikis is subject to open and democratic processes in editing and creating, and therefore many higher education institutions are looking for ways to handle such informal tools within the formalized structure of these institutions (Wheeler & Wheeler, 2009).

Another concern noted about the use of wikis is the idea of "hidden audience." In a study conducted by Wheeler and Wheeler (2009), they noted that students were aware of a hidden audience of visitors that would visit the wiki that could be tracked by the hit counter, but they had no knowledge of who these visitors were and they left very little feedback in the comment box. A simple solution to this problem is to create a password for accessing the wiki, thereby excluding outside visitors.

Some students were concerned about posting their writing in a public space and therefore put a lot of thought into their sentence structure, spelling (wiki lacks a spellchecker), and grammar, providing accurate citations to support their content, writing in small and manageable chunks of information, and also avoiding any type of content that would cause controversy among their peers (Wheeler & Wheeler, 2009). Another concern noted in an article posted by Educause Learning Initiative (2005) is that a wiki represents the collective perspective of the group that uses it, and therefore it has a collective bias.

While faculty need to consider how to address such concerns, each of these concerns also provide prime learning opportunities for teaching ethics, responsibility, privacy, Internet reputation, and more. Faculty may choose to establish ground rules and set parameters on the wiki form the start. Conversely, such decisions might be made through discussion with the students in each class using a wiki platform.

PEDAGOGICAL/ANDRAGOGICAL FOUNDATION

Powerful aspects of wikis in higher education are their collaborative and community-building power. Lave and Wenger first introduced the concept of a community of practice in 1991. Wenger (1998) states that communities of practice are groups of people who share enthusiasm or interest for something they do and learn how to do it better as they interact with each other. Wenger, McDermott, and Snyder (2002) similarly define communities of practice as "groups of people who share a concern, a set of problems, or a passion about a topic, and who deepen their knowledge and expertise in this area by interacting on an ongoing basis" (p. 7). Lave and Wenger (1991) argue that communities of practice are everywhere. They say that learning can happen in a social process in which people can participate at different levels. Wikis allow for much social interaction. Constructivist theorists believe that learning is a social process and that learning occurs through interactions (Bruner, 1996; Lave & Wenger, 1991; Vygotsky, 1978). Wikis allow students to problem solve and construct their own knowledge.

A community of practice provides an environment for social interaction between learners in which they can have a dialogue and discuss their learning and perspectives (Brown, 1994; Lave & Wenger, 1991). It is in participation in a dialogue with other learners that knowledge is shared, a community is formed, and dialogue occurs (Lave, 1988). Stein (1998) states that learning becomes a process of reflecting, interpreting, and negotiating meaning among the participants of a community.

While this concept may seem true for the faculty members in transition from face-to-face to online classrooms, many researchers believe that when in a new environment, teaching and learning assumptions must be renegotiated and what this means in the community of practice must be explored (Billett, 2001; Lave, 1988; Lave & Wenger, 1991; Wenger, 1998).

Clancey (1995) states that the situated learning discussions often refer to the idea of a community of practice. He explains that this is a way of describing any group of people who work together to accomplish some activity, which usually involves collaboration between individuals with different experiences.

Avis and Fisher (2006) state that engagement in communities of practice has increasingly been seen as an important aspect of adult learning. They believe that participation within such communities provides a dialogic space for learning. In the community of practice literature, learning is viewed as a social activity that occurs as new learners move through an established community's professional hierarchy toward expertise (Brown, Collins, & Duguid, 1989; Lave & Wenger, 1991; Wenger, 1998). Schlager Fusco, and Schank (2002) state that new practices and technologies are adopted by the communities of practice through their implementation over time. Lipponen (2002) believes that use of wikis in group work and collaboration assists in sharing knowledge and increases knowledge and expertise among the community of practice.

In using technology to create a community of practice, Carroll et al. (2003) suggest that using technology to connect learners when face-to-face interaction is not possible can be powerful and the ability to use such tools is growing among professionals. Schlager and Fusco (2003) note that formal structures such as WebCT are dominant in online education, and this type of environment takes away from creativity and spontaneity (Hartnell-Young, 2006).

Parker and Chao (2007) believe that there are two common approaches to learning in using wikis. The first is the cooperative/collaborative learning paradigm, and the second is the constructivist paradigm. In cooperative learning, students work in collaborative groups that support their individual learning. In these groups, there is interdependence between group members, but the individuals are held accountable for their contributions and collaboration. Johnson and Johnson (1986) state that individuals in cooperative teams will reach higher levels of thought and retain information longer than those who work alone. The second paradigm that Parker and Chao (2007) discuss is the constructivist paradigm. In this paradigm, knowledge is seen as constructed; the students engage in interaction with the learning materials, and by doing so, they can integrate new ideas and try to make meaning of the new information. In constructivism, learning is intentional through providing opportunities to the students to learn; this approach allows them authentic experiences where they can take away what they learned and apply it to new situations. Constructivism provides cooperative, collaborative, and conversational opportunities for the students, and this is what wikis are about.

Another approach to learning with wikis is narrative analysis. With this approach, text and online communication construct holistic learning experiences involving cognition, affect, and interaction (Yukawa, 2005). One can see how the complete recording of dialogue and editing in the wiki affords a prime platform for narrative analysis.

USES OF WIKIS FOR TEACHING AND LEARNING

Faculty can incorporate wikis into their curriculum in many different ways. They can be utilized in face-to-face or online classroom collaborative work and used for different aspects of course work. Warlick (2007) states that there are three major kinds of advantages to using wikis: (1) practical, as they allow for community collaboration; (2) political, as they offer freedom of participation; and (3) timely, as they can provide the most up-to-date content.

In an interview conducted by Briggs (2008) with Stewart Maden, Maden states that he believes that wikis can be a powerful tool in higher education in three areas: teaching, research, and administration. He states that in teaching, wikis may be used for faculty who teach different sections of the same course and are working together to develop or revise a curriculum and for course development. Another way to use wikis in teaching is as a collaborative tool for the students while working on group projects or lab reports. This also reduces the work load of the faculty who previously had to grade multiple projects and reports but now get fewer, as the wiki allows for more collaboration between students. This allows for sharing knowledge and experiences and also results in more in-depth and higher quality submissions. Wikis also allow the faculty to have a better sense of group participation, as wikis show the history of what content has been added and when, therefore making grading easier. Maden states that in administrative uses of a wiki, faculty, staff, and administration need to make a commitment to utilize the wiki as intended in order for it to be a successful medium.

In a research study conducted by the Center for Scholarly Technology (CST) at the University of Southern California on the uses of wikis in academic settings, Higdon (2005) identified six approaches to utilizing wikis in higher education. The first approach is student journaling, where the wiki allows "the students to journal for their own benefit, or for peer or instructor review" (Higdon, 2005, n.p.n.). The second approach is personal portfolios, in which the students electronically collect resources "such as course notes, images, Web resources, and PowerPoint slides" (Higdon, 2005, n.p.n.) in a wiki to assist them in making connections between these resources. Collaborative knowledge base is the third approach identified by Higdon; in this approach, wikis allow groups to create an environment in a wiki to share their information and knowledge while doing group work and projects.

Higdon (2005) suggests a fourth approach to wikis for use in research coordination and collaboration. A number of users at different locations may access the wiki, and within this environment they are given the opportunity to share ideas, documents, datasets, and other resources. Wikis also allow senior researchers to control the access permission to different parts of the wiki for other team members. The fifth approach to using wikis in higher education is for curricular and cross-disciplinary coordination purposes. As Higdon (2005) notes, "the wiki allows for departmental personnel, instructors, and teaching assistants to organize common course assets, such as syllabi, office hours, and assessments, without having an endless email chain or difficult to schedule face-to-face meetings" (n.p.n.). The sixth and final approach suggested by Higdon is to utilize wikis to coordinate and organize academic conferences and colloquia and also to permit the conference attendees to participate in discussions posted on a wiki and allow them to add or modify contents and share resources with other participants. Wikis can also be used as a medium for professional development by allowing faculty to post their resources, notes, research, and best practices about their field of study.

CASE STUDIES

This section presents two brief case studies to provide a close-up perspective of wikis used in higher education. To be certain, these are only a few of a myriad of possibilities; however, they provide details and specifics for you to translate and transform for your specific discipline and higher education context.

Athens State University

In a study conducted at Athens State University, Rich, Cowan, Herring, and Wilkes (2009) looked at the implementation of wikis in higher education and noted several pedagogical approaches to successfully incorporating collaborative technologies into online courses. These include student introductions, collaborative group work, project management, electronic portfolios (e-portfolios), a course bibliography, and a knowledge base of training materials about technology.

Wikis were utilized for student interactions in order to enable the faculty to build an environment for students to get together and create a knowledge warehouse of related information. Rich et al. (2009) state that wikis were often used to support group work and projects as well as to create personal student wiki pages so that the students could introduce themselves to the class and talk about their interests, hobbies, family, and likes and dislikes. Students used wikis to manage project timelines and content, and they were able to collaborate and share information about their project on their team wiki. The result of this collaborative work was an e-portfolio, which was a collection of information created as a result of this project. Wikis are living documents, so upon completion of a project, the resources may be shared with the next group to add and modify the content at hand (Raman, Ryan, & Olfman, 2005).

At Athens State University, in addition to using the wiki to create a collaborative work, students utilized this tool to create a course-specific bibliography of references and terms specific to the content matter. Rich et al. (2009) noted an additional use of wikis in creating a knowledge base of shared technology information. An example of the use of wikis in this manner was a wiki Web site created to serve as a repository of training materials related to Livetext, an e-portfolio software tool. To assist in training, a wiki (http://wendycowanlivetexttraining.pbwiki.com/FrontPage) was created to house a series of video tutorials and step-by-step guides for students and faculty members on how to use LiveText as well as instructional materials on accessing e-portfolios and assignments.

TikiWiki

In another case study, Raman et al. (2005) conducted research about whether wikis were effective tools to support knowledge creation and sharing in academia. In their study, they used an open source wiki called "Tiki-Wiki" with a class of 20 postgraduate students. They also interviewed these students. In their research, they understood that the students utilized this wiki that was set up as a knowledge management tool to create and extract information directly related to their class, such as summaries of recommended readings, only between 3–5 hours per week. However, the wiki was mostly used to follow up on what was discussed in their face-to-face class; it was used to a very limited extent to create new collaborative knowledge, and only two students used the wiki to facilitate group work. Raman et al. (2005) concluded that wikis are most used for managing and updating information rather than collaboratively creating new knowledge.

WIKI RESOURCES

There are several Websites that allow anyone to create wikis free of charge. These are open source, and others are commercial sites. However, you must note that free wikis typically include advertising. Some popular wiki sites include Google Docs (http://docs.google.com), Wetpaint (http://www.wetpaintcentral .com), PBWorks (http://pbworks.com), Wikidot (http://www.wikidot.com), TWiki (http://twiki.org), and Wikispaces (http://www.wikispaces.com).

WikiMatrix (www.wikimatrix.org) is a very useful tool for faculty, as it not only provides a comprehensive comparison of more than 50 types of wiki platforms, but also is set up as a Web site to assist in selecting the wiki most suitable to your needs. By clicking the Wiki Choice Wizard link (see Figure 8.1) and completing a set of questions, you receive a list of wikis that fulfill your specifications. For instance, as part of the questions asked, users choose whether they would like to choose free, open source, or commercial products.

In his book, *Wikipatterns*, Stewart Mader (2007) states that there is no single and correct way to using a wiki but notes the importance of patterns

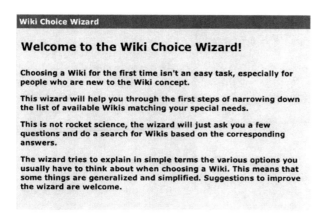

Figure 8.1 Wiki Choice Wizard (from www.wikimatrix.org/wizard.php) created by CosmoCode.

in building wikis. He explains that by using patterns, those new to using this media can benefit from other people's experiences and imitate what has been already created so as not to make the same mistakes. In the accompanying Web site http://wikipatterns.com/display/wikipatterns/Wiki-patterns, Mader introduces the user to the different types of patterns and how these patterns can be put to use to improve wikis.

EVALUATION

Kuropatwa (2006) reveals some of his wiki-related instructional strategies in a blog post in which he notes two specific types of wiki contributions that students could make while working together on a projects: (1) significant contributions and (2) constructive modifications. He defines *significant contributions* as "a new content addition to any wiki page" (Kuropatwa, 2006, n.p.n.). As part of the requirements for such contributions he asks his students to post at least 4–5 sentences of "accurate information and reflect a deep level of understanding about the topic that you are writing about" (n.p.n.). For grading purposes, he suggests the following questions: "Is the contribution related to current content? Is it accurate? Does it include an extensive amount of detailing? Is the language accurate enough to be understood easily?" (n.p.n.).

Furthermore, Kuropatwa (2006) codifies his instructional wiki use by defining a *constructive modification* as "when you [a student] edit someone else's work—not your own" (n.p.n.) by correcting or pointing out an error or noting grammatical errors or commenting on the interface and the way the wiki is structured. He states here that the idea is to guide the wiki content forward in a constructive way. He poses the following guiding questions for evaluating student contributions:

> Were the modifications done correctly? Did the corrected information need correction? Did the modifications clarify language that was confusing? Did the modifications make the language more interesting to read or more fluent? Did the modifications add to the piece in a meaningful way? Is the entry noticeably improved after the modifications? (Kuropatwa, 2006, n.p.n.)

Building upon examples such as Kuropatwa's, faculty can develop their personal criteria for wiki posting and the rubric or grading criteria they will use. As with all instructional assignments and their assessments, clearly stating requirements, expectations, and grading criteria will facilitate greater understanding of assignments and the expected potential learning outcomes.

ACTIVITIES FOR FACULTY

1. Review the possible uses of wikis in higher education classrooms from this chapter. Identify which courses will benefit from an online platform for student collaboration. Select the first one you will work on and check to see if your university has a wiki platform that they prefer you to use.
2. Review your group project instructions in one class. Consider how you could adapt it to a wiki format. Could each group have its own page to work on? Draft revised assignment instructions and then determine how you will describe your grading protocol with the wiki.
3. If you are able to select your own wiki platform, return to the section in this chapter about Wiki Choice Wizard. Visit the link and see which wikis will meet your next wiki project. (www.wikimatrix.org/wizard.php)
4. Search for several examples of classroom wikis. Make a list of best practices you see and would like to incorporate in your first wiki. Compare your list to those discussed in this chapter. Are there conflicts of purpose or practice? Have you discovered some new strategies? Keep evolving your practice by discussing with colleagues and posting to discussion boards of educational wiki users.

REFERENCES

Avis, J., & Fisher, R. (2006, July). Reflections on communities of practice, online learning and transformation: Teachers, lecturers and trainers. *Research in Post Compulsory Education, 11*(2), 141–151.

Billett, S. (2001). *Learning in the workplace: strategies for effective practice.* Crows Nest, Australia: Allen and Unwin.

Bonk, C. J., Lee, M. M., Kim, N., & Lin, M. G. (2009). The tensions of transformation in three cross-institutional wikibook projects. *Internet and Higher Education, 12*(3–4), 126–135.

Boulos, M. N. K., Maramba1, I., & Wheeler, S. (2006). Wikis, blogs and podcasts: a new generation of web-based tools for virtual collaborative clinical practice and education. *BMC Medical Education, 6*(41). Retrieved from http://www.ncbi.nlm.nih.gov/pmc/articles/PMC1564136/pdf/1472-6920-6-41.pdf

Boulos, M. N. K., & Wheeler, S. (2007). The emerging Web 2.0 social software: An enabling suite of sociable technologies in health and healthcare education. *Health Information and Libraries Journal, 24*(1), 2–23.

Briggs, L. L. (2008, August 20). The power of wikis in higher ed. *Campus Technology.* Retrieved June 15, 2009 from http://campustechnology.com/articles/2008/08/the-power-of-wikis-in-higher-ed.aspx

Brown, A. L. (1994). The advancement of learning. *Educational Researcher, 23*(8), 4–12.

Brown, J. S., Collins, A., & Duguid, P. (1989). Situated cognition and the culture of learning. *Educational Researcher, 18*(1), 32–42.

Bruner, J. (1996). *The culture of education.* Cambridge, MA: Harvard University Press.

Carroll, J. M., Choo, C. W., Dunlap, D. R., Isenhour, P. L., Kerr, S. T., MacLean, A., & Rosson, M. B. (2003). Knowledge management support for teachers. *Educational Technology, Research and Development, 51*(4), 42–46.

Chao, J. (2007, July). Student project collaboration using wikis. *Proceedings of the 20th Conference on Software Engineering Education and Training held at Dublin, Ireland* (pp. 255–261). Washington DC: IEEE Computer Society.

Chen, H. L., Cannon, D. Gabrio, J., Leifer, L., Toye, G., & Bailey, Y. (2005, June). Using wikis and weblogs to support reflective learning in an introductory engineering design course. *Proceedings of the 2005 American Society for Engineering Education Annual Conference & Exposition.* Portland, OR.

Clancey, W. J. (1995). A tutorial on situated learning. In J. Self (Ed.), *Proceedings of the International Conference on Computers and Education (Taiwan)(AACE)* (pp. 49–70). Charlottesville, VA. Retrieved July 30, 2010 from http://cogprints.org/323/1/139.htm

Educause Learning Initiative (2005, July). *Wikis.* Retrieved January 5, 2010 from http://www.educause.edu/eli

Evans, P. (2006, January/February). The wiki factor. *BizEd,* pp. 28–32. Retrieved from http://www.aacsb.edu/publications/archives/janfeb06/p28-33.pdf

Hartnell-Young, E. (2006). Teachers' roles and professional learning in communities of practice supported by technology in schools. *Journal of Technology and Teacher Education, 14*(3), 461–480.

Higdon, J. (2005, November 15). Teaching, learning, and other uses for wikis in academia. *Campus Technology.* Retrieved June 15, 2009 from http://campustechnology.com/articles/2005/11/teaching-learning-and-other-uses-for-wikis-in-academia.aspx?sc_lang=en

Johnson, R. T., & Johnson, D. W. (1986). Action research: Cooperative learning in science classroom. *Science and Children, 24,* 31–32.

Kirkpatrick, M. (2006). *The flu wiki: A serious application of new web tools.* Retrieved June 1, 2009 from http://marshallk.blogspot.com/2005/07/flu-wiki-serious-application-of-new.html

Knowles, M. (1984). *Andragogy in action.* San Francisco: Jossey–Bass.

Kuropatwa, D. (2006, April 29). Wiki solution manuals [Web log comment]. Retrieved from http://adifference.blogspot.com/2006/04/wiki-solution-manuals.html

Lave, J. (1988). *Cognition in practice: Mind, mathematics, and culture in everyday life.* Cambridge, U.K.: Cambridge University Press.

Lave, J., & Wenger, E. (1991). *Situated learning: Legitimate peripheral participation.* New York: Cambridge University Press.

Lipponen, L. (2002, January). Exploring foundations for computer-supported collaborative learning. *Proceedings of the Computer-supported Collaborative Learning Conference 2002, 72–81.* Boulder, CO.

Mader, S. (2007). *Wikipatterns.* New York: Wiley.

Madden M., & Fox, S. (2006). *Riding the wave of "Web 2.0": More than a buzzword, but still not easily defined.* Pew Internet Life Project. Retrieved from http://pewresearch.org/pubs/71/riding-the-waves-of-web-20

Mezirow, J. (1991). *Transformative dimensions of adult learning.* San Francisco: Jossey-Bass.

Moore, M.G. (1989). Editorial: Three types of interaction. *The American Journal of Distance Education, 3*(2), 1–6.

Parker, K. R., & Chao, J. T. (2007). Wiki as a teaching tool. *Interdisciplinary Journal of Knowledge and Learning Objects, 3,* 57–72.

Raman, M., Ryan, T., & Olfman, L. (2005). Designing knowledge management systems for teaching and learning with wiki technology. *Journal of Information Systems Education, 16,* 311–320.

Rich, L. L., Cowan, W., Herring, S. D., & Wilkes, W. (2009, March). *Collaborate, engage, and interact in online learning: Successes with wikis and synchronous virtual classrooms at Athens State University.* Paper presented at the 14th Annual Instructional Technology Conference, Murfreesboro, TN.

Richardson, W. (2006). *Blogs, wikis, podcasts, and other powerful web tools for classrooms.* Thousand Oaks, CA: Corwin Press.

Rogers, C.R. (1983). *Freedom to learn for the 80s.* Columbus, OH: Charles E. Merrill Publishing Company.

Schlager, M. S., & Fusco, J. (2003). Teacher professional development, technology, and communities of practice: Are we putting the cart before the horse? *The Information Society, 19,* 203–220.

Schlager, M. S., Fusco, J., & Schank, P. (2002). Evolution of an online education community of practice. In K. A. Renninger & W. Shumar (Eds.), *Building virtual communities: Learning and change in cyberspace.* New York: Cambridge University Press. Retrieved from http://tappedin.org/tappedin/web/papers/2002/TIEvolution.pdf

Stein, D. (1998). *Situated learning in adult eEducation.* ERIC Digest. Retrieved from http://www.ericdigests.org/1998-3/adult-education.html

Vygotsky, L. (1978). *Mind in society.* Cambridge, MA: Harvard University Press.

Vygotsky, L. (1986). *Thought and language.* Cambridge, MA: MIT Press.

Warlick, D. (2007). The executive wiki: Wikis can be a multitasking administrators' best friend. *Technology & Learning, 27*(11), 36.

Wedemeyer, C.A. (1981). *Learning at the back door: Reflections on non-traditional learning in the lifespan.* Madison, WI: University of Wisconsin Press.

Wenger, E. (1998). *Communities of practice.* Melbourne, Australia: Cambridge University Press.

Wenger, E., McDermott, R. A., & Snyder, W. (2002). *Cultivating communities of practice: A guide to managing knowledge.* Boston: Harvard Business School Press.

Wheeler, S., & Wheeler, D. (2009). Using wikis to promote quality in learning in teacher training. *Learning, Media and Technology, 34(1),* 1–10.

Wikipedia. (n.d.). Overview. Retrieved June 1, 2010 from http://en.wikipedia.org/wiki/Wikipedia:Overview_FAQ

Yukawa, J. (2005). Story-lines: A case study of online learning using narrative analysis. In T. Koschmann, D. Suthers, & T. W. Chan (Eds.), *Computer supported collaborative learning 2005: The next 10 years* (pp. 732–736). Mahwah, NJ: Lawrence Erlbaum Associates.

CHAPTER 9

VIRTUAL OFFICE HOURS

Thomas D. Cox
University of Houston–Victoria

April Williams
University of Tennessee–Memphis

INTRODUCTION

Research has shown that there are benefits of student–faculty contact out-side of the classroom. However, most studies have found that actual face-to-face communication between faculty and their students is infrequent and mostly limited to formal and structured situations such as classroom lectures (Pitts, 2009). The practice of holding traditional office hours has been a required part of professors' teaching responsibilities for a long time. It was designed to provide students with an opportunity for informal com-munication beyond the classroom in order to seek additional help and ask questions. The value of office hours has been widely viewed as a key aspect in facilitating the relationship between instructors and their students. How-ever, studies have shown that students rarely visit their instructors and when they do, the visits tend to be brief and concise. Studies performed by Jasma and Kopper (1999) and Fusani (1994) (as cited in Li & Pitts, 2009) found that fewer than half of the students in the study reported visiting their pro-fessor outside of the scheduled class session.

135

A key challenge for colleges and universities is to understand how to better engage students in the communication process that stimulates more substantial and frequent interaction with faculty. One such means for facilitating more frequent interaction is to utilize computer-mediated communications to enhance traditional office hours (as cited in Li & Pitts, 2009). In a study by CDW Government in 2008, college students indicatedthat they wanted more regular and immediate communication with faculty, and they rated online chat with professors as the capability they desired the most. Another study by Jafari, McGee, and Carmean in 2006 revealed that students preferred such means of communication as instant messaging and podcasts. College students want these tools integrated into the course environment for both communication and collaboration.

Such opportunities are where "virtual office hours" can accomplish many goals such as assisting students who miss in-person office hours; responding to individual questions publically so that all students can benefit; linking related facts through hypertext; making course materials available without building or library hours limitations; mapping student questions conceptually through FAQs (Frequently Asked Questions); and teaching concepts by linking to 3-D graphics, animations, and audio tracks. Chat rooms and instant messaging during virtual office hours also allows an opportunity for teachers to provide personalized encouragement to students who need it, motivation by commenting on strengths of student work, and clarifying for the student any previous feedback on their work. Chat and instant messaging also give the student a sense that there is a "real" warm-bodied person they are dealing with who is guiding their learning. In short, the use of these synchronous tools creates a more "robust" learning opportunity for students because teachers are meeting students where they are.

The word *virtual* can be defined as: that which is not real, but displays the full quality of the real. In other instances, it can be replaced with the word "almost" in a context such as "virtually impossible." The word *virtual* has been applied to computing and information technology with various meanings. In terms of "virtual office hours" and "virtual classroom," this chapter refers to computer-generated simulations of face-to-face meetings. Such virtual sessions include environments where users create entire virtual worlds and the real world is supplemented with computer images including words in various forms. This is a type of environmental habitation grounded in Web technology that allows interactions between individuals at different locations and at different times.

"Virtual office hours" often refers to set times when an instructor is available to learners for one-on-one or small-group consultations. For example, if an individual or several individuals are having difficulty understanding an assignment or want clarification of what the teacher wants for an assignment, the teacher can hold a virtual meeting to discuss only this assignment. Students can ask their questions for their own clarity and for the entire group's benefit.

Therefore, these hours may be scheduled individually or as a class. When a class is scheduled to meet at the same time, it may be through framed formats such as a webinar or a chat room. Virtual office hours may be used to offer individualized feedback for students regarding their work or as a group in regards to group projects. Such a format may be utilized to consult on academic or project planning with the learner. Virtual office hours may be used for "live performance" evaluations or consultations in live interactive simulation formats, or they may be used for learner supports for other specific needs related to instruction, tutors, or academic scheduling.

Virtual office hours aid in building and sustaining instructor–student bonding. This ongoing interaction humanizes the instructor to learners. Instructors may use live chat, live video, live audio, recorded video or audio, and webinar software to conduct virtual office hours. Table 9.1 provides just a few of the options for accomplishing this.

Instructors may use software such as those listed in Table 9.1 or even a telephone conference call to hold virtual office hours. The idea is to have multiple channels of communication between the instructor and the learner to form an optimum learning experience. Adult learners benefit from multiple communication forms and instructional strategies. Moreover, having multiple forms—or *redundancy*, as it is called in the technology world—is helpful when one form has technical disruptions or people do not access for other reasons.

TABLE 9.1   Virtual Office Hours: Technologies and Capabilities

Technology Format	Technology Service	Capabilities
Live Chat		Jabber Messenger is a full-featured Windows desktop instant messaging service for one-on-one and group chat. www.jabber.com
Live Audio/Video Webinar		Adobe Acrobat Connect allows screen sharing, whiteboard, chat, video, and audio conferencing. It also allows recording of sessions. www.adobe.com
Live Audio/Video/ Instant Messaging		Skype allows free video calls, free Skype-to-Skype calls, easy texting, and free instant messaging. www.skype.com

There are also some guidelines and imperatives for using virtual office hours to supplement face-to-face office hours. With more and more adults and non-traditional students attending college these days, we have to understand that many of them are balancing school, work, and families and cannot physically come to campus during the teacher's assigned office hours. Offering virtual office hours levels the "playing field" for all students to have interaction with the teacher. For instance, an unusual concern that has arisen in recent years is that some students consider that it is not "fair" that students who take classes online are in constant virtual contact with the teacher, while those who are in face-to-face courses only have an opportunity to interact with the teacher at the assigned course time or during assigned office hours. One has to teach online for but a short time to realize that, in a sense, because of email and the asynchronous nature of online courses, virtual office hours never cease. Therefore, faculty need to be sensitive and proactive in providing equal opportunities for interaction with all of our students.

Berger (1999) suggests that distance education professors set up online office hours and incorporate live chat sessions into their virtual classrooms. Similarly, Perreault, Waldman, Alexander, & Zhao (2002) recommend that professors strive to create distance education courses that promote interaction and collaboration by providing multiple means for communicating such as e-mail, discussion boards, online office hours, and flexible telephone access. Deciding which technology to utilize for virtual office hours is an individual decision for each instructor. However, having more than one option also supports and communicates a learner-centered climate.

Some instructors have very heavy workloads and may be scheduled in a face-to-face classroom or a clinic setting most of the week. This leaves precious few hours to complete lesson planning, test grading, and administrative responsibilities. It may be the best practice for these instructors to set specific times during the week for virtual office hours with students in the online class. If an instructor must set limited contact virtual office hours, however, he or she should take into consideration the fact that most online students today are non-traditional students and usually work during the daytime each week or they have other responsibilities that have caused them to choose the online setting for their education. The instructor may need to be flexible and set virtual office hours during an evening or two each week of the semester. This may be adjusted as the semester progresses for several reasons. Students tend to have more questions and concerns at the beginning of each semester and a week or two weeks before large projects are due.

Implementing virtual office hours into an online course can add synchronized communication for interaction among students and the professor. It also allows students to utilize different mass media sources. The environment can permit students to explore the learning materials organized in the virtual classroom such as hypermedia and online books, to conduct experiments in a virtual digital lab, to interact synchronously with student colleagues and/or the professor, and to evaluate their assessment through interactive tests (Bruselovsky, Schwarz, & Weber, 1996). This may prove to be an extraordinarily effective method to increase not only access to information and materials, but to augment and improve both faculty–student and peer contact, and ultimately to increase each student's depth and breadth of knowledge in his or her field of study (Skillicorn, 1997).

PEDAGOGICAL/ANDRAGOGICAL FOUNDATION: HOW DO VIRTUAL OFFICE HOURS ENHANCE LEARNING?

One cannot underestimate students' desire to communicate with an instructor, and learners in distance education environments are no exception (Leh, 2001). If an instructor is intending to integrate virtual office hour communication in the virtual classroom in the hopes of delivering timely and valuable feedback to students, the instructor needs to understand the concept of feedback and how it functions.

Bloom (1976) listed feedback, in addition to participation, cues, and reinforcement, as one of the four elements to determine the quality of instruction. It is generally agreed upon that feedback is an important aspect for improving student performance and instruction. Feedback is often subject to classification schemes outlining inherent characteristics. Carter (1984) describes feedback as having four characteristics: function, timing, schedule, and type. A review of the research surrounding the nature of instructor feedback and feedback's role in education reveals a multifaceted picture. This can be worsened if an instructor utilizes complicated means of communication that the instructor does not understand and cannot use properly, therefore failing to communicate frequently with students.

On the other hand, communication can be a wonderful means of delivering feedback to students. Once a basic understanding of feedback's role in learning is established by the instructor, he or she can begin to focus on strategies and methodologies to best take advantage of the pedagogical functions of communication forums. Tao and Boulware (2002) suggest that communication benefits faculty members by "identifying instructional focus and taking advantage of instructional moments to fit the developmental needs of their students in authentic situations" (p. 288). They also found that communication motivates learners, creates new learning opportunities, and encourages authentic communication. Therefore, feedback should not be underestimated by instructors.

Vonderwell (2003) found in a qualitative study of undergraduate students in an online course that online communication allows for improved communication and allows students an opportunity to ask more questions of the instructor. She also stresses that the use of online communication and feedback can create a sense of anonymity, which may cause increased participation from shyer students. In addition, three studies conducted by Smith, Whitely, and Smith (1999) concluded that online communication and feedback is a "viable alternative means of course delivery" (p. 24). Online instructors, therefore, need to utilize online feedback as much as possible with their students, and these findings point to likely benefits for face-to-face classes using the same communication tools.

DeBard and Guidara (2000) stress that better online communication and more frequent use of asynchronous communication in the higher education classroom is needed. They found that asynchronous communication can be utilized to meet Chickering's (as cited in Reisser, 1995) seven principles of effective teaching. DeBard and Guidara (2000) also point to online communication as a source of more intensive student interaction that can lead to more active, deeper, and more engaged learning. They note that "an average response in an electronic discussion was found to be 106 words while the average in-class response was only twelve words" (DeBard & Guidara, 2000, p. 225).

Leh (2001) conducted a study that found that "computer-mediated communication was beneficial for communication and learning and that participants were in favor of the use of computer-mediated communication" (p. 126). A follow-up study performed found the positive impact of computer-mediated communication increased over time as well. The more students were comfortable using the technical forms of communication, the more they used it. This speaks to building 21st-century workplace skills and information literacy into all classes.

Carswell, Thomas, Petre, Price, & Richards (2000) at The Open University in the United Kingdom performed a large-scale trial study of undergraduate students solely taught via online communication. They provided a summary of online advantages as perceived by the students:

- Faster assignment return
- More immediate feedback
- Robust model for questions with greater perceived reliability
- Increased interaction with instructor and other students
- Extended learning experiences (such as problem-sharing with other students) beyond the lecture
- Internet experience

They also discovered that students' experiences were largely favorable and "they wished to repeat the experience—a major factor in maintaining the enthusiasm and motivation of distance education students…" (Carswell et al., p. 45). In addition, online communication can be seen as an "ideal tool for building and maintaining social relationships" (Carswell et al., p. 45).

As we have just seen through reviewing the research, there are many advantages to online communication. From a methodological and pedagogical perspective, Roblyer and Knezek (2003) stress the importance of improving technology implementation methods of adult educational instruction. Not all adult learners are the same, however. Not all online students will be open, willing, and able to implement all forms of online technological communication, such as webinars, instant messaging, chat rooms, and so forth. Therefore, it is the instructor's responsibility to aid any students who are not able to utilize the mediums of online communication for virtual office hours.

This task of providing guidance in using the technology may be very difficult if the student is in need of intense tutoring. What does an instructor do with a student who is not able to learn how to operate the technical varieties of virtual office hour communication? An instructor should have step-by-step instructions or instructional Web site links for the technology used in virtual office hours available for all students in the class. Moreover, an instructor who is utilizing many different forms of virtual office hour communication may select the most appropriate technology option available to tutor a student who is having a difficult time with curriculum concepts.

In relation to this discussion, we need to remember that faculty do not want to enable students' abdication of responsibility. Knowles (1970, 1980) proposed that one of the hallmark assumptions of adult learning is that learners become increasingly self-directed as they mature. According to Merriam and Cafferella (1999), three of the major goals of instructors of adult learners are (1) to enable students to be lifelong and self-directed learners, (2) to foster transformational learning as central to self-directed learning, and (3) to promote emancipatory learning and social action as an integral part of self-directed learning. Virtual office hours should be utilized to encourage self-learning. This goal can be achieved by educators as they encouraged adult learners to be able to plan, carry out, and evaluate their own learning through metacognition. Such learning can be facilitated and accomplished individually or through online group communication. For example, in the independent pursuit of learning, instructors might provide feedback to individuals or groups of students regarding locating resources or mastering alternative learning strategies.

Garrison and Baynton (1987) assert that learner control is a chief factor in establishing positive or negative instructional interactions between the online learner and the instructor. Learner control implies independence, competence, and support during distance interactions. Garrison and Baynton (1987) further point out that communication between learner and instructor is recommended not only when instruction is taking place, but also in the planning stage in order to allow students an opportunity to negotiate objectives, content, and learning activities. Therefore, if an instructor is going to stress self-directed learning for adult online students and allow for learner control, then many technical means of accessing virtual office hours is imperative for such a classroom setting. By having many forms of virtual office hours media available to the adult online student, the instructor allows students to choose the medium that is most comfortable for him or her to utilize in order to access instructor feedback.

BEST PRACTICES, INCLUDING CAUTIONS

Virtual office hours also serve the purpose of creating a sense of community. Merriam and Caffarella (1999) mention others' claims about the importance of "community." Sissel (1997, as cited in Merriam and Caffarella, 1999) observed that "the creation of community and the promotion of participation with learners require concrete steps.... Questioning and reflection are but the first steps . . . that can be increasingly responsive to the needs of learners" (p. 85). According to Cunningham (1988, as cited in Merriam and Caffarella, 1999) community "means encouraging expression by the individual through dialogue, writing, and public expression" and promoting the skills necessary in "creating knowledge and action" (p. 85). Critical pedagogy, or critical practice, is most useful when it originates with and from community-based social action groups with an interest in changing social structures.

In addition, using various forms of online communication for virtual office hours, for both face-to-face and distance online learning, comes with some caveats. Carswell et al. (2000) discovered that inexperience is a major obstacle for online-based classroom settings. They found that online cultural inexperience was a larger obstacle than technical inexperience, contrary to what most people would expect. This is because asynchronous online environments require a shift in communication norms, such as sensitivity and attunement to online etiquette and rules as well as appropriate communication expectations, such as how long it should take an instructor to respond to a question or discussion board post.

In addition, online communication can be time consuming, and it often means extra work for instructors (DeBard & Guidera, 1999). However, utilizing best practices can help save time. The use of online chats and instant messaging to facilitate student interaction and virtual office hours has been found to increase workload for faculty and result in student expectations of "ubiquitous instructor access" (Li & Pitts, 2009, p. 179). A solution for this problem is to set ground rules and limitations for the professor's time commitment and help. This will assist in student expectations. For example, teachers should clearly outline times for virtual office hours. It might be useful to include this in the syllabus or emails at the beginning of class, including days and times, and mention that other opportunities will be scheduled as needed. Doing these things will make it clear to students when they can expect to have access to the teacher.

Organizational support of faculty members to provide virtual office hours is important. Training and online access are also factors to consider. Both instructor and students need to be oriented to each form of online communication that will be utilized in the classroom. The campus must have a hardware and software infrastructure already in place (Yu & Yu, 2002). This is because the utilization of multiple online communication mediums requires a certain level of technical expertise and a considerable amount of technical support (Carswell et al., 2000).

Vonderwell (2003) discovered that some students can be uncomfortable interacting with people they do not know and have never met. She also found that some students are uncomfortable in the delay of immediate instructor and student feedback. Some students also perceived a sense of separation from the instructor. In contrast, virtual office hours are a chance for the faculty member to use a variety of tools for meeting different learning and communication needs of students. Video, chat rooms, live audio, and webinar software may be used to ease the negative feelings listed above.

For example, virtual office hours can be a collaborative and community-building experience instead of being potentially isolating. Furthermore, collaborative learning can be facilitated through the use of online chats. The following tip sheet (Table 9.2), adapted from Paloff and Pratt (2007), identifies the challenges associated with online chat and highlights key strategies for implementing effective and engaging chat experiences.

Deciding how to best utilize different forms of online communication mediums for a particular class is not an exact science. However, the literature and your own personal experience teaching your discipline and knowing your student needs can help guide you. Listed below are some suggestions or guidelines from research for effectively using online communication means in order to utilize virtual office hours to their full potential.

Getting Started With Virtual Office Hours

According to Tao and Boulware (2002), instructors must take an active role in encouraging active student participation in virtual office hour technology. One way to accomplish this is to have collaborative exercises early in the semester or quarter that require synchronous and asynchronous components in order to promote a sense of community. Yu and Yu (2002) also sug-

TABLE 9.2   Tips for Effective Online Chats

Challenges to Effective Chats
- Facilitating a chat is typically much more difficult than facilitating a face-to-face discussion.
- Typing ability affects one's ability to participate in the chat.
- Students without a high-speed Internet connection may experience additional lag time between postings and responses, thereby disrupting the synchronous nature of the chat.
- Chats are generally more conducive to extemporaneous discussion rather than reflective and critical thinking.

Overcoming the Challenges
- Limit chat groups to four or five students.
- Keep chat sessions to an hour or less.
- Provide specific questions for students to consider prior to the chat.
- Be clear about chat room rules, including who will facilitate portions of the chat, the instructor's role throughout the chat, how often and when students should post comments, civility expectations, and acceptable shorthand notation.
- Instruct students to break up lengthy posts by typing ellipses (...) after the first portion of a post.

Strategies for Structuring Effective Chats
- Jigsaw: The purpose of the jigsaw is for each student to share relevant highlights from an assigned text with classmates who reviewed different texts. Through this technique, the group gains familiarity with a broader array of sources.
- Role Play: In a role play, student postings take the perspective of a type of person (example: Union Leader) or an actual person (example: Ulysses S. Grant).
- Debate: Students respond by taking a specified position on an issue. Clear guidelines on the structure of the debate and content of postings are critical to a successful debate.
- Guest Speakers: Outside experts can join the discussion and field student questions. Alternatively, the "guest speakers" could consist of selected students playing the role of an expert.
- Office Hours: Instructors can use online chats as the medium for holding office hours. This can be especially helpful since all students can reference the archived chat at later dates.

Other Possible Resources

Acrobat Connect	Google Talk*
Adobe Connect	Instant Messaging *
Audacity *	iTunes *
BlackBoard Chat (electronic Whiteboard)	MOO
Blog or Threaded Discussion to Frequently Asked Questions on Discussion Board	Moodle*
Collaborate!	Pronto (Wimba)
Dimdim*	Quick Time Player *
Email (with video or audio attachments if possible)*	RealPlayer*
Elluminate Live!	SharePoint (Microsoft)
Facebook *	Skype*
Gizmo*	Twitter*
Google Buzz*	Yugma*
	WebEx (Cisco Systems)
	Windows Media Player*

* Indicates resource is free

Note: Adapted from *Collaborating Online: Learning Together in Community* (p. 121) by R. Palloff and K. Pratt (2007). San Francisco: Jossey-Bass. Copyright 2007 by Wiley & Sons. Adapted with permission.

gest using icebreaker activities the first week to start dialogue and familiarize students with the technology and with each other. An introduction and orientation to all available communication technology features is also needed. One specific suggestion is to run a "test exercise" (and require attachments, if applicable) for each medium of technology to be used in the class. This approach could include posting a photograph and short biography to the class roster page. In this manner, students not only practice the technology, but also become acquainted with one another (including the instructor!).

VIRTUAL OFFICE HOUR CORRESPONDENCE AND ETIQUETTE

Warm and friendly virtual communication is the preferred mode for faculty members. Keeping correspondences and chat replies with students as personal, friendly, and positive as possible has many benefits. Cold and impersonal online communication can alienate online students and detract from the online community. As the instructor, you set the tone of the class. Use students' names as much as possible. This helps put students at ease, especially in the asynchronous means of online communication. Another suggestion is to use emoticons to provide social cues (Skillicorn, 1997). In addition, research has shown that audio clips from the instructor or video attachments of related content may foster a sense of community and strengthen social relationships (Woods & Keeler, 2001). A good plan is to use these frequently, but to spread them out over time to balance the workload.

Some additional virtual communication etiquette rules for faculty include the following:

- Be aware of and sensitive to students who are not native speakers of the language.
- Instructors are liable for everything in writing when posted online in virtual office hours and in the discussion board. Therefore, be cautious and succinct, but thorough.
- Be aware of each online student's physical location. Students may experience emergencies, inclement weather, or natural disasters during the semester, which can cause a student's computer server to go down. Therefore, having an instructor telephone number posted in the classroom for the students to reach the instructor in case of such an incident is imperative.
- Maintain a sense of professionalism by watching spelling and grammar in all forms of written online communication. However, this rule may be relaxed in chat sessions due to the nature of the chat room, where typing speed needs to be dramatically increased.

- Instructors should treat distance students with the same respect as face-to-face students. This includes family emergencies and other issues. Prior to the first day of class, guideline statements should be placed in the syllabus or within the online classroom that discusses how student emergencies, natural disasters, inclement weather, and inoperable servers will be handled by the instructor.

CASE STUDIES

The following are examples of unique case studies about how some universities and faculty are using virtual office hours. You are encouraged to explore the cases first-hand as well as read about them here.

1. The University of California in Los Angeles (UCLA) Biochemistry department has posted a Virtual Office Hours Web site for their students at http://voh.chem.ucla.edu. They state that 96% of sophomore chemistry students polled voted "Yes" to virtual office hours. If you visit the Web site, there are many different links to aid students and faculty. There is a "Frequently Asked Questions" link, a specific link for faculty members, a specific link for online students, a "Virtual Office Hours Handout" link, a "How To" link, a software link, and many more. It is worth reviewing to develop ideas for how you might want to implement and document virtual office hours into the curriculum.
2. Purdue University has a Web site link at http://www.education.purdue.edu/edit/officehours/, where the university's Educational Information Technology department holds virtual office hours by using Adobe Connect every Wednesday afternoon during a specific time slot to answer student and faculty member questions. This Web site allows visitors and instructors with Adobe Connect capabilities to visit the Web site in order to learn more about this kind of software.

DISCUSSIONS FOR FURTHER USE

Virtual office hours and advances in online communication mediums are growing as powerful educational and communication forces. With this integration also comes a wonderful opportunity for refurbishment of the educational delivery to adult learners. With all of the new technology available to adult learners, faculty must make a commitment to integrate technology into the curriculum. There are many potential advantages of virtual office hours over technical office hours. These include speed of delivery,

TABLE 9.3   Comparison of Virtual Office Hours to Traditional Office Hours

Advantages	Disadvantages
More time and location flexibility for instructor and students.	If no video, no face-to-face cues. More likely to misinterpret something written or said if video is not utilized.
Introvert students may be more willing to communicate with instructor.	Some students feel isolated from the instructor.
Every student gets an opportunity to ask questions and participate in the classroom.	Time consuming for instructor and students without specific strategies for best practices.
Students able to utilize a wide variety of technology.	Instructors must manage their time commitments and boundaries.
Instructor able to thoroughly think about feedback and make changes before posting.	Technology use may heighten anxiety for some students.
When using text, improves student writing skills.	Some instructors and students find learning new technology frustrating and difficult.
Additional forms of communication available for students to contact instructor in case of extended illness or absences, a natural disaster, or inclement weather.	

improved and more immediate communication, freedom from constraints of location and time, potential for increased interaction, development of writing skills, decreased social isolation, increased Internet experience, and extended learning opportunities (Huett, 2004). However, without firm commitment and concerted effort, the potential of this latest technology will not be utilized (Leh, 2001).

Table 9.3 is a comparison of the current advantages and disadvantages of conducting virtual office hours compared to traditional office hours. Remember, in face-to-face and hybrid classes it does not have to be either/or—it can be both.

SAMPLE EXERCISES

The purpose of the following exercises is for students and faculty members to explore virtual office hour technologies.

1. Email a welcome letter to each student in the class prior to the first week of class. The welcome letter may include such items as a short biography of the instructor to help the students to feel welcomed, a video or audio attachment of the instructor welcoming the class, a copy of the syllabus, a link to the classroom sign-in page, an

invitation to students to get acquainted with the online classroom, instructions for the first week's course requirements, and a request for students to respond to the email by a specific date. This usually reminds students about the class, makes them feel more at ease because the instructor is aware that they are registered for the course, and ensures that the students know how to contact the instructor.

2. If teaching an online class, have students post a home page in the online classroom during the first week. This information should include a photograph, and be sure to emphasize that it should be a tasteful photograph but may include family members or pets. The Home page should also include contact information so that the instructor and other classmates may contact the student. The student should include some personal information to aid fellow students and the instructor in remembering him or her. This may include where the student is located, where the student was born, where he or she grew up, if the student has any other degrees, family information such as children or spouse, where the student is employed, et cetera. The shared information should ultimately be the student's decision because some students may not want to share such personal information. Another possibility for a home page is for students to attach a short video of themselves telling fellow classmates about themselves or to produce a Facebook home page where classmates may interact with one another.

3. Establish virtual office hours.
   a. Implement virtual office hours in a face-to-face class.
   b. Provide written instructions for students to select a virtual office hour medium. Provide a written schedule and written ground rules.
   c. Ensure that the technology works successfully prior to implementing it in the course.
   d. Test the medium a few days before the first virtual office hour session and whenever you change software or equipment.
   e. Gather feedback from students. Use feedback and your experience to improve your virtual office hour practice, policies, and expectations.

4. Using the "pedagogy-up" approach, set up clear instructional objectives for each course week, select the types of learning experiences appropriate for achieving these goals, and select (or build) the essential technologies to achieve these goals. Be sure to incorporate virtual office hours into this equation.

REFERENCES

Berger, N. (1999). Pioneering experience in distance learning: Lessons learned. *Journal of Management Education, 23*(6), 684–691.

Bloom, B. S. (1976). *Human characteristics and school learning.* New York: McGraw-Hill.

Brusilovsky, P., Schwarz, E., & Weber, G. (1996). A tool for developing adaptive electronic textbooks on the world wide web. *Proceedings of the WebNet'96 Conference,* San Francisco, 64–69. Retrieved from http://www.eric.ed.gov/PDFS/ED427649.pdf

Carswell, L., Thomas, P., Petre, M., Price, B., & Richards, M. (2000). Distance education via the internet: The student experience. *British Journal of Educational Technology, 31*(1), 29–46.

Carter, J. (1984). Instructional learner feedback: A literature review with implications for software development. *The Computing Teacher, 12*(2), 53–55.

DeBard, R., & Guidera, S. (1999). Adapting asynchronous communication to meet the seven principles of effective teaching. *Journal of Educational Technology Systems, 28*(3), 219–239.

Garrison, D. R., & Baynton, M. (1987). Beyond independence in distance education: The concept of control. *American Journal of Distance Education, 1*(3), 3–15.

Huett, J. (2004). Email as an educational feedback tool: Relative advantages and implementation guidelines. *International Journal of Instructional Technology & Distance Learning 1*(6), n.p.n. Retrieved from http://www.itdl.org/Journal/Jun_04/article06.htm

Jafari, A., McGee, P., & Carmean, C. (2006). Managing courses, defining learning: What faculty, students and administrators want. *EDUCAUSE Review, 41*(4).

Leh, A. (2001). Computer-mediated communication and social presence in a distance learning environment. *International Journal of Educational Telecommunications 7*(2), 109–128.

Li, L., & Pitts, J. P. (2009). Does it really matter? Using virtual office hours to enhance student–faculty interaction. *Journal of Information Systems Education, 20*(2), 175–186.

Merriam, S. B., & Caffarella, R. S. (1999). *Learning in adulthood: A comprehensive guide* (2nd ed.). San Francisco: Jossey-Bass.

Palloff, R., & Pratt, K. (2007). *Collaborating online: Learning together in community.* San Francisco: Jossey-Bass.

Perreault, H., Waldman, L., Alexander, M., & Zhao, J. (2002). Overcoming barriers to successful delivery of distance-learning courses. *Journal of Education for Business 77*(6), 313–318.

Reisser, L. (1995). Revisiting the seven vectors. *Journal of College Student Development, 36,* 505–511.

Roblyer, M. D., & Knezek, G. A. (2003). New millennium research for educational technology: A call for a national research agenda. *Journal of Research on Technology in Education, 36*(1), 60–71.

Skillicorn, D. B. (1997). *Using collaborative hypermedia to replace lectures in university teaching.* Retrieved on September 20, 2009 from www.cs.queensu.ca/achallc97/papers/a012.html

Smith, C. D., Whitely, H. E., & Smith, S. (1999). Using e-mail for teaching. *Computers and education, 33,* 15–25.

Tao, L., & Boulware, B. (2002). Issues in technology email: Instructional potentials and learning opportunities. *Reading and Writing Quarterly, 18,* 285–288.

Vonderwell, S. (2003). An examination of asynchronous communication experiences and perspectives of students in an online course: A case study. *Internet and Higher Education, 6,* 77–90.

Woods, R., & Keeler, J. (2001). The effect of instructor's use of audio e-mail messages on student participation in and perceptions of online learning: A preliminary case study. *Open Learning, 16*(3), 263–278.

Yu, F. Y., & Yu, H. J. (2002). Incorporating e-mail into the learning process: Its impact on student academic achievement and attitudes. *Computers and Education, 38,* 117–126.

Steven Aragon (2003) said it best: "Social presence is one of the most significant factors in improving instructional effectiveness and building a sense of community" (p.). The role of technology in building and cultivating learning communities has been more researched and discussed since online education went mainstream. Richardson and Swann (2003) noted that in online education, the roles of teacher and student have metamorphosed into more socially effective positions. They concluded that online instructors have become more like facilitators than lecturers, and students are becoming more active learners, participating in their own educational process (Richardson & Swann, 2003). While these roles play a part in the transformation of online learning, a larger contribution is made by more immediate teacher accessibility and social presence for all types of classes.

In settings where they are used as integral parts of courses, instructors and students communicate more regularly in asynchronous learning environments, often responding daily to each other's posts on discussion boards and blogs. This immediate response system also fosters the development of social presence and blurs the lines of teacher and student. Teachers are guides and students are pioneers, moving into learning areas that they can explore and develop as a team. Regardless of its cause, developing a social presence remains an important criterion for student success in the online environment.

Having taught for many years in a face-to-face classroom setting, I often noted the lack of communication between students and faculty beyond the subject matter at hand. Consider the following situation, which many of us who teach required courses encounter. Students entered the classroom— some grudgingly, since required English courses are not their favorite classes to take—and could not wait for the end of the period to make their quick exit. Most did the required work, and despite my best efforts to engage them with multiple intelligence approaches to composition and literature, they did not share my enthusiasm and creative efforts. So, how can we encourage them to want to learn, to become partners in their own education?

My online classes offered me insights for changing my face-to-face classroom approach. Once I began teaching online, an entire new world of possibilities emerged. While students were no longer physically visible, their online presence became more personal, more immediate, and more vital. Because online classes demand more communication to fill the void of physical anonymity, I noted that the online courses also enabled students to share much more personal information. My students answered their asynchronous, open-ended weekly Discussion Board questions with greater honesty. They responded to each other's posts, which was a requirement, but they seemed to develop a genuine concern and empathy for each other. They shared personal stories and responded with compassion and feeling.

It was at that point that I realized how important, even imperative, it was to continue to build more of these classroom communities in my classes.

The synchronous components, audio seminar, and office hours on AOL Instant Messenger (AIM) became valuable communication points in the technology choices I made. These vehicles corresponded to face-to-face classroom functions when everyone was engaged in a lively discussion about the subject matter at hand. My hope became to continue that formula with every class, and even beyond into office hours.

Online classes use email for quick communication. One of the most effective tools for building classroom community is responding quickly and frequently to student questions, something most face-to-face classes do not offer. Students either have to wait for class, the professor's office hours, or hope that a professor will see the email they sent and respond in a timely manner. How, therefore, can we address student needs and questions in a timely and effective way?

SYNCHRONOUS CONFERENCING OFFERS NEW DIMENSIONS TO VIRTUAL COLLABORATION

When professors and/or learners use synchronous virtual collaborative practices, it reinforces the sense of social presence we so importantly need in dialogue. We need to feel connected to others, of course, but this need goes much deeper than merely wanting to talk with people and exchange information. It is an inherent human need to feel part of a whole. Synchronous conferencing helps us complete tasks for our jobs, but more importantly allows us to connect as whole beings, satisfying the innate need for camaraderie.

Yamado and Akahori (2007) note that when people share both audio and video communication (as synchronous conferencing can allow with Skype), it can have a "significant effect on perceived consciousness of language learning in communication, productive performance and consciousness of learning objectives" (p. 35). In essence, we become more productive and learn how to apply what we learned more effectively.

According to Glyn Thomas (2008), facilitators are effective both face-to-face and online when using person-centered approaches. This means that it is important for a facilitator of either a classroom (online or face-to-face) or a conference with colleagues to have "strong personal qualities and /or presence" (Thomas, 2008, p. 175). Once discovered in themselves, then they can convey this to students and colleagues. This facilitation is demonstrated in master teachers in dynamic face-to-face classrooms; it is also apparent in virtual environments. Different tools, distances, and techniques need to be used, but the results can be very similar and may take on new dimensions of possibilities (global reach).

Skype Connections: Voice Over Internet Protocol

One such tool that can be used with great success in both face-to-face and online classes came with the advent of VOIP (Voice Over Internet Protocol). I often call students on Skype if they are willing to download the software and participate. Recently, a student asked me to phone her to review some material she was confused about. Instead of phoning, I asked if she had Skype, so not only could we chat, but perhaps video chat as well. She indicated that she had a webcam and was eager to try it. She downloaded the Skype program in a few minutes and sent me an instant message saying that she was ready to try the connection. I provided my Skype contact name, and within seconds we were chatting with clear video about her project. She was amazed at the simplicity and clarity of communication. From that day forward, she preferred to contact me using Skype rather than any other means.

VOIP allows users to communicate quickly and easily via their computers or other Internet devices. It takes usual analog audio signals and turns them into digital data, thus enabling the signal to be to be transmitted over the Internet (Valdes & Roos, n.d.). VOIP can be used from a regular land line phone by using (1) an analog telephone adaptor (ATA); (2) an IP phone that has a built-in Ethernet adaptor; or, the easiest method, (3) a computer-to-computer connection.

Skype is one of the easiest and most fun VOIP technologies to use. It allows both video and audio two-way communication in real time directly from anyone's personal computer, laptop, or mobile device (see Figure 10.1). As with my previously mentioned student, if the users have a webcam, they can even see each other at the same time. Last century's science fiction video phones have become this century's reality.

Figure 10.1 Student video chat example. *Note:* Used with permission.

There are two types of Skype accounts: one that is free and one with more features, and still reasonably priced. By far, there are more free users than paying customers. With the free account, one can chat with any member of the Skype community at any time, with or without video. The paying customers can call any phone (cell or land line) at any time, whether the recipient is a member or not. Depending on the range of countries called, the monthly fees for unlimited calls to landlines tend to be more reasonable than most long distance phone companies'. Skype also has a pay as you go feature, allowing the subscriber to pay for calls, voicemail, text messages, and other services as needed.

Required Hardware

The requirements are not outlandish. Basically, a standard microphone ($10–$30) or headset ($15–$60) will be fine, as well as the standard speakers most computers come with today. A webcam ($20–$100) will enable video as well, though it is not necessary for clear audio communication. When in a personal Skype screen, one has the option of initiating or receiving a Skype call. A ringing sound signals an incoming call request. The user just clicks on the icons for phone or video and the parties are connected. It may take a few moments for the video to appear, but voice is immediate once connection is established.

PRACTICAL USES FOR SKYPE IN CLASSROOM CONFERENCING

I have found Skype especially useful for both student and colleague conferencing. It is an easy process to download the software and register. To begin, one goes to www.Skype.com and follows the simple directions to set up an account. Once the software is downloaded and installed to the user's computer, it only requires selecting a username and password to be accepted into the Skype community. Once there, the user can add new contacts, receive invitations from other Skype users, and selectively add or reject those contacts that they wish. One can use the email feature to send messages back and forth to Skype contacts as well as set up phone and/or video communication.

For classroom application, I invite my students to register on Skype. Once they do, I ask them to add me to their contact list by sending me an email in Skype or sending their username to my college email account. The user can then add the names to the contact list and communication can begin!

Group Discussions: Voice and Text

Skype has many features that can be used for classroom purposes. More than one person can be included in the chat, but video may be limited by the monitor size. This can be very useful when the professor needs to chat with small groups of students, like cohort or study groups. When incorporating group projects in the course, the professor can monitor or check in with group members on Skype, connecting all parties at the same time. Regular phone connections can only accommodate three-way calling. The free version of Skype can accommodate up to five people on calls. Therefore, conferencing with several students at the same time is possible.

Recording and Archiving Discussion or Events

One can even record the call with the "Pamela" feature. This might be a helpful feature for recapping group decisions and providing a record for the professor should future miscommunication become an issue. Accessed from the Skype toolbar, any Skype user can access Pamela and create an MP3 recording of the conversation. Like most additional features on Skype, the Pamela feature requires another download with user agreement, but it can be accomplished almost immediately. From the toolbar, click on "Conversation," select "Extra," then "The Pamela Recorder" and save the file. The basic Pamela application is free but is limited to 15 minutes. For a one-time purchase price of about $23, unlimited length recordings can be made.

Community and Entertainment to Explore Connections for Learning

Additional tools are useful and fun to include in student conversations—creating avatars, doing virtual makeovers, playing music that will mute when a call comes in, customizing emoticons, and even allowing screen captures. Students will even enjoy the games that are part of the site. Each requires a separate download.

Virtual Office Hours

I also use Skype to hold virtual office hours, along with AOL Instant Messenger. The more ways a student is able to reach the professor, the more comfortable he or she will feel. Even face-to-face students appreciate live contact with an instructor at times other than set office hours. This can be arranged by mutually agreeing to meet at a convenient time using online conferencing tools such as Skype.

Guest Speakers for Traditional Classrooms

If one's school has the necessary video equipment, Skype can also be used in the classroom to invite guest speakers from another location. As often seen on popular television shows, live video connections with special guests are often arranged via Skype. Students may also conduct interviews with experts for projects using Skype audio or video connections. The range of possible uses in the classroom is amazing.

Group Project Collaboration

Students can collaborate after class via Skype for projects or study groups. I often assign students to small groups, calling them *cohorts.* Group members are only asked to help each other during the course. This provides students with a support team of peers who share ideas, ask questions, and generally serve as "study buddies." Communicating on Skype has become a popular means of contact for these smaller groups.

Extended Absence Connections

Further, when students are ill or have been incapacitated for a length of time, Skype can provide a wonderful connection to the classroom and professor. Students can become virtual participants in the class activities. Often students with physical disabilities are unable to attend classes. Many of these students prefer online universities for this reason, but with software like Skype, many of these handicapped students could attend face-to-face classes as well.

Hybrid Courses

Taking this one step further, many colleges and universities today offer hybrid courses, combinations of face-to-face and virtual class attendance and activities. Skype can be a wonderful tool to link students from a distance to their classmates and instructor via the virtual space.

Some teachers hold on-campus classes with local students, while the distant students connect via Skype voice and text to hear and participate in synchronous sessions. In addition, in between on-campus classes, the group or individuals can connect for discussions through a medium described above, such as Skype, IM, email, et cetera. The broader representation of perspectives from diverse locations and the multiple opportunities for communication streams can only create a better, more diversity-aware learning community.

ACTIVITIES: TRY SKYPE WITH YOUR CLASSES

1. As a first Skype class activity, I encourage you to try the following activity in your classroom. Interview an expert in your course content area with a Skype video connection.
2. In another session, try some additional features, selecting one or more from the following list:
   a. Take screen shots of the expert at varying times.
   b. Using the Pamela feature, record the interview, save it as an MP3 file, and make it available after the interview.
   c. Make a complete archive of the event. Share the recording along with a PowerPoint presentation in which you incorporate screen shots of the interview with your guest expert.
   d. Using email or the "Doc Sharing" tool, online educators can also share the completed PowerPoint and MP3 with students. This multi-media presentation should appeal to many students and provide another dimension to your teaching.

SKYPE IN ACTION: CASE STUDY

In my July, 2009 term, out of four online classes with a total of 120 students, only five students were willing to try Skype to communicate with me. Several indicated that they had webcams but still were not willing or able to meet me on Skype to conference. However, the five students who bravely agreed to chat with me on Skype to review class work became enthralled. After my first "chat" with each of them, two students using audio/video and three using audio only, it became clear that they liked the way we communicated. However, only two of the students felt comfortable enough to continue contacting me during office hours to chat on Skype. They preferred to meet me there rather than on our usual AIM (AOL's Instant Messenger). These *digital immigrants* (Prensky, 2001) were more like *digital pioneers* and were willing to make the leap and trust the new technology. As with any new idea, it takes a certain adventurous spirit to experiment and learn the new technique.

COLLEAGUE INTERACTION

While many of my online colleagues are digital immigrants, they are still infused with a desire to learn these new ideas. I suppose that their willingness to work online also drives them to learn the new tools that can enhance their effectiveness as facilitators and teachers. I often have Skype chats with these colleagues, preferring Skype format to email or even phone conversations. Some of my colleagues whose families or friends live in other countries are already using Skype since they have learned that it is the most economical way to communicate with loved ones abroad. In addition, being able to see loved ones in real time is a huge plus that cannot be achieved without this video technology.

I have discussed joint projects with colleagues on Skype, often connecting with two and three at the same time. In this format there is no longer a need to have three-way calling or schedule a conference call, since Skype can connect up to four recipients as well as the host. Skype 3.8 for Windows can accommodate up to 25 callers, but if any are not Skype members, they will incur a charge for this service.

All in all, Skype offers a free, quick, and easy synchronous experience to confer, chat, and socialize with students and colleagues. Once these contacts can overcome the fear of trying this relatively new technology, they will quickly learn to use it effectively and often. At this point, the focus shifts to cultivating community and collaborating through virtual dimensions with new tools.

MORE ADVANCED SKYPE FEATURES

There are many other Skype features, including Skype Prime, Skype SMS (Short Messaging Service), and SkypeFind. Skype Prime contains a directory list of advisors who offer a wide variety of advice or skills training over the free Skype software. Anyone who uses Skype and is over 18 can call an advisor, but calls are charged at a rate both callers and advisors agree to.

Skype SMS is a text messaging feature that allows the Skype user to send text messages up to 160 characters to any texting device. The cost to send SMS messages from Skype varies depending on the country to which the text messages are sent. SkypeFind is a service that enables the user to locate businesses that other Skype users have recommended. The user can also recommend businesses to this database. While some of these features might not appear to be immediately valuable for educational purposes, they may apply to different disciplines as ways of creating simulations or potential further personal and business communication formats.

DIFFICULTIES AND CONCERNS

A popular paradigm has been proposed by Marc Prensky (2001) that identifies younger students (Generation "Y" and younger) as *digital natives.* They have the innate ability to process information faster, can multi-task on their computer screens and mobile devices, and prefer "graphics before their text" (Prensky, 2001, p. 2). While some college-age students (ages 18–22) fit this description, it is not so with nontraditional students and those in online environments. Most online students are much older, probably came from Generation X backgrounds, and do not have the advantages that younger college counterparts may have. As such, these nontraditional online and face-to-face adult learners may find the growing technology difficult to comprehend. They struggle with these new technologies. As Prensky noted,

> Digital Immigrants typically have very little appreciation for these new skills that the Natives have acquired and perfected through years of interaction and practice. These skills are almost totally foreign to the Immigrants, who themselves learned—and so choose to teach—slowly, step-by-step, one thing at a time, individually, and above all, seriously. (2001, p. 2)

That is not to say that digital immigrants cannot learn the new technology. They most certainly can, but the learning curve is steeper. It requires learning by following the same step-by-step learning style to which they are accustomed. Of course, they must also have the desire to learn it, which brings us back to using Skype and other synchronous tools to communicate in their classes. Many digital immigrant learners are simply not willing to try this new communication approach. In my experience, however, they can be encouraged to give it a try.

Motivation: New Opportunities

Motivation is a key element for taking risks in learning something new. In the case of learning Skype, if I have students who are hesitant to try it, I share stories with them of grandparents using Skype to visit in real time with distant grandchildren or how business people conference with each other from remote locations. I even share my own personal stories of how I chat with friends who are far away, some in other countries, and how good it makes us feel to see each other in real time. These examples can introduce practical and motivating examples. Modeling is also valuable and demonstrates how connecting on Skype is simple and easy.

Low-Cost Equipment, if Needed

Some students may also be concerned about the cost of equipment. Faculty should remind students that there are a variety of solutions that can allow them to participate using Skype. Ear buds, headphones, or inexpensive speakers they have from other activities may work fine with Skype. If they do not have any of these, the investment can be as small as $2–$10 for this equipment and can be considered a justified learning expense. Further, there are many ways to obtain low-cost hardware to enable audio or video chat. Technology discount stores, online stores, and online auctions are some sources where all kinds of equipment can be purchased for much less than they sell for at retail. As technology becomes more and more ubiquitous, costs associated with hardware and software continue to drop. Most hardware needs for Skype are small expenditures, less than $50.

Privacy Concerns

Another reason why some students might hesitate to use or like Skype could be that most digital immigrants do not like the possibility of having someone "see" them in their home environment. They perceive it be an invasion of their privacy, even a source of possible embarrassment. This can be easily addressed by explaining that Skype is no more invasive than a telephone call and it is much cheaper. Therefore, another rationale to encourage them to try to use Skype is to explain how economical and convenient it can be. There is no requirement to use the video component when communicating on Skype and there is no dial-up. People should always be encouraged to work at their comfort level.

OTHER SYNCHRONOUS CONFERENCING TOOLS

There are several other conferencing tools available that can be used for different teaching and learning activities; their costs vary greatly. Aside from online platforms that often utilize live chat and seminar rooms (such as Blackboard or Desire2Learn), there are a few free services that can enable instant communication tools:

- Yugma: www.yugma.com
- Wiziq: www.wiziq.com
- Vyew: www.vyew.com
- Dimdim: www.dimdim.com
- ooVoo: www.oovoo.com

All of the above Web sites offer free conferencing and/or calling features. Some offer shared screen capability, recorded sessions, and easy access for multiple users.

Learncentral

Another noteworthy platform is Learncentral, a free conferencing site in its beta stage from Elluminate. Learncentral is easy to download, install, and use for anyone who has used an Elluminate platform. It offers the same features that Elluminate does—whiteboard, screen sharing, VOIP microphone access, et cetera—but will only allow up to three people in an Elluminate vRoom. I use it for conferencing with students to go over course work, review projects, present additional material, and have them demonstrate their question or knowledge. The whiteboard allows interactive teaching and learning (see Figure 10.2).

Learncentral's Elluminate vRoom can also be used to conference with colleagues, go over collaborative projects, and discuss upcoming presentations. The whiteboard allows easy loading of any PowerPoint or screen share. The whiteboard editing tools allows users to employ pointers, text boxes, and so forth so that conferring has a real conference room feel with complete media and virtual access. The platform supports videos and Web browsing. With these capabilities, faculty can show a video to a small group or take the group with them to view different Web sites together. Much like the full version of Elluminate, it has a polling feature, text chat box, microphone, raise hand signs, private messaging, emoticons, et cetera.

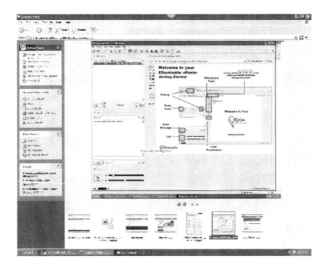

Figure 10.2 Learncentral's Elluminate vRoom. Note: Used with permission.

More importantly, Learncentral's Elluminate vRoom gives colleagues an immediate opportunity to conference and share materials. Whether students collaborating on a group project or professors working on a departmental report or book chapter, we do not have to wait for an available conference time to schedule our meetings. We can use IM (instant messaging) to communicate and decide that we need to meet immediately. Then we can arrange to go to a virtual conference room at a time that is convenient for all of us because we do not have to pre-schedule a room and time slot. This virtual conference room is always available to us, a distinct advantage of such technology. According to Netspoke (Reshape Communications, 2005), this kind of immediate conference communication eliminates the need to wait for conference room availability and provides colleagues a chance to discuss immediate and pressing issues. Spontaneous educational pursuits not being crushed by room availability or bureaucratic processes—that *is* a great advancement!

When facilitators find this ability in themselves, it can be the key component of any successful communication, whether individual or group. The synchronous tools available now to teachers and students can be highly successful in building better learning communities. Continued research and development of VOIP will only enhance learning and conferencing for all education. Students and their teachers will not have to be tied to a classroom space or even seated behind a computer screen at home to participate in learning. More frequently, they will use their advanced mobile devices to connect, participate, and apply what they learn to their area of study or their assigned projects. Such connections will also alter the way they do business while in school and afterward. Working from public laptop stations, Wi-Fi hotspots, home offices, even while traveling has become commonplace.

Skype, Learncentral, Elluminate, WebEx, Yugma, Vyew, DimDim, WizIQ, ooVoo, and many others are the forerunners of the next wave of digital technology designed to connect us at almost any time to almost anywhere. The world of digital media communication is just dawning. The programs mentioned previously are the pioneers and we are the digital generation, poised and ready to meet the future at home, in the classroom, or anywhere. Such innovations in interpersonal communication have only just begun.

REFERENCES

Aragon, S. R. (2003). Creating social presence in online environments. *New Directions for Adult and Continuing Education, 2003*: 57–68. doi: 10.1002/ace.119.

Comer, J. (2005). The human development gap. *Connection: The Journal of the New England Board of Higher Education, XX*(2), 35–36.

CHAPTER 11

FACEBOOK GOES ON "PRAC"

Using Social Networking Tools to Support Students Undertaking Teaching Practicum

Jennifer Howell
Australian Catholic University

Rebecca English
Queensland University of Technology

INTRODUCTION

The use of discussion forums within educational settings has been steadily gaining in popularity of use. Of particular interest to this chapter is their use while students are on teaching practicum in schools (Barnett, Keating, Harwood, & Saam, 2002; Rye, & Katayama, 2003). The focus of these earlier projects has been upon extending applications within learning management systems (LMSs), such as Blackboard®, within a currently enrolled unit. This has meant the use of discussion lists, chat rooms, and other communicative tools located within these programs.

The Professor's Guide to Taming Technology, pages 165–179
Copyright © 2011 by Information Age Publishing
All rights of reproduction in any form reserved.

The high adoption rate of LMSs within higher education has often re-sulted in students being members of a number of formal online learning discussion groups. The enthusiasm with which these applications are used by students is often low. LMSs are often active at the start of a unit as students seek clarification of key issues; however, this initial activity often diminishes over time, which has left lecturers pondering why these discussion forums cannot be sustained across teaching terms. The lack of participation may lie with the LMSs themselves, however: Could these tools provide environments that lead to sustained social collaboration away from formal learning environments?

It was this question that guided the following study. Rather than use an existing LMS application, it was decided to try a Web 2.0 social networking program. During the 2008 semester, one teaching practicum period, it was decided that the Facebook behavior and activities of an undergraduate co-hort, would be studied. The cohort was comprised of fourth-year business education students who had "friended" their lecturer (a term for a higher education instructor in other countries) on Facebook. Closer examination revealed that the majority of students had Facebook accounts, hence this Web 2.0 application appeared to have a high adoption rate among this cohort. Thus, a Facebook group was created for the project during the students' four-week teaching practicum. An initial analysis revealed that 63% were active participants, posting a total of 100 messages, thus it would appear that the Web 2.0 application might offer more sustained interactions over a longer period of time than the LMS-based applications more traditionally used.

Web 2.0 technologies have made an impact in the communicative behaviors of individuals. Abbitt (2007) stated that there has been "tremendous growth in the popularity of websites focusing on social activities and collaboration" (p. 1); this would include online applications such as Facebook. Facebook (2008) describes itself as a "social utility that connects people with friends and others who work, study and live around them" (p. 1). Somewhere among its "more than 80 million active users" (Facebook, 2008, p. 2) were the fourth-year business education students ($N = 30$), and this prior experience helped to naturalize its use by them while on practicum. This paper will describe the process of adopting a Facebook group for students while on practicum and discusses the affordances such accessible social networking communities may bring to educational environments. It will describe the pedagogical strategy adopted by staff to use Facebook as a means to connect with students while they are on practicum and will conclude with an analysis of the findings. Further, it will hypothesize the advantages and disadvantages of using this kind of freely available social networking application to support classroom learning.

This chapter provides an overview of the Facebook instructional application within a higher education class. Additionally, the chapter provides recommendations and activities for faculty to explore how this practice may have benefits for use in their contexts and disciplines. As we will discuss, there is an increased adoption of technology and social media communities among students. The ultimate question is, *How and why would we leverage these for the purposes of teaching and learning?*

THE INCREASING DIGITALIZATION OF STUDENTS

Who are our students today? What are their typical behaviors and expectations? Today's students use technology (for example, instant messaging, Facebook, Flickr, Skype) to be constantly connected with more people, in more ways, more often. Members of the current generation seamlessly transition between "real" and digital lives (British Educational Communications and Technology Agency [BECTA], 2008, p. 12). Educators face the constant challenge of adopting teaching and learning techniques to keep up with the increasing demands and expectations of students who in this chapter have been labeled as *Generation C.*

The characteristics and behaviors of these students are distinctly different from those of an aging faculty who closely resemble Prensky's (2001) *digital immigrants*—those who have not embraced the use of information and communication technology (ICT) in the instructional process. As a consequence, the impact of Generation C students on how higher education institutions function over the next few years will be particularly stressful for faculty. In order to reach these students more effectively, like it or not, educators will have to stay in tune with these students in order to realize pedagogical benefits.

Generation X and Y: Where We Have Been

Educationalists have had to grapple with new generations of learners, each with a particular label and distinctive characteristics, for many years. The Baby Boomers were the first such labeled generational cohort and were largely born during the 1960s and 1970s and are regarded as entrepreneurial and technology friendly (see Table 11.1). Generation Y, born during the 1980s and early 1990s, have also been labeled The Internet Generation (see Table 11.1) and have grown up in an increasingly digital and Internet-driven world.

From an educational perspective, these two generational cohorts have seen dramatic change within the classroom. Generation X would have experienced computers in their schools, mainly in mathematics, limited to basic programming and iterative loop-type exercises. Generation Y would have experienced the most dramatic changes within the classroom and at

TABLE 11.1   Comparison of Generation X, Y and C

Which generation?	When were they born?	What are they characterized by?	What innovations have they seen?
Generation X	Born during 1960s and 1970s	These are the children of the baby boomers. They are regarded as entrepreneurial and technology friendly, as the majority of technology innovations and developments has been driven by this generation.	The development of the WWW, email, mobile phones, and computer games.
Generation Y	Born during the 1980s to early 1990s	Also known as The Internet Generation. They have grown up in an increasingly digital and Internet-driven world.	The use of the Internet in all spheres of life, both personal and business. The development of digital technologies such as high-speed broadband and digital cameras.
Generation C	Not limited to a particular time	Digital content creators who use Web 2.0 and habitually and fluently create user-generated digital content. The first digitally native generation.	The use of Web 2.0, digital communication, mobile technologies, WiFi, digital editing, MP3, podcasts, RSS streaming, and vodcasts.

home. The pervasiveness of personal computers would have meant that more homes had PCs. Schools were using computers across subject areas, making use of CD ROMs, software programs, and the Internet.

Generation C: Where We Are Going

Who, then, is Generation C? This generational grouping has been prophetically theorized by many researchers but had not been formally labeled (Lessig, 2002; Papert, 1993; Prensky, 2001) until 2004. Who the learners of the future may be and how they might be characterized has been suggested by Lessig (2002): "Technology could enable a whole generation to *create*—remixed films, new forms of music, digital art, a new kind of storytelling, writing, a new technology for poetry, criticism, political activism—and then, through the infrastructure of the Internet, *share* that creativity with others" (p. 9).

Generation C was a term first offered by the Internet site Trendwatching. com in 2004 and builds on the work of Lessig (2002). Here, members of Generation C are defined as those who typically produce and share digital content (Trendwatching.com, 2004) such as blogs, digital images, digital audio or video files, and SMS (short message service) messages. They are digitally fluent and fearlessly use new forms of technology as they are released. They fluently use computers, mobile telephones, the Internet, and other associated technologies (see Table 11.1). As Dye (2007) states, "[T] hey aren't categorised by age, they're categorised by behavior. And it's very much about content-centric communication, how they share, store, and manage content" (p. 38). They are a "generation that spans across the age divide to encompass the growing population that creates, shares, and is connected by its own user-generated content" (Dye, 2007, p. 38).

This generational cohort of digital content creators uses Web 2.0 habitually and fluently to create user-generated digital content. But what types of innovations or digital technologies is this generation using? This behavioral group, courtesy of Web 2.0 technologies, is fluent in social and mobile digital technologies, WiFi, digital editing, MP3s, podcasts, RSS streaming, and vodcasts. These composite characteristic make Generation C the first digitally native generation. Its members typically build networks, relationships, and their very identities around and through content (Dye, 2007, p. 38). Lenhart, Madden, Rankin Macgill, and Smith (2007) reported that "44% of US adult internet users (53 million people aged 18 and over) have created content for the online world through building or contributing to web sites, creating blogs, and sharing files" (¶5).

Perhaps one of the most distinguishing characteristics that marks Generation C as significantly different from predecessors is that there has been a shift from straightforward consumption of digital technologies to customization and coproduction (Trendwatching.com, 2004, ¶14). This is an active and creative cohort, thus the amount of user-generated content is expected to increase significantly (Dye, 2007). Generation C has grown up in a world dominated by technology.

As Generation C is digitally fluent, the impact of technology is apparent in all spheres of its members' lives; no longer is life neatly divided into personal, business, or education categories. What is apparent is that their social network is both physical and digital, often a hybrid blend of both. It is neither separated nor distinguishable. Relationships are maintained both face-to-face and via SMS, email, online chat, MMS (multimedia messaging service), and so forth, regardless of where the other person may be (Goldberger, 2007). The impact of technology on social networks has resulted in a significant shift; according to Dye (2007), it is simultaneously larger and narrower: "[T] he entire globe is their new local, and niche communities are the new mass audience" (p. 40). The online tools and programs available to users mean that geographical and time constraints are increasingly irrelevant.

IMPACT ON PEDAGOGY: HOW WILL GENERATION C EFFECT LEARNING?

As Mark Prensky (2001) has suggested, today's students are no longer the people the current educational systems have been designed to teach. Today's students exhibit digital fluency, have enormous access to digital technology, and display characteristics such as ability and familiarity with new technologies never before imagined. *Digital fluency* here refers to their level of ability to interact with ICTs. *Digital expectancy* is a term that refers to the digital expectations of the learner. The learner expects that her or his education, from primary through to tertiary, will continue to develop her or his digital fluency by both teaching how to use and exposing them to new digital technologies as they emerge.

Digital expectancy also refers to the pedagogical approach employed by teachers. Specifically, Generation C expects to be instructed via digital technologies. Teaching via traditional approaches will no longer satisfy these learners; they want to be taught and engage in teaching and learning that makes use of new technologies. Meeting the expectations of these new learners is the challenge facing educational systems at present.

Thus, tertiary institutions need to consider the imperatives digitally fluent and digitally expectant learners place on current and future teaching and learning. The following questions need to be taken into consideration:

- How do we meaningfully develop the digital fluency of our students?
- How do we incorporate digital expectancy within our teaching and learning strategies?

It is an exciting time for tertiary education. Generation C is the first cohort that will present a student body that is digitally fluent. The challenge, therefore, is to develop teaching and learning strategies that will meet the anticipated digital expectancy of this group.

ONLINE COMMUNITIES: DOES FACEBOOK HAVE EDUCATIONAL APPLICATIONS?

Online communities offer pre-service teachers a forum to discuss their developing pedagogy and gather information, resources, and support as they develop their classroom skills while on practicum. Participants can decide, based on discussions in chat rooms (Galland, 2002) and through other online media, whether to try the strategies and use the resources or approaches suggested by their peers. Collaboration is thus widely identified as an important activity in encouraging learning and can be applied to preservice teachers. Boyle et al. (2004) proposed that collaborative networks are effective since they are often conducted over a long period of time, allowing teachers to learn and reflect on their teaching practices. Networking offers teachers the opportunity to be exposed to new ideas and practices (Huberman, 2001; Strehle, Whatley, Kurz, & Hausfather, 2001), and by establishing critical communities of teachers, pedagogy may be improved via a process of critical reflection (Kemmis, 1989).

Several recent papers examining the building of online communities have dealt with different aspects of online community building in classroom environments. In a paper on the use of social content strategies in an undergraduate educational technology course, Abbitt (2007) used a Coldfusion system to allow students to add resources and have these rated by their peers. In another example, Roper (2008) utilized an asynchronous online discussion tool to allow students to participate in her online undergraduate labor/management relations class. Similarly, McElrath and McDowell (2008) examined Brown's theory of community building in their online distance education course. Reil (2000) argues for the use of discussion forums in classroom interaction, stating that the effectiveness of a discussion forum to build community is its ability to create a shared interest and learning goal for students. The students are involved in an inquiry process that produces knowledge shared with a group and made public, usually through the LMS, and is available to the whole group of learners. While each of these provides a useful background to the project, their methodologies and outcomes were slightly different. In this paper, the authors are examining how pre-existing online community software can be used to develop a community among students who are in a quasi distance mode as a result of their practicum placements but who are already part of a classroom-based community and know each other in the "real world."

The current student cohort within tertiary institutions is typically more digitally fluent than previous cohorts. These students use Web 2.0 habitually and fluently to create user-generated digital content, which they produce and share via tools such as blogs, digital image repositories (e.g., Flickr), digital audio or video files, and SMS messages. Perhaps a distinguishing feature of this cohort is its participation in community. The behaviors these students exhibit are generally collaborative and communicative; they share their digital content, ideas, opinions, and experiences *online*. Community appears to be an increasingly online or virtual behavior. As Bishop (2007) concluded, "[O]nline communities are increasingly becoming an accepted part of the lives of Internet users, serving to fulfill their desires to interact with and help others"

(p. 1881). It is the desire to build communities that leads to the implementation of a discussion forum in tertiary classes. How, then, can academics harness this increasingly accepted behavior? Wellman, Boase, and Chen (2002) explored how the Internet or being online has changed the sense of community—if it had weakened, enhanced, or transformed it in some way. Opinion will remain divided, but what is clear is that the use of social networking tools and their popularity among users continues to increase.

As the authors have previously suggested, our current student cohort is digitally fearless and uses new forms of technology as they are released. These are powerful behaviors and ones that institutions have been slow to utilize. Typically, as these behaviors have been identified, LMSs have sought to replicate them via the addition of discussion lists, blog tools, and wikis on platforms such as Blackboard. However, what has been noted is that there is marked difference in the way these have been used by students. This project sought to use a Web 2.0 tool, Facebook, that was a habitual digital tool of the cohort involved in the study.

CASE STUDY: UNIT Z GOES ON PRACTICUM

The group was set up by the lecturer and was "closed," meaning that potential members had to request permission to join the group through Facebook. Two "administrators" were nominated, the lecturer and a colleague who was to teach the unit in the following semester. The students were encouraged to join the group in a face-to-face classroom setting two weeks before practicum placements started.

The members of the Facebook group were an undergraduate cohort of students who had met before in a subject in second year and may have had other contact throughout the other four years of their degree. The majority of activity was on the "wall," described by Facebook (2008) as "a forum for your friends to post comments or insights about you" (p. 1). The wall is a front page application in Facebook that is available when you open the group page. Its ease of use and its availability on the front page probably contributed to its high level of use by the students.

Preparation of Environment/Wall

Posts to the wall required a substantial amount of seeding by the lecturer who acted as one of the administrators of the group. This meant that the vast majority of posts (31) were posted by the lecturer acting as the group's administrator, with one of the rural and remote students posting the second largest number of seeds (17). Four administrator posts were a result of a student who was on an international practicum placement having difficulty accessing the site from China. One student who was on a rural and remote placement was not able to access the site at all, which necessitated that I post for her (her school had blocked the Facebook application). Two discussion forums were started by one rural student who also posted 32 photographs and two of the three video posts to the group page.

Analysis of Posts

Posts to the wall were analyzed by the two administrators. Five themes were deduced from the posts: *Excitement, Problem, Joke, Solution,* and *Other.* The *Other* category was the largest theme. It included group reinforcement such as encouraging more posts, advice on teaching resources or behavior management, checking on others, and making links; this included talking to students who were on a practicum placement in a school with which another student had involvement. *Excitement* was the second largest theme and was most prevalent at the beginning of the four-week period (before practicum placement, expressing excitement about going on the practicum) and at the end of the four-week period (students expressing excitement about their careers as teachers).

Discussion

Three discussion topics were set up and attracted 15 posts. Two of these discussion topics were requested by a member of the group via email to the administrator/lecturer since he was unable to create the discussion forums, as he was not an administrator of the group. The lack of activity in this section of the group page can probably be seen to be a result of the steps required to access these. The wall is available on page one, and the box to input a thread is accessed from the front page of the group's site; the discussion forum, by contrast, requires three steps to access. The first involves clicking on the discussion topic, the second requires you to select "reply to [poster]," then students are able to post to the discussion. The discussion topics were not heavily seeded by the administrator/lecturer, which might also explain their lack of use.

FACEBOOK FURTHER USE AND POSSIBILITIES: BUILDING RAPPORT THROUGH SOCIAL NETWORKING?

The accessibility and popularity of Facebook among the student cohort at this institution would imply that there are many ways that the technology can also be used for building rapport with students. Communicative tools are well designed to encourage rapport, and the popularity of Web 2.0 social networking applications has helped to establish the types of communicative behaviors that education can build upon. This seems to be consistent with the findings of Huberman (2001) and Strehle, Whatley, Kurz, and Hausfather (2001) that social networking tools such as the Facebook group offer teachers the opportunity to be exposed to new ideas and practices, to assist with critical reflection, and to access new information and ideas. Put simply, it is realizing the potential identified earlier with technological networks. Connecting people together, such as education students on teaching practicum, is powerful due to the communicative potential such connections offer.

Previously, we would connect via applications purpose-built, but the explosion of social networking programs means that we can how harness what is popular, what is commonly used, and hopefully encounter less resistance. Rapport building is more simple and effective using these types of programs. In one example of a Facebook application that can be used to build rapport, the students post their activities through the "status bar." The status bar is described by Facebook (2008) as a means to connect with what is happening with friends and family. If a user posts an update to her or his status—for example, "sooo going to FAIL tomorrowwwwww !!! :'(" (CR, 06/18/09), or, "is fuming" (AW, 04/09/09)—the update is visible on her or his friends' Facebook home page. The status bar can be used to access the students' experiences and feelings. Students who post status updates create opportunities for the lecturer and others in their social community to follow up on what is happening and to provide advice and assistance beyond the classroom. Perhaps a further lesson here is for LMS designers: Capitalize on the usability of social networking programs and try to incorporate elements such as the status bar into LMS programs.

Another example of this is the wall feature, which appears on every Facebook profile page. The wall allows friends to post messages that are visible on the home page and can be seen by all other Facebook users who are friends. This can also be used to build rapport with students. Importantly, it is also visual. You are not identified by a username, but by your name and picture. The images chosen to be linked to profiles on Facebook are varied, but they personalize the online community that you are a member of. Previous manifestations of online communities were text-based, and members were identified by either usernames or email addresses.

Perhaps a key to building rapport online is to combine visual and textual cues. One student, CR, was a first-year undergraduate student enrolled in the lecturer's class in early 2009. She was also studying Physical Education teaching, which required her to do a subject in anatomy. CR's post, "i have a rash .. i think it's rabies .. enough to get me out of my exam today you think?" (CR, 06/19/09), created an opportunity for the lecturer to ask all students who are also enrolled in the anatomy subject to how they were progressing in their preparations for the exam. When the exam was completed, the lecturer was able to post messages such as, "How'd you go with the anatomy exam today?" (RE, 06/19/09) onto the students' home pages on Facebook, which provided an opportunity to discuss the students' progress and maintain contact and sustain the relationship after the close of the semester.

Similarly, the IM (instant message) function on Facebook is useful for having a conversation in real time with students, but it is not a feature unique to this program, as many LMSs have chat tools. However, its use and effectiveness was higher due to the fact that the majority of students regularly (i.e., daily) logged on to Facebook, and thus informal chats were more popularly used. Perhaps it is the informality of these timely and opportunistic chats that lies at the heart of their effectiveness. For example, one student while on practicum placement in a school in the country initiated an IM conversation about how to teach a particular aspect of her syllabus. The student described this as a useful opportunity to have a "proper" conversation about the topic of study that would not have been facilitated through regular email messages.

The "Inbox" function is also useful for private conversations with students. In one example, a student wrote, "Hey Rebecca, Can i please have an extension till monday for Assignment 2? Thank you" (LB, 05/23/09).

Coping with Complications and Limitations

However, there are some problems with the use of Facebook in an educational setting. This is because the lecturer can become a 24-hour, seven day a week resource for students. The students in this study tended to use Facebook rather than regular university email channels. This can be seen in the example from the student who applied for an extension through Facebook rather than using the university email function. This seemed to support Prensky (2001), who stated that students in today's classrooms are not the students the current educational systems are designed to teach. They seem to want to access lecturers in different ways and through different channels, any time of the day or night.

When asked about his choice of Facebook over the university email, the student referred to above stated that he never checked his university email so was loathe to use it. Similarly, the IM conversation with the student on practicum occurred very late on a Saturday night. The connectivity that is a major benefit of using social networking to communicate and connect with the students can also create a situation in which lecturers are constantly working. The experience of using Facebook in this study seemed to support Dye's (2007) assertion that time is a premium for this generation, which wishes to be able to access content wherever they go. It could be extended that they also wish to access information and advice through various means and at different times.

A problem that arose due largely to the friction between the formal and informal learning environments was inappropriate uses of the technology. The idea of such a Facebook group as we established appeared to result in a negative manifestation. Students created and joined a group titled "anti [unit code] has poo assignments." All students who were friends with the lecturer on Facebook and enrolled in the unit joined the group. It was a vehicle for students to complain about the assignment: "does [subject code] not realise we reflect enough in their bloody weekly textbook readings and journal reflections. why demonstrate these stupid things again in a 3500 word essay. UGH." (DL, 03/31/09).

The majority of the students were not active within the group (out of the six students who were both members of the group and friends with the lecturer), with only two students actively writing on the wall. The ease with which students were able to create a group, which was a vehicle for complaining about a subject at the university, demonstrated the public nature of the social networking medium and the risks it posed to the university environment. The coordinator of the unit was not a member of Facebook, so he would have had no access to the site or its comments among students. Considering this example, it is a risk that educators have to weigh to determine whether it is worth taking. It is the opinion of the authors that the positives do outweigh the negatives and further uses for Facebook are encouraged.

CONCLUSION

This paper has described the use of social networking tools, most fully Facebook, to support students undertaking teaching practicum. It described a project that involved a cohort of business education students who used a Facebook group page as a support tool during their teaching practicum placements. The results have indicated that the digital behaviors and habits of students enrolled in tertiary studies may be used in developing supportive tools that can be harnessed during practicum periods.

However, it should be noted that this is a pilot study for a larger body of work examining undergraduate education students' usage of Web 2.0 tools and their engagement with ICTs. The small number of students and their relationships that had been established in second year and over their involvement in other subjects throughout the four years of their degree may have skewed the data in favor of the Facebook group, creating an enthusiasm and a community that might not otherwise have been present. It would be interesting to replicate this study with the postgraduate cohort, the members of which are not known to each other and who meet for the first time when they enroll in their first Business Education Curriculum Studies subject. A comparison between the data reported here and this cohort of students might provide a different analysis of the data. Similarly, the cohort size for this group was quite small. A study that examined the use of Facebook groups among much larger cohorts of students might provide another perspective on the building of community among students who are away on practicum placements and who rely on Facebook to connect with their peers.

SELECTED SOCIAL MEDIA RESOURCES

- Facebook: http://www.facebook.com/
- Twitter: http://www.twitter.com/

ALTERNATIVE WAYS TO COMMUNICATE WITH STUDENTS

- Tumblr: http://www.tumblr.com/
- Blogger: https://www.blogger.com/start

QUESTIONS FOR REFLECTION

1. What Web 2.0 behaviors have you identified in your current student cohort? (This might be informally through conversations you have participated in or overheard or in formal discussions with your students.)
2. Have the digital behaviors of your students had an impact on your teaching? Compare your teaching now with the teaching you may have undertaken/experienced three to five years ago.
3. Are there any imperatives for you to increase the digitalization of your teaching?
4. Do you feel that your students exhibit digital expectancy?

IDEAS FOR ACTIVITIES

1. If your university's LMS (Web CT or Blackboard) has discussion lists or chat rooms, think about ways you can include those applications in formative assessment activities with your students. This might in-

clude planning of assignments, discussing readings, group work, and online presentations.

2. Try using online tools for assignments. For example, you could ask students to create a blog or a wiki. Alternatively, ask students to do presentations using a blog or a wiki tool. Set up a Facebook site for a unit and explore the possible uses for that Web 2.0 tool for example support and resource exchange. Start slowly and increasingly upscale your activities to the point where you are incorporating those behaviors into your unit in a meaningful way.

REFERENCES

Abbitt, J. (2007). Exploring the educational possibilities for a user driven social content system in an undergraduate course. *MERLOT Journal of Online Learning and Teaching, 3*, 437–447. Retrieved from http://jolt.merlot.org/Vol3_No4.htm

Barnett, M., Keating, T., Harwood, W., & Saam, J. (2002). Using emerging technologies to help bridge the gap between university theory and classroom practice: Challenges and successes. *School Science and Mathematics, 102*(6), 299–313.

Bishop, J. (2007). Increasing participation in online communities: A framework for human–computer interaction. *Computers in Human Behavior, 23*(4), 1881–1893.

Boyle, B., While, D., & Boyle, T. (2004). A longitudinal study of teacher change: What makes professional development effective? *The Curriculum Journal, 15*(1), 45–68.

British Educational Communications and Technology Agency (BECTA). (2008). *Technology strategy for further education, skills and regeneration: Implementation plan 2008–2011*. Retrieved November 18, 2009 from http://foi.becta.org.uk/display.cfm?cfid=1476190&cftoken=29154&resID=40511

Duncan-Howell, J. (2008). *Digital expectancy: The impact of Generation C on tertiary education*. Paper presented at the Australian Association for Research in Education (AARE) Annual Conference, November 30–December 4, 2008, Brisbane, Queensland.

Dye, J. (2007, May 1). Meet Generation C: Creatively connecting through content [Electronic Version]. *EContent: Digital Content Strategies and Resources*. Retrieved November 19, 2009 from http://goliath.ecnext.com/coms2/gi_0199-6764528/Meet-generation-C-creatively-connecting.html

Facebook. (2008). *About Facebook*. Retrieved August 10, 2009 from http://www.facebook.com/bout.php

Galland, P. (2002). Techie Teachers—Web-based staff development at your leisure. *TechTrends, 46*(3), 11–16.

Goldberger, P. (2007, February 22). Disconnected urbanism. *Metropolismag*. Retrieved November 28, 2009 from http://www.metropolismag.com/story/20070222/disconnected-urbanism

Huberman, M. (2001). Networks that alter teaching: Conceptualisations, exchanges and experiments. In J. Soler, A. Craft & H. Burgess (Eds.), *Teacher development: Exploring our own practice* (pp. 141–159). London: Paul Chapman.

Kemmis, S. (1989). Critical reflection. In M. F. Wideen & I.Andrews (Eds.), *Staff development for school improvement: A focus on the teacher* (pp. 73–90).New York: The Falmer Press.

Lenhart, A., Madden, M., Ranking Macgill, A., & Smith, A. (2007). *Teens and social media*. Retrieved December 1, 2009 from http://www.pewinternet.org/pdfs/PIP_Teens_Social_Media_Final.pdf

Lessig, L. (2002). *The future of ideas*. New York: Vintage Books.

McElrath, E., & McDowell, K. (2008). Pedagogical strategies for building community in distance education courses. *MERLOT Journal of Online Teaching and Learning, 4,* 117–127. Retrieved 22 November 2009, from http://jolt.merlot.org/vol4no1/mcelrath0308.htm

Papert, S. (1993). *The children's machine*. New York: Basic Books.

Prensky, M. (2001). Digital natives, digital immigrants [Electronic Version]. Retrieved 22 November 2009, from http://www.marcprensky.com/writing/default.asp

Riel, M. (2000). *New designs for connected teaching and learning*. Retrieved November 2, 2009 from http://www.gse.uci.edu/mriel/whitepaper

Roper, C. (2008). Teaching people to bargain online: The impossible task becomes the preferred method. *MERLOT Journal of Online Learning and Teaching, 4,* 254–260. Retrieved from http://jolt.merlot.org/vol4no2/roper0608.htm

Rye, J., & Katayama, A. (2003). Integrating electronic forums and concept mapping with a science methods course for preservice elementary teachers [Electronic Version]. *Electronic Journal of Science Education, 7.* Retrieved from www.unr.edu/homepage/crowther/ejse/rye.pdf

Strehle, E. L., Whatley, A., Kurz, K. A., & Hausfather, S. J. (2001). Narratives of collaboration: Inquiring into technology integration in teacher education. *Journal of Technology and Teacher Education, 10*(1), 27–47.

Trendwatching.com. (2004). *Generation C.* Retrieved from http://trendwatching.com/trends/GENERATION_C.htm

Wellman, B., Boase, J., & Chen, W. (2002). The networked nature of community: Online and offline. *IT & Society, 1*(1), 151–165.

PART III

SPECIAL TOPICS

CHAPTER 12

REVELATIONS OF ADAPTIVE TECHNOLOGY HIDING IN YOUR OPERATING SYSTEM

Kathleen P. King
University of South Florida

SCENARIO 1: ADAPTIVE TECHNOLOGY NEED

Bryce had had a work accident that greatly damaged the functioning of his hands. He was unable to grasp small objects well and his coordination was erratic. The neuromuscular condition became debilitating in many aspects of his life. Through physical and occupational therapy, he had learned to cope with the ongoing pain enough to be able to have an active and productive life. He equipped his car with assistive devices to be able to drive, and he returned to school to finish his associate's degree and possibly pursue a bachelor's degree. He really wanted to become a counselor and help people through the difficulties in their lives; it had been a tough two years, and many people had done so much work with him, he wanted to give back just like that and knew he could now.

The roadblock to his dream was school work and technology. How was he going to be able to read books if he could not hold them steady? How could he type on a computer when his movements were erratic? But he had come through so much already, he finally figured that today there must be some solution.

The Professor's Guide to Taming Technology, pages 183–199

He discussed the matter with the Admissions Office even before applying, so he knew he needed to head to the Student Services Office and talk with the special needs staff there. Long story short, they had a simple video series he could sit and watch or take home on a DVD to watch that explained the adjustments or adaptive resources which that were now included in Windows or Mac personal computer or laptop systems. He had had no idea that these features were available! Moreover, the videos guided him step by step through finding the features and configuring them on his own computer to meet his specific needs.

In Bryce's case, the keyboard sensitivity features were essential. They allowed him to have the computer not respond unless he really pressed hard on the keys. His multiple taps—or "flitters," as he nicknamed them—over the keys during spasms and tremors would no longer create the usual paragraphs full of typos that had been so frustrating. Then there was the text to audio feature: His computer could read the books to him if he could get an electronic copy of the text or scanned the pages in first. That meant that he did not have to constantly wrestle with trying to read a book and could instead focus on content.

Bryce was thinking, "If I found this much free assistance in just one week, imagine what else is out there. Why did I delay in coming back to school and pursuing my dream? My life is opening up."

INTRODUCTION TO PREMISE AND DEFINITION

This chapter is about people like Bryce, in situations both less and more severe, "normal" people, any graying generation, you, and me. We will be focusing on simple and free technology resources and programs that are provided with the major operating systems (OS) (Windows Vista, Mac OS X, and Linux). The fortuitous and startling point of this situation is that other than the original cost of your OS, there are no additional fees, nothing additional to install before using the features and programs we include. Certainly, you cannot compare the features of these free tools to high-end products, but it is surprising how people who are familiar with the resources and tools in detail can determine unique ways to meet many physical learning challenges. Easy to use, requiring no additional cost, and easy to learn, these parameters also create a rapid learning curve. Up and running, plug and play, adaptive technologies meet the needs of our diversely and differently-abled society (People's Movement for Human Rights Learning, 2008).

DIFFERENTLY-ABLED

The phrase differently-abled has become a positive synonym for the older terms disabled and handicapped. In the field of special needs, the phrase has been adopted because it emphasizes the point that people have different abilities and, while some people have limitations, that does not mean they have no abilities. By using this phrase, we are building a more positive approach to understanding the abilities and desire for self-sufficiency that these people possess and communicating how the general public, the educational system, and training and medical systems can best support them in the quest for independence (Bausch, Ault, Evmenova, & Behrmann, 2008; People's Movement for Human Rights Learning, 2008; United Nations, 2008).

The following quote from Hitchcock and Stahl (2003) describes how special education curriculum purpose and design have changed: The emphasis is now on bringing these students into the same goals and objectives for all learners:

> Traditional special education was designed to provide specialized educational services to achieve what too often was a set of goals that differed from those of general education. Today, special education services align the skills and abilities of students whom [sic] are perceived to be different than most learners within the existing general education curriculum. The student is at the center of defining the problem, although it is becoming apparent that the barriers that exist within the general education curriculum itself are what need to be examined and minimized. To achieve this goal, materials, methods, and assessments must be designed from the start to be flexible and supportive of diverse styles and abilities. (Hitchcock and Stahl, 2003, p. 48)

It is widely documented that a positive attitude in medical and educational settings reaps positive results in motivation, perseverance, and outcomes (Bausch, Ault, Evmenova, & Behrmann, 2008). While it is not easy to change current language conventions, the benefits of this small language change can be significant for the individuals who are in the situation and all people involved in the support system.

Differently-abled can included a wide variety of conditions and different levels/extents of limitations. From large and small (gross and fine) motor skills in hands, feet, arms, and legs to differences in vision, hearing, speaking, and comprehension, the scope of challenges is wide and the degree of limitations varied. Some people might be able to hold a cup and pick up a book but not be able to control detailed movements with a traditional pencil, mouse, or keyboard. Therefore, many different types of tools and adaptations are needed to address these situations and build confidence and self sufficiency. Solutions range from free technologies and adjustments included in computer software and simple daily modifications of routines to moderate to extensive modifications or extra resources. Because the needs and solutions are widely overlooked, this chapter introduces and highlights those solutions that can help everyday people and the differently-abled at no additional cost.

DIFFERENTLY-ABLED DOES NOT MEAN NOT ABLE

In this brief self-disclosure, I use myself as an example to explain the difference between what you might see when looking at a differently-abled person and what might be the real situation. I offer this real-life example because it will be more meaningful to our readers and the example may help break down preconceptions that are not often thought about by people not afflicted with these daily limitations.

When you see me in public, I am usually using a 3-wheeled motorized scooter. People assume I cannot walk, but they also jump to conclusions such as, "She cannot hear, she cannot think for herself, and she is on disability." When I ride up to the podium at a conference keynote or session, many people look puzzled.

Certainly, this reaction is compounded by the fact that I am widely published and my name is well-known in my field, yet I do not often talk about my physical condition. So they have assumed that I am "like everyone else." Guess what: I really am!

Besides the issues of ability I have addressed, let us turn to the actual limitations. I cannot walk long distances (around the block, a conference center, mall, university). On good days, my spinal condition and chronic pain are well enough managed that I can walk around the room, stand intermittently, teach for about 30–45 minutes, and greet people at my door. The scooter keeps me from becoming homebound and helps me able to enjoy being in public instead of suffering severe pain and muscle spasms for days afterwards. No-brainer: This is pretty essential, right?

As mentioned, I have an invisible condition called chronic pain that is under the control of myself and several highly specialized doctors. I have an internal device that drips medication into my spine 24/7. I use mindfulness, meditation, relaxation, and music therapy to control some minor pain myself, and I manage my schedule to not be overly active frequently. However, this chronic pain comes from several spinal conditions that could be debilitating: I do have to work hard to keep it under control. Yet the only evidence to the outside world is the scooter and my cane when I walk across a room.

It might appear to be arthritis or bone disease, isolated to walking. Instead, it is a life-consuming difficulty that I have to manage daily and hourly. I choose not to discuss it with most people, as there is no need to, and since no such slogan emblazoned t-shirts fit with my stylish suits, I cannot broadcast it. And why would I?

The point is that often what we see with a differently-abled person is not the whole story. We should never make assumptions about what a person can or cannot do or what the condition is. Most people would not overtly assume to do these things, I know, but it comes through in the ways we interact with people and the choices we sometimes make for people. I hope this sharing has guided you to reflect on the actions you can take in the future and to think about those people in your life you might have made assumptions about. Give them a chance to tell you what they need and want, if they desire to do so. They will likely respect you for respecting them and asking.

REVELATIONS AND PREMISE
OF OS ADAPTIVE TECHNOLOGY

Premise

The premise of this chapter is that there are many people who have needs for adaptive technologies that might never even consider, much less avail themselves of, specialized software. However, as people who continue to learn across our life spans, our vision, coordination, and hearing change due to temporary physical conditions, aging, and disease (Merriam, Caffarella, & Baumgartner, 2006). An added benefit of this broad group of people becoming more familiar with adaptive technologies is that it also reveals an entirely new world of technology accommodations for people with minor to severe needs.

As illustrated in Figure 12.1, building awareness of solutions, raising awareness of needs, and realizing that solutions are readily available can

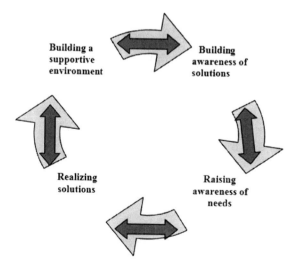

Figure 12.1 Relationships among awareness, solutions, and support.

culminate in building a more supportive environment for everyone. More-over, in this diagram, the different shaped arrows are purposefully designed in two shapes: unidirectional for the overall flow of the diagram, and yet simultaneously bidirectional.

This design reveals a progression of connection and experience. For ex-ample, as people grow and change, they are exposed to new information constantly, and the process is continually rotating and feeding information throughout the wheel. It is not a rigid or strictly linear growth of under-standing and awareness. Instead, this development is much more dynamic, fluid, and ever-growing in terms of the possibilities of application across current and future situations.

The diagram helps us understand the process we experience as educa-tors and lifelong learners become aware of adaptive technologies, thereby expanding our worldview of differently-abled people, resources, support needs, and solutions. It is a diagrammed process that builds upon mod-els of transformative learning (King, 2003, 2005; Mezirow, 1978) and the changes people experience as they encounter new ways of making sense with their world as well as culturally responsive teaching (Wlodkowski & Ginsberg, 1995), which affords ways to examine needs and information from multiple perspectives. Both are widely accepted models but are not often connected to how we comprehend and view the changing ability needs of learners of all ages.

Revelations

While another chapter in this book will go into detail about more ad-vanced and diverse options for adaptive technology, this chapter serves more as an introduction to the mostly hidden treasures of onboard solutions. All of the resources shared in this chapter are included at no additional cost in the original OS. Yet, through experience, we know that very few people know that the adaptive technologies are there or how they might be used. This is a chapter of revelations!

In many situations, it is an extraordinary discovery that the computer already has solutions like these:

- magnification of part of or the entire screen for those who are hav-ing visual difficulties;
- reading of the screen aloud with a click of a mouse button when one cannot sit upright or see the pages well;
- use of the mouse as a keyboard so that hand tremors do not create constant, frustrating typographical errors.

In these cases, it is a screen magnifier, narrator, and on-screen keyboard (respectively) that are supplied with the Windows OS. These features can each be all found in the "All Programs" menu, subheading "Accessories," and folder "Ease of Access." On the Mac OS X, the "Text to Speech," "Cursor Magnification," and "Screen Magnification" features among other accessibility tools are available in "Finder." These very simple examples just scratch the surface of what is available and the possible needs that might be fulfilled!

NEEDS THAT CAN BE ADDRESSED AND RELATED OS TECHNOLOGIES

Consider the wide variety of needs that might exist or arise that can be addressed with adaptations to your computer system. These adjustments or mini-programs (applets) not only assist in computer use, but also make it possible to do other functions with the computer's aid that people could not accomplish otherwise. In this section, the needs that might be addressed are listed and briefly explained in non-technical terms to demonstrate the scope of assistance. This section provides illumination by also revealing those needs that might have been invisible, unnamed, or forgotten; in this case, it is empowering to name these cognitive and physical needs. Several categories provide clarity and frame this overview: ergonomics, motor skills and related pain, visual and hearing difficulties.

Ergonomics

The issue of ergonomics has reached a critical level in our society. Examining the catalogs, stores, and Web sites of office supply stores reveals a copious variety of ergonomic office chairs, keyboards, mice, trackballs, and devices because of demand and supply. The field of ergonomics has evolved to become what is called human-centered, as it is the user who is the center of the efforts and studies (Kroemer, 2006). Ergonomics incorporates many disciplines including a host of medical science specialists, policy makers, human resource specialists, trainers, and research and development specialists.

As early as 2001, the Department of Labor recognized the serious trend already evidenced in the 21st century:

> The new data released today by the Bureau of Labor Statistics covering 1999 shows us where our efforts are succeeding and where we need to direct our focus as we move toward developing a 21st Century Workforce.

> One interesting point in the study is that as more Americans were in the work-force than ever before, the number of ergonomics-related injuries continued to decline. However, musculoskeletal injuries accounted for nearly one-third of all the injuries. This finding demonstrates the need for a solid, comprehensive approach to ergonomics. (U.S. Department of Labor, 2001, ¶2–3)

Recommendations for practice are supported now by the Department of Occupational Safety and Health Administration (OSHA). Yet, despite the soaring number of cases of bad backs, repetitive strain injury (RSI), and carpal tunnel syndrome, private citizens seem uninformed regarding the seriousness of and recommendations for ergonomic best practice (King, 2008). Even though the U.S. Department of Labor has developed a Web site, educational materials, and literature describing concept of "neutral body positioning," few people are reading or listening until they are in great pain. Information on that site describes how to check for more correct body alignment and diagnostic tools. The concepts described in the following explanation provide a starting point for building understanding. This information should be regularly included in personnel orientation and personal medical checkups:

> To understand the best way to set up a computer workstation, it is helpful to understand the concept of neutral body positioning. This is a comfortable working posture in which your joints are naturally aligned. Working with the body in a neutral position reduces stress and strain on the muscles, tendons, and skeletal system and reduces your risk of developing a musculoskeletal disorder (MSD). (U.S. Department of Labor, 2006, n.p.n.)

Motor Skills

While ergonomics applies to everyone who uses technology, equipment, furniture, devices, and machinery, the difficulties that arise from not learning appropriate ergonomics are realized through many sources of pain, conditions, and ailments. In addition, hereditary, degenerative, and infectious disease as well as trauma can result in physical damage that impairs motor skill function.

SCENARIO 2

Grant is finding that checking student emails, grading papers, and conducting correspondence, the absolute minimum of computer use for teaching, is becoming excruciating. He is fearful that mentioning this will raise attitudes of ageism and reveal his decades-long struggle against arthritis in his shoulders, elbows, hands, and now fingers. But he knows that with all those gadgets he sees the students and some faculty use, there must be a way to gain some technology-related help.

- Can he stand the risk of saying he has pain?
- To whom does he speak about the situation?
- Will his conversation be held confidential?
- How much does such extra equipment cost?

While this might sound melodramatic to some people, the fears and consequences are all too real for people of all ages. Unfortunately, most cultures, especially Western, do not respect medical illness or regard it as suffering. In the workplace, countries and organizations have had to institute laws to protect people from discrimination based on illness, disability, and the like because of the abuse they have experienced (Americans with Disabilities Act, 2009). So while in our scenario Grant is developing many fears without solid information, it is based in reality. Certainly confirming confidentiality in the discussions and then seeking assistance and guidance from the university's human resources office for accommodations, disability services, or the information technology department are in order rather than feeling trapped.

Usually, the basis for motor skill difficulties that many people experience can be related to any one or more of the following: the skeletal, muscular, or nervous system. The symptoms can be evidenced in arm, wrist, and hand pain; stiffness; and malfunction (medically termed dysfunction). The causes are familiar to us: arthritis, rheumatoid arthritis, carpal tunnel, RSI (Ergoweb, Inc., 2006), neuropathy (often related to diabetes), and more. With so many common causes, one can see that it is helpful that assistance to reduce pain and suffering is only a few clicks away, hidden in your current computer!

Options for coping with difficulty typing range from changing the responsiveness of the keyboard, to clicking an on-screen keyboard, to dictating into a microphone attached to your computer and having it type for you ("Speech to Text" in Windows OS, "Voice Over" in Mac OS). At this time, all these features are in the "Ease of Access" subfolder in the "Programs" menu in Windows Vista (Microsoft, 2009). The adjustments and programs listed in Table 12.1 can provide substantial assistance. For additional details and video tutorials about these and other features, visit the respective Microsoft and Apple accessibility Web sites:

- http://www.microsoft.com/enable/
- http://www.apple.com/accessibility/

TABLE 12.1 Mapping Motor Skills and Pain to OS Adaptive Technology Adjustments

Motor Skills and Pain Symptoms	OS Adaptive Technology Adjustments and Ergonomics
Difficulty hitting only one key; keyboard adjustment	• Change keyboard responsiveness • Change the pressure speed of key clicks • Change keyboard responsiveness • Windows Filter keys
Difficulty with fine mouse movements	• Change sensitivity of mouse responsiveness • Use mouse pad with a wrist rest
Difficulty with too rapid mouse movements	• Change the speed of the mouse of the screen • Change the speed of the cursor
Need more shortcuts for keystroke combinations	• Reprogram function keys, create macros, or program an extra mouse button or wheel • Windows Sticky Keys, also macro/recorder • Apple Automator
Difficulty typing; pain, stiffness in arms, hands, and/or fingers	• Use speech to text features/programs for long or short passages • Change angle of keyboard • Use wrist rest for keyboard
Difficulty with mouse control	• Use speech recognition to basic command computer functions

SCENARIO 3

It was the 3rd week of his junior year in college, and Brendan called home: "Mom, I think something is wrong with my eyes, and I need to go for a checkup. I have narrowed down the blurriness and headaches to when I use the computer a lot. These advanced classes in engineering require a lot of design time on my computer and I think that is how it is kicking off even more than usual. Does it make sense to you? Where do I go to get my eyes checked?"

VISUAL DIFFICULTIES

Medical experts say that it is no coincidence that vast numbers of people are seeking medical help for headaches, blurry vision, stinging sensations in their eyes, and neck aches. The fact is that the devices we use and the nature of tools we use to do most of our work in the 21st century has shifted to a range of 1–3 feet (Anshel, 1999; Reed, 2004). Whereas for centuries homo sapiens had done work and activities at varied focal lengths (distant, mid-range, and near), today recreation and work alike are pursued at a close range (Anshel, 1999). For instance, consider how many hours per day we are engaged with any of the following: computers, cell phones, iPhones, iPads, netbooks, PDAs, MP3 players, handheld gaming devices, and close-range TV viewing for gaming. Moreover, this trend is regardless of one's age group or demographics situation. The result is that our change in habits is expanding and accelerating visual problems for larger numbers of people.

The condition described above has several names at this time to differentiate causes and symptoms. Variously known as visual fatigue, visual fatigue syndrome, or computer vision syndrome, there has been a surge in recognizing and being able to treat people who suffer from these frustrating and painful visual, neurological, and sometimes muscular disturbances (Reed, 2004). Indeed, many health professionals will discuss ergonomics and lighting for patients but then also consider whether corrective lenses may be of assistance. This chapter also poses the possibility that adjustments made to computer use could assist in mitigating the problems and could be included in the first, no-cost round of corrections advised.

In addition to this growing phenomenon of eyestrain, there are many other problems people experience with their sight. For example, some people may have difficulty seeing certain types of figures or details based on neurological conditions; others have difficulty with contrasts of color (or color blindness), differentiating visual spatial relationships (or following moving objects), or lights on screens. The reality is that these situations can be invisible to other people unless the individual has severe impairment that disrupts their interaction with others. Making assumptions about what people see on a computer screen, book page, or poster can be detrimental and embarrassing in these circumstances. We need to recognize that learners with special needs can be addressed with dignity and support in our classes (King & Griggs, 2007).

Building greater awareness of the variety of visual difficulties people have and all people may encounter over years of work with close range devices and as maturing adults provides a platform to inform about resources to help all. As listed in Table 12.2, several significant tools "hidden" in the OS toolbox can help alleviate some of the struggle that visually impaired individuals may experience.

The Screen magnifier software and browser zoom features as well as the screen contrast settings are fundamental features that all readers should explore. Based on their operating system (Windows, Mac, or Linux), the settings might be named differently, but the features will be available. Certainly, each of us has received documents that need to be magnified for ease of viewing. A wise strategy is to employ the two or three keystrokes to zoom in on the text, chart, or figures in order to reduce eye strain. It is not surprising that most people are not in this habit and will incur extra strain unnecessarily because few of us have had formal instruction in computer ergonomics and visual ergonomics.

TABLE 12.2 Mapping Visual Difficulties to OS Adaptive Technology Adjustments

Visual Difficulties	OS Adaptive Technology Adjustments
Difficulty seeing details on screen, video, text	• Use Windows Narrator, Apple Text to Speech, or other to read text aloud • Use screen magnifier to zoom in on sections of screen • Use software zoom features • Use the screen contrast feature • Use the screen resolution adjustment
Visual fatigue, visual fatigue syndrome, or computer vision syndrome symptoms: headaches, eyestrain, blurry eyes, neck pain, dry eyes, stinging eyes	• Use Windows Narrator, Apple Text to Speech, or other to read text aloud • Use screen magnifier to zoom in on sections of screen • Use software zoom features • Use the screen contrast feature
Difficulty reading text	• Use Windows Narrator, Apple Text to Speech, or other to read text aloud
Difficulty seeing menus for computer operation	• Use speech recognition for basic command computer functions

The screen reader tools are also invaluable for providing some visual reprieve for all users. Are there times you can have a report read aloud to you, rather than reading yet another document? Can you time your work so that you can listen to one document while doing something else in the office? This promotes good ergonomic habits as well, as you might be able to stand up and move around while still listening to the reading you need to accomplish. It is not always working harder that is needed. In these cases, it is clear that working smarter is the means to running the longer race! Using the free OS tools and considering different work habits may breathe new strength into weary professionals.

DEAFNESS AND HEARING IMPAIRMENT

Hearing impairments can be frustrating in personal and professional settings. Indeed, with age comes a standard progressive increased ossification of the tiny bones in the inner ear, which will result in hearing loss. However, many people suffer neurological, congenital, or trauma- or disease-related hearing damage that will disrupt their lives to different degrees.

While most of the work done on computers can be conducted without hearing as a primary sense, it is surprising how different it is to interact

TABLE 12.3 Mapping Hearing Difficulties to OS Adaptive Technology Adjustments

Hearing Difficulties	OS Adaptive Technology Adjustments
Difficulty hearing video, audio, audio books, music, computer system alerts	• Use Sound Settings to increase volume • Use speakers, earbuds, or headphones to magnify volume • Need to find materials with closed captioning features • Need to find transcripts
Difficulty keeping up with speed of audio	• Use media player to slow down playback: Windows Media Player, iTunes—both free
Difficulty hearing computer system alerts	• Use light and popup balloons for basic command computer functions

with computers if you cannot hear the click of the keys and mouse, the system warning signals, and the audio and video circulating on the Web or for training functions in the workplace. Fortunately, the OS again provides some degree of assistance in these areas. Table 12.3 reveals how different functions can be adjusted or used to bridge the gap of hearing impairment or lack of hearing.

Indeed, by adjusting the sound setting controls, some people may be able to amplify sound enough to hear sounds that are usually muffled for them. Probably the three most valuable on-board features are, however, (1) the ability to set your computer to pop up windows and make the screen flash when an error message occurs (Apple names this "Visual Alert") (Apple, 2009), (2) using the media players to speed up or slow down the playback of audio and video, and (3) "Talking Clock" (Apple, 2009). In the case of video, this might afford the opportunity for people to more easily lip read the video actors. In addition, if the impairment is not too severe, the slower pace can aid in discerning the words. Some players such as QuickTime include close captioning capability if the audio or video are recorded with this information (Apple, 2009).

This review highlights the fact that hearing impairment is at least addressed through the OS adaptive tools. On-board features and tools that can transcribe reliably need to be moved into the OS. Moreover, generating transcripts for video and audio needs to be a mainstream feature rather than an add-on and a difficult process. There are many other excellent applications for which such transcript-creating software could be used. Proprietary products have advanced greatly over the years, but we need the integration with the OS and more reliable 100% transcription.

RECOMMENDATIONS FOR HANDLING INSTRUCTIONAL AND PROFESSIONAL NEEDS

This final section suggests how faculty might begin to incorporate adaptive technologies into their instructional and professional roles. Given the relentless work of the clock on our bodies' health, developing good habits early in our careers and learning about strategies that may be adopted as needed may preserve our well-being and participation in our careers longer!

Give Your Back a Break Today

On those days when you are doing an extraordinary number of hours of computer work, consider how you can break up the routine of your day and work in blocks of time. Medical experts say that we need to shift our position at the computer every 20 minutes, and we need to look away from the computer about as often. Evaluate and reconsider how you might plan your time and space. Three different configurations among which one might rotate during a long computer use day are described below. Completely changing positions every two hours makes a substantial difference in all the body systems and reduces back, neck, eye, and muscle strain.

Multiple Computer Work Area Configurations

Station 1: Desk with ergonomic chair at correct height, monitor and keyboard aligned

Station 2: Couch with lumbar cushion and lap desk to have laptop positioned at correct height

Station 3: Sitting at the dining room or conference table, using a laptop lift to align the laptop screen more fully with your eyes and using a proper chair

Be Kind to Your Eyes

Another viable strategy is to consider whether some tasks can be done with a different input mode. If you have a lot of information to input, are working on a draft of an article or a book, responding to correspondence, or writing a report, for instance, why not use voice-to-text software to do the typing for you? Inputting the first large draft can greatly reduce the number of hours at the keyboard and provide a change in body use, which aids wellbeing.

Moreover, as mentioned previously, get into the habit of using the magnification and zoom features in your software and the OS. Learn the hot keys so that you can click a few buttons to zoom in (Windows version:

Ctrl + PLUS; Apple version: Apple Key + EQUAL) and zoom out (Windows version: Ctrl + MINUS; Apple version: Apple Key + MINUS) on a browser screen and many other programs. Determine if your major programs have quick ways to make the adjustments; if not, use the zoom function or computer screen magnifier. Once people start breaking the habit of squinting at small print, they never turn back and their eyes will be less strained.

Buy Back Your Free Time

The final recommendation addresses file management and streamlined planning of the work we do as professors. Evaluate the file planning system you have on your hard drive or server. Are you using the file folders so that you can find the documents you need easily? Do you need to consider a different layout? Again, we are so busy with our work that we often do not pause for these housekeeping essentials, but if we have predictable filing systems, the time at our computers can be reduced. The other aspect of this suggestion is to create folders that can be templates for many of the repetitive tasks you perform in your professional role. This tactic will decrease redundant typing and improve efficiency.

We are familiar with form letters, and most of us will build references from portions we have written before, but let us expand the model further. When students hand in certain types of assignments, there are many similar comments you make on papers about errors, research, writing, content, et cetera. Are there instructions, help sheets, or assistance that they need every semester? Consider developing a few templates and master sheets each semester, such as the following:

- How to do a literature review for Professor Mudd
- The critical eye for historical research by Dr. Choi
- Grading comments for mid-term essay exams
- Research-related comments for Psychology 501 final paper

Another important time-saving feature is to think in terms of repeatable keystrokes or frequently used long phrases. In Apple, this application is called "Automater" and in Windows it is found in the function called "Recorder" or macros.

These strategies will assist all educators in working more efficiently and being able to minimize the eye, muscle, and back strain that is becoming synonymous with computer use.

CONCLUSION

This chapter describes not only the copious number of free assistive technology tools that are "hidden" in our computer OSs, but also the host of physical difficulties we encounter in the Information Age. This information is empowering for all people because it reveals how to make computer use and professional work more accessible and efficient for all of us. The chapter has also developed critical concepts of differently-abled individuals, ergonomics, invisible disabilities, physical impairments, empowerment, and independence. By discussing these topics, we bring to light topics that are too often solely relegated to special education discussions instead of everyday consideration.

The focus of the chapter is on all people becoming aware of the free tools and functions available through their current computer's OS. Additionally, we have approached how all people can work more efficiently to reduce computer time. Ultimately, as time passes, joints are sore, or eyes more strained, we will all benefit from these features. In the meantime, reading this chapter empowers all educators to recommend free adaptive technologies for students and colleagues immediately. We are mobilizing the masses to be advocates for wellbeing and empowerment of differently-abled individuals.

REFERENCES

Americans with Disabilities Act of 1990, Including ADA Amendments Act of 2008, Pub. L. No. 101-336, § 2, 104 Stat. 328 (2009). Retrieved September 12, 2009 from http://www.ada.gov/pubs/ada.htm

Anshel, J. (1999). *Visual ergonomics in the workplace.* Philadelphia: Taylor & Francis, Inc.

Apple. (2009). *Accessibility.* Retrieved June 12, 2010, from http://www.apple.com/accessibility

Bausch, M. E., Ault, M., Evmenova, A., & Behrmann, M. M. (2008). Going beyond AT devices: Are AT services being considered? *Journal of Special Education Technology, 23*(2), 1–16.

Ergoweb, Inc. (2006). *Glossary of ergonomic terms.* Park City, UT: Author. Retrieved September 12, 2009 from http://www.ergobuyer.com/resources/faq/glossary

Hitchcock, C., &, Stahl, S. (2003). Assistive technology, universal design, universal design for learning: Improved learning opportunities. *Journal of Special Education Technology, 18*(4), 45–53.

King, K. P. (2008). Ergonomics. In L. Tomei (Ed.), *Encyclopedia of information technology curriculum integration I: A–interactive videoconferencing* (pp. 286–291). New York: IGI Information Science Reference. Retrieved July 12, 2010, from http://www.igi-global.com/reference/details.asp?id=7304

King, K. P. (2005). *Bringing transformative learning to life.* Malabar, FL: Krieger.

King, K. P. (2003). *Keeping pace with technology: Educational technology that transforms.* Cresskill, NJ: Hampton Press.

King, K. P., & Griggs, J. K. (Eds.). (2007). *Harnessing innovative technologies in higher education: Access, equity, policy and instruction.* Madison, WI: Atwood Publishing.

Kroemer, K. H. E. (2002). *Definition of ergonomics.* National Safety Council. Retrieved February 7, 2010 from http://www.nsc.org/issues/ergo/define.htm

Merriam, S., Caffarella, R., & Baumgartner, L. (2006). *Learning in adulthood* (3rd ed.). San Francisco: Jossey-Bass.

Mezirow, J. (1978). *Education for perspective transformation.* New York: Teachers College, Columbia University.

Microsoft. (2009). *Microsoft accessibility: Technology for everyone.* Retrieved March 8, 2010 from http://www.microsoft.com/enable/

People's Movement for Human Rights Learning. (2008). *The human rights of differently-abled persons.* Retrieved January 12, 2010, from http://pdhre.org/rights/disabled.html

Reed, P. (2004). *The medical disability advisor* (5th ed.). Westminster, CO: The Reed Group.

United Nations. (2008). *Resolution adopted by the General Assembly: 63/173 International Year of Human Rights Learning.* New York: Author.

United States Department of Labor OSHA. (2001). *OPA Press Release: Secretary of Labor Chao.* Washington, DC: Author. Retrieved May 12, 2010 from http://www.dol.gov/opa/media/press/opa/opa2001074.htm

United States Department of Labor OSHA. (2006). *Computer workstations: Good working positions.* Washington, D.C.: Author. Retrieved November 1, 2010 from http://www.osha.gov/SLTC/etools/computerworkstations/positions.html

Wlodkowski, R., & Ginsberg, M. (1995). *Diversity and motivation: Culturally responsive teaching.* San Francisco: Jossey Bass.

CHAPTER 13

ACCESSIBLE TECHNOLOGY FOR ONLINE AND FACE-TO-FACE TEACHING AND LEARNING

Sheryl Burgstahler
University of Washington

Alice Anderson
Mike Litzkow
University of Wisconsin–Madison

INTRODUCTION

It has been estimated that more than 10% of college students have disabilities, of which the largest and fastest growing group is those with learning disabilities (National Center for Education Statistics, n.d.). When compared to their nondisabled peers, individuals with disabilities experience less success in college and careers, including the pursuit of science, technology, and engineering fields (National Science Foundation, 2009). These facts are particularly troubling since securing a postsecondary degree is a critical juncture toward success in many lucrative careers.

Teaching practices, including those that employ digital media, impact the learning of all students. However, physical spaces, technological tools,

The Professor's Guide to Taming Technology, pages 201–218
Copyright © 2011 by Information Age Publishing

201

and engagement strategies typically used in face-to-face (on-site) and online learning can erect barriers for some students with disabilities. For example, the content of a video that is not captioned is inaccessible to a person who is deaf; a cluttered computer lab is inaccessible to a wheelchair-user; graphic images on a projection screen are inaccessible to a student who is blind unless the images are described using audio. Instructors are often unaware of challenges that students with disabilities face, what specific accommodations are appropriate, what their own role is in making accommodations available to students, which teaching strategies work best, and what resources are available (Burgstahler & Doe, 2005; Dona & Edmister, 2001; National Center for the Study of Postsecondary Educational Supports, 2000).

The objectives of this chapter are to increase the knowledge of postsecondary instructors and technology specialists as they integrate information technology (IT) into face-to-face and online instruction, of professionals who promote the use of technology in learning environments, and of researchers identifying topics for further study. The authors present legal issues, technology access challenges, approaches for ensuring that technology-rich learning environments are inclusive of everyone, a case study of the design of an instructional tool that promotes the use of accessible media, and recommendations.

LEGAL ISSUES

Establishing an institution-wide goal to ensure that students with disabilities have full access to all offerings may be motivated by a commitment to make learning opportunities fully inclusive of all students. Accessible practices may also be motivated by legal mandates. For example, almost all institutions of higher education are covered by both Section 504 of the Rehabilitation Act of 1973 and the Americans With Disabilities Act of 1990 (ADA). These and other laws prohibit discrimination on the basis of disability (U.S. Department of Justice Civil Rights Division, 2005). They are generally interpreted to require that educational entities plan for, purchase, and use IT that is accessible to students and faculty with disabilities (Patrick, 1996). Disabilities covered by relevant legislation include conditions that affect sight, hearing, mobility, learning, attention, and social interactions.

APPROACHES FOR ADDRESSING DISABILITY-RELATED ACCESS ISSUES

Accommodations

The typical approach to dealing with access challenges encountered by a student with a disability is for the student to present documentation of his/her disability to a student service office; that office determines what accommodations are reasonable and informs instructors of approved accommodations for the student. Examples of accommodations include providing printed materials in Braille or electronic text for a student who is blind, relocating a class to an accessible room for a student with a mobility impairment, allowing extra time on tests for a student with a learning disability, offering alternative testing locations for a student with an attention deficit, and providing specialized technology for a student who cannot operate the computer configuration used by other students. Thus, accommodations are reactive and address access issues for a specific student.

The accommodation model is not always effective and efficient. Imagine trying to accommodate a deaf student enrolled in an online course where a significant amount of content has been embedded in video and audio clips that are not captioned or transcribed. The institution offering the course might be required to develop transcripts of audio content, provide a sign language interpreter wherever student is located, or offer sign language interpreting via an online system. In contrast, being proactive in addressing such potential access barriers as a course is being developed—in this case, by captioning video and transcribing audio clips—can allow an institution and/or instructor to avoid accommodations that need to be made at the time a student enrolls, at (potentially) greater expense.

Universal Design

To fully serve all students in an instructional setting, the cultures, native languages, reading levels, technical skills, and other characteristics of potential students should be considered as each instructional tool and strategy is developed. This proactive approach is called *universal design*. The term—coined by Ron Mace, a professor of architecture who founded the Center for Universal Design—is defined as "the design of products and environments to be usable by all people, to the greatest extent possible, without the need for adaptation or specialized design" (CUD, 2008, p. 1). First practiced in architecture, universal design has more recently been applied to information technology and instruction (Burgstahler, 2008a, b, c; The Center for Universal Design in Education [CUDE], n.d.). The UD approach benefits students with disabilities, but others as well; captions, for example, are useful to students accessing the course content in both noiseless and noisy environments, to students for whom English is not their first language, and to everyone who wants to search the audio for specific information.

The Center for Applied Special Technology (CAST) has taken a leadership role in promoting the development of educational technology that includes "rich supports for learning, and reduces barriers to the curriculum, while maintaining high achievement standards for all" (CAST, n.d.b, p. 1). Specifically, CAST applied the results of brain research and the capabilities of IT to create three universal design for learning (UDL) "principles that together form a practical framework for using technology to maximize learning opportunities for every student" (Rose & Meyer, 2002, p. 5):

- *Multiple means of representation* to give learners various ways of acquiring information and knowledge.
- *Multiple means of action and expression* to provide learners alternatives for demonstrating what they know.
- *Multiple means of engagement* to tap into learners' interests, offer appropriate challenges, and increase motivation (CAST, n.d.a, p. 1) UDL software has built-in features that address the needs of students with diverse cultural and language backgrounds; interests; and abilities and disabilities associated with learning, attention, mobility, sensory perceptions, spelling, reading, and handwriting.

Access Challenges and Solutions

Universal design offers inclusive solutions that benefit all students, including those with disabilities, with respect to the physical environment, IT, and engagement strategies in online and on-site instructional settings.

Physical Environments

Access Issues. Students and instructors who face physical barriers to technology-rich on-site activities include those who use canes, walkers, and wheelchairs and/or have visual impairments.

Access Solutions. To ensure their full participation, design features such as the following should be considered.

- Provide work surfaces and chairs that are adjustable in height.
- Connect all resources in a facility via wheelchair-accessible routes of travel.
- Place computer equipment in areas that are uncluttered; where lighting can be adjusted; and where large-print, high-contrast signs and labels are installed.
- Provide spaces for students who work best in locations where visual and auditory distractions are minimized.
- Provide adequate room for both right- and left-handed users. (Burgstahler, 2009; Thompson, 2008)
  Such proactive efforts toward access and usability benefit many users, not just those with disclosed disabilities.

Interaction

Access Issues. Some students face challenges when interacting with instructors and student cohorts in technology-rich instructional environments. For example, students for whom English is a second language and those with learning disabilities that affect reading skills (e.g., dyslexia) may have difficulty understanding messages that are long and use vocabulary with which they are unfamiliar and/or composing their thoughts into text messages. In addition, students who have conditions that affect social skills (e.g., Asperger's syndrome) may have difficulty interpreting social cues inherent in face-to-face and electronic communications. Even in online environments that lack observable social distinctions, race, ethnicity, and other factors can affect interactions between students and instructors as they make assumptions about social distinctions from the tone, content, vocabulary, and grammar of online messages (Guy, 2002).

Access Solutions. Strategies that may help students with a variety of characteristics communicate effectively include giving very specific instructions, modeling appropriate communications, using multiple communication styles, making content relevant to students with many backgrounds, avoiding or defining jargon that might not be familiar to some students, and providing constructive feedback to specific individuals.

Technology

Access Issues. Instructors, IT developers, and support staff can no longer assume that a student is using a traditional desktop computer, monitor, keyboard, and mouse to access technology-based content. Cell phones and other mobile devices, televisions, and gaming systems provide options for accessing digital media. In addition, a student with a visual impairment may use adjusted color combinations, enlarged font sizes, and other individualized settings within their operating systems and software applications. Some may employ specialized hardware and software called *assistive technology* (Closing the Gap, n.d.). For example, screen reader software—which includes products such as JAWS, Window-Eyes, VoiceOver, and a growing number of free and open-source products—allows a student who is blind to access text content presented on the screen using a Braille display or speech synthesizer (Anderson & Ewers, 2001). A student with a learning disability may use products that enlarge font sizes, highlight words on the screen, or read text in a synthesized voice. A person who cannot operate a standard keyboard or mouse may use a track ball or a device controlled with speech or eye movement.

Access issues will likely arise when instructors, technology specialists, and product developers design, select, or use digital media after considering only a narrow range of characteristics of potential students and the technology they use. This applies to both asynchronous technologies (e.g., email and discussion lists, Web-based forums, social networking applications, and video presentations) and synchronous tools (e.g., telephone and audio-video conferencing, virtual worlds, and interactive Web-based collaborative tools).

Access Solutions.   In 1992, technology leaders published guidelines for the design of accessible displays, input devices, and other ITs that address issues related to a wide range of sensory, physical, cognitive, seizure, and language abilities (Vanderheiden & Vanderheiden, 1992). About this time, the World Wide Web was introduced as a tool for education and research and, in 1993, informal specifications for Hyper-Text Markup Language (HTML), the primary language used for creating Web sites, were developed. Even these first HTML specifications supported universal design by providing Web developers the option to include text descriptions of images (called alternative or "alt" text) that can be accessed by screen readers (Berners-Lee, 1993). According to Berners-Lee (1993), the Web inventor, "The power of the Web is in its universality. Access by everyone regardless of disability is an essential aspect" (World Wide Web Consortium [W3C], n.d.).

W3C, directed by Berners-Lee, was founded in 1994 to develop and promote protocols that ensure interoperability of the Web worldwide. To address accessibility concerns, the W3C launched a special Web Accessibility Initiative (WAI), which recommends practices that make it possible for everyone to use the Web—regardless of physical and sensory abilities, language, culture, and other characteristics; regardless of technology used; and regardless of bandwidth available (W3C, 2007). Under a mandate of Section 508 of the Rehabilitation Act, as amended in 1998, the U.S. Access Board (n.d.) developed accessibility standards for IT used by federal agencies (Office of the Federal Registrar, 2000). Similar to those developed by W3C, the Section 508 standards have had an impact beyond federal agencies as they have been voluntarily adopted by some state agencies, schools, and other organizations as one way to meet their Section 504 and ADA obligations.

Even with the availability of accessibility legislation and guidelines, many educators are unaware of their legal obligations for making products accessible, which IT design features are inaccessible to some users, and guidelines for universal design. As a result, they erect barriers to potential users (Golden, 2002; National Council on Disability, 2004).

Distance Learning Courses and Programs

Practitioners and researchers have addressed the accessibility of online (or distance learning) programs as well as of specific courses to individuals with disabilities.

Overall Program Accessibility.   A recent study explored overall policies and practices related to the accessible design of distance learning programs (Burgstahler, 2006) and developed, tested, and refined a list of Distance

Learning Program Accessibility Indicators with input from 16 programs nationwide that delivered online instruction. Each accessibility indicator relates to one stakeholder group:

- *For students and potential students:* Distance learning programs committed to accessibility ensure that students and potential students know of the program's commitment to accessible design, how to report inaccessible design features they discover, how to request accommodations, and how to obtain alternate formats of printed materials; the distance learning home page is accessible and all online and other course materials of distance learning courses are accessible to individuals with disabilities.
- *For distance learning designers:* Distance learning programs that are committed to accessibility ensure that course designers understand the program's commitment to accessibility, have access to guidelines and resources, and learn about accessibility in training provided to course designers.
- *For distance learning instructors:* In distance learning programs committed to accessibility, publications and Web pages for distance learning instructors include a statement of the distance learning program's commitment to accessibility, guidelines regarding accessibility, and resources; training for instructors includes accessibility content.
- *For program evaluators:* Distance learning programs committed to accessibility have systems in place to monitor accessibility efforts and make adjustments based on evaluation results (Burgstahler, 2006).

Accessibility of Instructional Technologies. Some practitioners continue to address accessibility issues related to new technologies as they become available to support on-site and online instruction. Such technologies include social networking, such as Facebook (n.d.) and Twitter (Lembree, 2009; Randall, 2009), and virtual worlds, such as Second Life (International Business Machines, 2008; Linden Research, n.d.). However, a recent study of the accessibility of Facebook, MySpace, YouTube, Yahoo, and Bebo reports that "they are effectively 'locking out' disabled visitors, the majority of whom cannot even register, let alone participate in the on-line communities they wish to join" (AbilityNet, 2008, n.p.n.). Accessibility problems include the inability to create user accounts on MySpace, Friendster, or Facebook without sighted assistance because of the use of CAPTCHAs, those abstract renderings of random characters that ask users to retype the word they see on the screen; cluttered Web pages with many links; and unlabeled links (American Federation for the Blind, 2009).

Accessibility of Course Authoring Tools. Authoring tools—sometimes called learning management systems (LMS) or course management systems

(CMS)—are used by instructors and course designers to make Web pages and organize course content. To ensure that accessible curricula are created, tools selected to develop the presentation of course content should be easy for course authors to use and designed for those who have little or no knowledge of and motivation to address accessibility issues. Developers of a content authoring tool must take the needs of students with many different types of disabilities into account to ensure that digital materials created with the tool are accessible to all learners. For example, captions of video presentations are needed by students who are deaf; keyboard access to all functions is needed by students with limited motor skills and those who are blind or rely on screen readers; students with learning and language challenges can benefit from the ability to control the pace and timing of the presentation.

Accessibility problems can be found in authoring tools such as Mediasite (Sonic Foundry, n.d.), Articulate (Articulate Global, n.d.), Adobe Acrobat Connect Pro (Adobe Systems, 2009), and Tegrity (n.d.). Issues relevant to a screen reader user include:

- onscreen buttons (e.g., pause, forward, stop) are not labeled,
- hot keys conflict with screen reader keystrokes,
- presenter and screen reader volumes cannot be controlled separately, and/or
- slide changes are outside the screen reader's control and, thus, may occur before a student is ready.

A CASE STUDY:
CREATING ACCESSIBLE DIGITAL MEDIA WITH ETEACH

This section presents a case study of how the multimedia authoring tool eTEACH was developed to meet accessibility goals. Highlighted are mechanisms used to ensure access to blind users who use screen reader software, because these are the most difficult accessibility problems to address and their solutions often benefit others as well. The case study documents the process of discovering disability-related access barriers and the application of universal design. The experiences shared may be useful to course developers and instructors as they plan online activities.

The University of Wisconsin–Madison (UW–Madison) began developing the free authoring tool called eTEACH in 1999. Ten years and three upgrades later, it continues to evolve. eTEACH creates Web-based presentations that combine video, audio, and animations with slides, captions, and other instructional content to enrich or replace traditional on-site lectures and lab demonstrations (Foertsch, Moses, Strikwerda, & Litzkow, 2002). The video presented may be a "talking head" of an instructor presenting

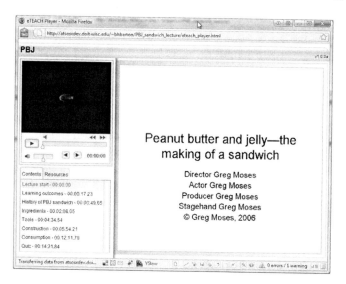

Figure 13.1 Screen shot of presentation created with eTEACH Authoring Tool.

PowerPoint slides or it may be more directly related to the subject matter. PowerPoint animations allow the instructor to direct students' attention to particular details on a slide. Some eTEACH presentations contain self-assessment quizzes.

eTEACH is used to present classroom lectures and lab demonstrations online so that instructors can save in-class time to engage students in interactive discussions or problem-solving activities. It is also used to deliver distance learning courses. In both cases, students can choose where and when they view lectures. Feedback from students taking courses delivered with eTEACH is predominantly positive (Moses & Litzkow, 2005).

Accessibility Challenges in eTEACH

The first version of eTEACH was developed by Professor Gregory Moses and researcher Mike Litzkow. Early in the development of their project, Moses and Litzkow became aware of Web accessibility issues and, specifically, the UW–Madison Web Accessibility Policy (UW–Madison, 2009a). They quickly responded by incorporating new capabilities for captioning and transcripts of the lectures. However, eTEACH's reliance on video content was an immediate concern. In particular, making such a complex multimedia tool accessible to blind and visually impaired students would be difficult.

Testing eTEACH presentations with a blind student using a screen reader quickly revealed that he was unable to make much sense of the presentations without help from a sighted person. Litzkow then sought help from Neal Ewers, a blind researcher working at the Trace Research and Development Center (UW–Madison, 2009b). With help from Ewers, Litzkow began to realize that individuals who are blind have trained themselves to learn from lectures without being able to see visual cues, such as the instructor's face, content presented on a whiteboard, and slides projected onto a screen. He envisioned that the eTEACH interface could be modified to make online lecture content at least as accessible to blind students as on-site attendance in a lecture hall. In retrospect, this made a lot of sense and was in alignment with eTEACH's general goal of replicating the best features of classroom lectures while adding value in terms of convenience, search ability, and reusability.

Ewers helped Litzkow understand why simply meeting minimum accessibility standards did not result in a satisfactory experience for a screen reader user. He learned that viewing eTEACH lectures is a more complex task than viewing simple Web pages that contain only static text, graphics, and links. Multimedia typically used in lectures—video, audio, and images—contribute significantly to the students' lecture experience, as each medium contains important components of the information presented by the lecturer. Students need to be able to navigate within a lecture using a table of contents or other controls. Because audio and video are time-based and slides and animations are synchronized with audio and video, timing is a significant issue. For example, even if a play/pause button is available, if the access method is slow and awkward, the student who wants to pause the audio so that the screen reader can "speak" the text on a PowerPoint slide may be unable to do so before the slide changes. By addressing in the design of eTEACH the complex issues of video, PowerPoint slides, control of "reading" versus "listening," and math content from a blind user's perspective, the developers resolved accessibility issues encountered by users with other disabilities as well. In the following sections, we detail some of the critical issues in making multimedia lectures accessible to blind students.

Video

When important content is presented visually, students who are blind need an audio or a text-based description of the visual information. They cannot see video, but they can hear the associated audio (provided they do not have disabilities that affect hearing). In fact, the audio is often the most information-rich part of a multimedia lecture. Students who are blind need a mechanism to effectively control the pace of the video—that is, with "play," "pause," "rewind," and other functions—in order to make sense of the related audio. They need quick and convenient access to these functions so that they do not miss the audio while they are trying to locate the proper controls. They also need a clear and synchronized association between the portion of the video that relates to a particular slide and the textual content of that slide. Having the capability to control the pace of the content and to return to content for review is critical for all students.

PowerPoint Slides

Most PowerPoint slides consist of text and images; some also contain animations. In some cases, the animations are gratuitous (i.e., they are just "eye candy" that does not convey essential content). However, in other cases, they highlight particular parts of the slide as the instructor discusses them. At minimum, blind users should be able to read all of the text and access the content of images on a slide. It is important to be aware that when slides are created by using images that contain characters or words, they appear as text to sighted users but screen readers interpret them as images and therefore cannot access the words presented. For screen reader software to access the content of a slide, it must be presented in a text-based format and images or animations must be tagged with "alt text" that describes the content.

Control of "Reading" Versus "Listening"

Sighted users access textual content on a slide by simply reading it. Most can easily integrate listening to the lecturer's comments about a slide with reading the slide's text. This is possible because two different sensory inputs are used (visual and sound). In contrast, screen reader users who are blind must use the same sense (hearing) to gain information from both the slide and the lecturer's comments. They must listen to the slide's textual content spoken by a synthesized voice at the same time they are listening to the instructor's comments about the slide. Consequently, content should be presented so that the screen reader's "reading" does not conflict with the student's "listening" to the instructor's spoken words. Ideally, the student should be able to choose to read the slide text first, listen to the audio content first, or jump back and forth between the two. The student also needs a way to balance the volume of the spoken audio with the volume of the screen reader so that one does not dominate the other.

Math Content

Since mathematics is a component of many disciplines, authoring tools must be able to support the presentation of mathematical expressions and formulae in multimedia presentations. For a blind user to make sense of the mathematical content presented in a lecture, math symbols need to be presented in a structured format supported by screen readers.

Addressing Accessibility Issues in eTEACH

Each new version of eTEACH incorporates more accessibility features than its predecessor. The current version facilitates the presentation of content that is accessible to students with a wide variety of disabilities. Captioning capabilities are included for students who are deaf or hard of hearing and interaction through the keyboard alone is available for those who have fine motor limitations and/or use alternative input devices.

Carefully following the principles of universal design made eTEACH accessible to most students with disabilities. However, analyzing the specific and complex access issues for screen reader users discussed earlier and recognizing that some specific features desirable for these students can add unnecessary complications for others, eTEACH developers decided that having a separate version designed for students who are blind would be the best approach to ensuring equal access. The "regular" version employs universal design principles so that it is accessible to most students, and the "screen reader" version facilitates use with screen readers. So that the two versions remain equally functional and equally up to date, developers incorporated a feature in eTEACH to automatically generate two versions of every lecture. Blind students are led to the screen reader version by a link that is "visible" with screen reader software, but invisible to those not using screen reader software. In this way, eTEACH provides versions of a lecture tailored to students who are blind and to visual learners, yet does not depend on instructors providing special links and instructions for students.

The screen reader version of eTEACH lectures capitalizes on the strengths of screen readers by creating a highly structured version of the lecture for blind users. Although students who are blind cannot navigate through a Web page by recognizing visual cues, their screen readers are very good at navigating structural elements like headers, lists, and internal links. Many blind students are highly skilled at using this structure to quickly find the content they seek. The audio part of the lecture is simply the audio track from the regular video, but it is broken up into a slide-by-slide format.

Use of eTEACH

Since 2000, the UW–Madison College of Engineering has used the Web as a tool to deliver lectures in large undergraduate classes. Traditional lecture hall sessions with hundreds of students who meet weekly have been replaced with online rich-media presentations. eTEACH lectures have replaced traditional lectures in such diverse departments as Computer Sciences, Nuclear Engineering, Nursing, and Business Education on the UW–Madison campus, as well as on several other campuses nationwide. eTEACH was selected by University of Wisconsin–Whitewater's online MBA program as the delivery method for their distance education courses (University of Wisconsin–Whitewater, n.d.). Because of built-in features that promote universal design, as the use of eTEACH expands so does the creation of courses that are automatically accessible to and usable by students with a wide range of disabilities.

Christopher Blaire Bundy, a Senior Learning Technology Consultant for DoIT, used eTEACH to create "The Storyteller with Professor Harold Scheub," an account of Sheub's remarkable experience with African storytellers (UW–Madison, 2007). Bundy started with a slide carousel of about 130 images from Sheub's journeys spanning 40 years and thousands of miles of walking along the southeastern coast of Africa recording native storytellers of the Xhosa. The images were digitized into jpeg format and inserted into PowerPoint. Once in PowerPoint, each slide was given a unique title, which served as the navigation structure in eTEACH. Professor Scheub was filmed responding to several questions about his experiences. iMovie was used to edit the video and it was converted to Streaming Flash. eTEACH was used to synchronize the video to the slides, making the content as accessible to as many audiences as possible.

Critical to the success of this project was the planning and storyboarding Bundy did ahead of time to map out the presentation before transferring the content into eTEACH. In addition to the benefits of eTEACH acces-

Figure 13.2 eTEACH ability to shift focus in large video area from content to professor.

sibility, the capabilities to stream at multiple connection speeds for those using slow bandwidth and to bundle the transcripts (both in English and Xhosa) in the presentation were essential to meeting the needs of intended audiences. Another benefit of eTEACH was the ability to shift the focus and size of images and video clips to highlight the most engaging elements of the presentation at any one time.

DISCUSSION

This chapter describes challenges that must be addressed to ensure the full inclusion of postsecondary instructors and students with disabilities in technology-rich online and face-to-face learning environments. The authors discussed potential barriers to participation that relate to access to physical environments, IT, and engagement. They propose solutions to address these challenges that incorporate both proactive and reactive approaches—that is, universal design and accommodations, respectively.

As increasing amounts of academic content are being presented using digital media, as our postsecondary student bodies are becoming more diverse overall, and as growing numbers of students with disabilities are attending colleges and universities, the importance of providing digital content that is accessible to and usable by students with a wide variety of characteristics, including disabilities, is hard to overstate. Products that are universally designed support the institution's compliance with the ADA and other legislation and welcome the participation and promote the success of all students in courses that employ digital media. Authoring tools that promote and support the creation of accessible content can help course developers and content authors develop instructional media that is accessible to and usable by all students.

Key steps in the process of incorporating accessibility features into a course authoring tool, as illustrated in the case study presented in this chapter, include understanding and implementing Web accessibility standards, providing the capability to include captions and transcriptions for students who are deaf, ensuring access to all features and content with the keyboard alone for students who cannot use a mouse, and making courses completely accessible for students who use screen reader and other assistive technologies. Instructors and developers are also encouraged to address accessibility issues in early design stages and to incorporate accessibility features into the mainstream lessons and products whenever possible, and, if a separate version is needed for a specific audience such as screen reader users, the product itself should automatically create the special version from the most current version of the main product.

RECOMMENDATIONS

Most practitioners are in the position of choosing a course authoring tool rather than creating one. In this case, they should look for a product that encourages authors to create accessible content, creates accessible content with little or no extra work by content authors, and meets accessibility standards. They should keep in mind that product-marketing claims about accessibility could be misleading. Administrators are encouraged to have tools evaluated by both experts on accessibility issues and by individuals who use assistive technology, especially screen readers, to ensure both accessibility and usability before selecting a course authoring tool.

Areas for future research include exploring the value of captioning beyond accessibility compliance (e.g., its value for content searches and index creation); supporting multi-modal learning; addressing challenges of learners with language differences; and identifying content presentation and supports that improve comprehension for students with a wide range of abilities with respect to reading, content processing, and attention, as well as those with various learning styles and other characteristics. An additional area for further study is to analyze the challenges and solutions in making course authoring tools themselves fully accessible to developers with disabilities, including those who are blind and using screen reader software.

ACKNOWLEDGEMENTS

This chapter is based on work supported by the National Science Foundation under grant #HRD-0833504 in Research in Disabilities Education (RDE) and #CNS-0540615 and #CNS-0837508 in Computer and Information Science and Engineering (CISE). Any opinions, findings, and conclusions or recommendations expressed in this material are those of the authors and do not necessarily reflect the views of the National Science Foundation. This chapter includes excerpts, with permission, from a chapter originally written by A. Anderson and M. Litzkow (2008) in the book *Universal Design in Higher Education: From Principles to Practice.*

REFERENCES

AbilityNet. (2008, January 18). *State of the eNation reports: Social networking sites lock out disabled users.* Retrieved December 1, 2009 from http://www.abilitynet.org.uk/enation85

Adobe Systems. (2009). *Elearning with Adobe Acrobat Connect Pro: Easy, effective, enjoyable—and memorable.* Retrieved December 1, 2009 from http://www.adobe.com/products/acrobatconnectpro/elearning/

American Federation for the Blind. (2009). *Are social networking sites accessible to people with vision loss?* Retrieved December 1, 2009 from http://www.afb.org/Section.asp?SectionID=4&TopicID=167&DocumentID=3153

Americans with Disabilities Act of 1990. Pub. L. No. 101-336, § 12101 et seq. (1991).

Anderson, A., & Ewers, N. (2001). *Accessibility: Introduction to the screen reader* [video and transcription]. Retrieved December 1, 2009 from http://doit.wisc.edu/accessibility/video/intro.asp

Anderson, A., & Litzkow, M. (2008). Problems and solutions for making multimedia web-based lectures accessible: A case study. In S. E. Burgstahler & R. C. Cory (Eds.), *Universal design in higher education: From principles to practice* (pp. 225–233). Boston: Harvard Education Press.

Articulate Global. (n.d.). *Articulate.* Retrieved December 1, 2009 from http://www.articulate.com/

Berners-Lee, T. (1993, June). *Hypertext Markup Language (HTML).* Retrieved December 1, 2009 from http://www.w3.org/MarkUp/draft-ietf-iiir-html-01.txt

Burgstahler, S. (2006). The development of accessibility indicators for distance learning programs. *Research in Learning Technology, 14*(1), 79–102.

Burgstahler, S. E. (2008a). Universal design of instruction: From principles to practice. In S. E. Burgstahler & R. C. Cory (Eds.), *Universal design in higher education: From principles to practice* (pp. 3–20). Boston: Harvard Education Press.

Burgstahler, S. E. (2008b). Universal design of physical spaces: From principles to practice. In S. E. Burgstahler & R. C. Cory (Eds.), *Universal design in higher education: From principles to practice* (pp. 187–197). Boston: Harvard Education Press.

Burgstahler, S. E. (2008c). Universal design of technological environments: From principles to practice. In S. E. Burgstahler & R. C. Cory (Eds.), *Universal design in higher education: From principles to practice* (pp. 213–224). Boston: Harvard Education Press.

Burgstahler, S. (2009) *Equal access: Universal design of computer labs.* Seattle: University of Washington. Retrieved December 1, 2009 from http://www.washington.edu/doit/Brochures/Technology/comp.access.html

Burgstahler, S., & Doe, T. (2005). Improving postsecondary outcomes for students with disabilities: Designing professional development for faculty. *Journal of Postsecondary Education and Disability, 18*(2), 135–147.

Center for Applied Special Technology [CAST]. (n.d.a). *CAST: Transforming education through universal design for learning.* Retrieved December 15, 2009 from http://www.cast.org

CAST. (n.d.b). *What is universal design for learning?* Retrieved December 10, 2009 from http://www.cast.org/research/udl/

CUD. (2008). *About UD.* Raleigh, NC: Author. Retrieved July 15, 2009 from http://www.design.ncsu.edu/cud/about_ud/about_ud.htm

The Center for Universal Design in Education [CUDE]. (n.d.) Retrieved December 1, 2009 from http://www.washington.edu/doit/CUDE

Closing the Gap. (n.d.). *Closing the Gap solutions: Producers.* Retrieved December 10, 2009 from http://www.closingthegap.com/solutions/producers/

Dona, J., & Edmister, J. H. (2001). An examination of community college faculty members' knowledge of the Americans with Disabilities Act of 1990 at the fifteen community colleges in Mississippi. *Journal of Postsecondary Education and Disability, 14*(2), 91–103.

Facebook (n.d.). *Accessibility and assistive technology.* Retrieved December 1, 2009 from http://www.facebook.com/help.php?page=440

Foertsch, J., Moses, G., Strikwerda, J., & Litzkow, M. (2002). Revising the lecture/homework paradigm using eTEACH web-based streaming video software. *Journal of Engineering Education, 91,* 267–274.

Golden, D. C. (2002). Instructional software accessibility: A status report. *Journal of Special Education Technology, 17*(1), 57–60.

Guy, T. (2002). Telementoring: Shaping mentoring relationships for the 21st century. In C. A. Hansman (Ed.), *Critical perspectives on mentoring: Trends and issues* (pp. 27–38). Columbus, OH: Center on Education and Training for Employment. Retrieved from www.calpro-online.org/eric/docs/mott/mentoring1.pdf

International Business Machines. (2008). *Virtual worlds user interface for the blind.* Retrieved December 1, 2009 from http://services.alphaworks.ibm.com/virtualworlds/

Lembree, D. (2009). *Accessible Twitter.* Retrieved from http://www.accessibletwitter.com/

Linden Research. (n.d.). *Second Life accessibility.* Retrieved December 1, 2009 from http://wiki.secondlife.com/wiki/Accessibility

Moses, G., & Litzkow, M. (2005, October). In-class active learning and frequent assessment reform of nuclear reactor theory course. *Frontiers in Education Proceedings: 35th Annual Conference.* Retrieved December 1, 2009 from http://ieeexplore.ieee.org/xpls/absprintf.jsp?arnumber=1612006

National Center for Education Statistics. (n.d.). *Fast facts: What proportion of students enrolled in postsecondary education have a disability?* [Data source: U.S. Department of Education, National Center for Education Statistics. (2006). *Profile of undergraduates in U.S. postsecondary education institutions: 2003–04* (NCES 2006-184)]. Retrieved December 1, 2009 from http://nces.ed.gov/fastfacts/display.asp?id=60

National Center for the Study of Postsecondary Educational Supports. (2000). *National survey of educational support provision to students with disabilities in postsecondary education settings.* Honolulu: University of Hawaii.

National Council on Disability. (2004). *Design for inclusion: Creating a new marketplace.* Washington, DC: Author. Retrieved December 1, 2009 from http://www.ncd.gov/newsroom/publications/2004/online_newmarketplace.htm#afbad

National Science Foundation [NSF]. (2009). *Women, minorities, and persons with disabilities in science and engineering.* Arlington, VA: U.S. Government Printing Office. Retrieved December 1, 2009 from http://www.nsf.gov/statistics/wmpd/disability.htm

Office of the Federal Register, National Archives and Records Service, General Services Administration. (2000, December 21). Electronic and information technology accessibility standards. *The Federal Register, 65*(246), 80499–80528.

Patrick, D. L. (1996, September 9). [Correspondence to Senator Tom Harkin]. Retrieved December 1, 2009 from http://www.usdoj.gov/crt/foia/cltr204.txt

Randall, S. (2009). *Jawter: Twitter from Jaws with no software in the middle*. Retrieved July 15, 2009 from http://randylaptop.com/software/jawter-2/

The Rehabilitation Act of 1973, Pub. L. No. 93-112, 29 U.S.C. §§ 504 & 508 (amended, 1998).

Rose, D. H., & Meyer, A. (2002). *Teaching every student in the digital age: Universal design for learning*. Alexandria, VA: Association for Supervision and Curriculum Development.

Sonic Foundry. (n.d.). *Your know-how, online now*. Retrieved December 1, 2009 from http://www.sonicfoundry.com/mediasite/

Tegrity (n.d.). *Integrity*. Retrieved July 15, 2009 from http://www.tegrity.com/

Thompson, T. (2008). Universal design of computing labs. In S. E. Burgstahler & R. C. Cory (Eds.), *Universal design in higher education: From principles to practice* (pp. 235–244). Boston: Harvard Education Press.

U.S. Access Board. (n.d.). *Section 508 home page: Electronic and information technology*. Retrieved December 1, 2009 from http://www.access-board.gov/508.htm

U.S. Department of Justice Civil Rights Division. (2005). *A guide to disability rights laws*. Washington, DC: Author. Retrieved from http://www.ada.gov/cguide.pdf

University of Wisconsin–Madison [UW–Madison]. (2007). *The storyteller*. Retrieved December 1, 2009 from http://africa.wisc.edu/thestoryteller/

UW–Madison. (2009a). *Accessibility: Understanding the UW policy*. Retrieved December 1, 2009 from http://www.doit.wisc.edu/accessibility/policy.asp

UW–Madison. (2009b). *Trace Research and Development Center*. Retrieved December 1, 2009 from http://trace.wisc.edu/

University of Wisconsin–Whitewater. (n.d.). *Online MBA*. Retrieved December 1, 2009 from http://www.uww.edu/cobe/distance/onlinemba/

Vanderheiden, G. C., & Vanderheiden, K. R. (1992). *Guidelines for the design of consumer products to increase their accessibility to people with disabilities or who are aging (Working Draft 1.7)*. Madison, WI: Trace Research and Development Center. Retrieved December 1, 2009 from http://trace.wisc.edu/docs/consumer_product_guidelnies/toc.htm

World Wide Web Consortium [W3C]. (n.d.). *Web Accessibility Initiative (WAI)*. Retrieved December 1, 2009 from http://www.w3.org/WAI/

W3C. (2007). *About W3C: Future*. Retrieved December 1, 2009 from http://www.w3.org/Consortium/future

CHAPTER 14

INCORPORATING 3D VIRTUAL LABORATORY SPECIMENS TO ENHANCE ONLINE SCIENCE

Examples from Paleontology and Biology

Kevin F. Downing
Jennifer K. Holtz
DePaul University

INTRODUCTION

This chapter provides an introduction to and case study of how digital media can be used in a specific discipline, science. The more specific focus in the use of three-dimensional (3D) imaging is to create engaging and meaningful learning experiences. The broad acceptance of e-Learning by students and the proliferation of online schools and colleges have created an increasing demand for diverse online science learning activities. From an instructional and technological standpoint, designing an effective e-Learning environment for science, as with other disciplines, presents many

The Professor's Guide to Taming Technology, pages 219–238
Copyright © 2011 by Information Age Publishing
All rights of reproduction in any form reserved.

general challenges (see Downing & Holtz, 2008 for a full discussion). One of the most prominent instructional challenges in the development of online science course activities is to provide students with practical learning experiences that approximate the informational richness of a laboratory or field investigation.

Many online science courses limit themselves to conceptual treatments of subjects and rely on simple graphics. However, there are extensive limitations to 2D scientific representations, as many essential in-class learning activities rely on a student's investigation of authentic material objects such as everyday items, artifacts, representative physical models, and scientific specimens. How can such learning activities be translated to and/or embellished by online learning environments? One means is to provide online students comparable virtual study items called *3D learning objects*.

Essentially, any real object that can be scanned in three dimensions can be rendered into a 3D learning object for use in K–16 distance education. 3D learning objects (or 3D knowledge objects) are digital representations of the surface morphology of objects (real or inanimate) constructed of a mesh of polygons in various 3D file formats (e.g., VRML, DXF, 3DS). Corresponding 3D browsers afford students the ability to manipulate a 3D object's size, perspective, and lighting as well as analyze its characteristics quantitatively via linear measurements, basic volume analysis, and so on. For this reason, 3D learning objects can provide the requisite informational depth to substitute for real objects to support online inquiry, experimentation, and visualization.

KEY TERMS

3D Learning Objects (or 3D Knowledge Objects)
   Digital representations of the surface morphology of objects (real or inanimate) constructed of a mesh of polygons in various 3D file formats (e.g., VRML, DXF, 3DS).

3D Browsers
   Software viewers, like Web browsers, which enable users to manipulate a 3D learning object's size, perspective, and lighting as well as analyze its characteristics quantitatively via linear measurements, basic volume analysis, and so on.

INSTRUCTIONAL FOUNDATIONS: THEORY AND PRACTICE

There are many examples of the use of animations, simulations, and other kinds of 3D imaging that help many students learn science material more quickly and more thoroughly; what is critical is strategically determining the learning conditions under which the majority of students benefit (e.g., Gazit, Yair, & Chen, 2005; Korakakis, Pavlatou, Palyvos, & Spyrellis, 2009; Steinkeuhler & Duncan, 2008). Practical work and the benefit of hands-on experimentation is well documented in history, most commonly as the apprenticeship model that continues in multiple learning environments, from trade schools to medical residency to doctoral fellowships. Moreover, practical work is appropriate for multiple levels of learning. Woolnough and Allsop (1985) define four categories of tasks: (1) *exercises* that demonstrate theory or teach functional procedure, (2) *experiences* to provide insight into observable science, (3) *investigations* that apply scientific reasoning to test hypotheses, and (4) *illustrations* that make clear scientific laws and theories.

Criticisms of practical work focus on the extent to which claims are met. Jenkins (1999) cites the difficulty in replicating scientific methods in the school setting, maintaining that insufficient modeling of authentic practical work may not be as effective as alternatives that emphasize construction of knowledge. Millar (1998) and Jenkins (1999) concur, crediting practical work with a conveyance of general meaning rather than insight into practice. Further, online practical work activities are even less effective than on-site practical work, "since real events contain more information then representations of them (videos, computer simulations, etc.)" (Downing & Holtz, p. 85; See also Millar, 2004). In our experience, these arguments are negated by implementation of scaffolding systems that are sufficiently flexible to support the greatest possible range of novice to expert learners. In sum, practical work activities such as scientific laboratory investigations are fundamental to science as a way of knowing (Hofstein & Lunetta, 2003; Singer, Hilton, & Schwiengruber, 2005) whether a student is on-site or online.

ANIMATIONS AND SIMULATIONS

Use of animations and simulations in science learning environments represents emergent best practice, regardless of educational philosophy or the type of student engaged. Both modalities can serve as powerful scaffolding for novice learners and can provide *practical work experience*, arguably the most important development for online science learning (Ross & Scanlon, 1995). Simulations that are done well—from those in which learners input or change variables to those that incorporate state-of-the-art haptic design—mimic the hands-on experience of laboratory, field, and experimental work, as does incorporation of manipulative 3D learning objects (Ross, & Scanlon, 1995; Van Marion, 1999).

SCIENTIFIC VISUALIZATION AS A TOOL
FOR ONLINE LEARNING

One approach to designing and engaging students in an interactive lab or field trip for on-site or online courses is through the use of scientific visualization. Two-dimensional visualizations may effectively accomplish learning objectives as in the example of computer-aided visualization and animation of ocean waves of Gould and Whitford (2000); however, scientific visualization is commonly three-dimensional, as in the case of the virtual fruit fly described by Kusnick (2001). Scientific visualization typically involves the representation of data and objects in 3D images in order to navigate through them more quickly as well as access, interpret, and understand information in a more natural manner (El Saddik, 2001).

Scientific visualization became expansively useful as a learning tool with the advent of the Virtual Reality Modeling Language (VRML). VRML and its successor, X3D, provide the user an opportunity to navigate through 3D worlds, visualize information, and inspect 3D models (Vacca, 1996). The complete extent of 3D scientific visualization is a virtual reality environment where a user-learner is immersed in a 3D environment with a head-mounted display providing vision, headphones providing sound, and tactile feedback provided by a haptic device.

It is expected that within the next few decades the general public will have ordinary access to scientific data depositories and the software tools for modifying and viewing 3D scientific visualizations through the Internet (Rhyne, 2000) such as the emerging cyberinfrastructure in earth science described by Ramamurthy (2006). The presence and use of scientific visualization and 3D objects on the Web is slowly escalating for both research and teaching purposes; however, a standardized scientific visualization approach for online labs and field trips using 3D learning objects is largely unrealized.

BENEFITS OF SCIENTIFIC VISUALIZATION

If designed with sound attention to pedagogical best practices, learning exercises employing the technology of scientific visualization are highly effective in supporting inquiry-based learning (Edelson, 2001; Edelson, Gordon, & Pea, 1999). El Saddik (2001) summarized the specific benefits of employing visualization tools in teaching as improvement of a student's understanding, skill mastery through additional practice opportunities, development of analytical skills, motivation enhancement, and as a presentation aid in the classroom. Further benefits of scientific visualization can also be recognized:

- Enhancing learning and practice, plus opening up new ways to view science and going about solving problems (McGrath & Brown, 2005)

- The development of mental models, *metavisual capacity*, and deeper understanding of scientific models through 2D and 3D representations (Gilbert, 2005)
- Students generate the visualizations themselves (El Saddik, 2001)

Teaching abstract concepts is proven to be enhanced with quality 2D and 3D visualizations, for instance, electromagnetism (Dori & Belcher, 2005), genomics (Takayama, 2005), and geology (Reynolds & Mason, 2005). We view the relationship of visualization levels from 2D through 3D graphics to be one of general increasing opportunity for scaffolding, interactivity, and multifaceted inquiry (Figure 14.1). Where 2D graphics are static and limited to one perspective, passive 3D graphics can provide multiple perspectives, including the circumnavigation of an object. Active 3D is an even more sophisticated instructional design tool providing the user-learner the ability to self-direct motions through the 3D environment such as zoom, pan, and rotation perspectives about an object. Adding measurement tools to the active 3D interface provides the user-learner with greatly expanded abilities to undertake quantitative inquiry. Finally, if a haptic interface is coupled with the 3D graphic environment, responsive touch feedback is added and the investigative possibilities are further enhanced. In Table 14.1, we categorize the relationships between graphic level, user control, and visualization characteristics, including examples of each, and in Appendix A we provide links to select examples. The 3D learning objects (i.e., virtual specimens) described in this study center on the active 3D level with coupled browser tools for quantitative inquiry.

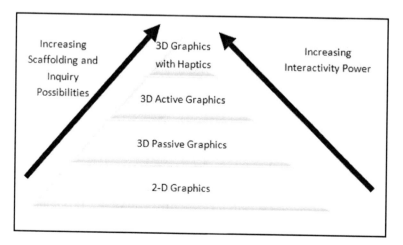

Figure 14.1 Hierarchy of online graphical types in relation to scaffolding, interactivity, and inquiry.

TABLE 14.1

Graphic Type	User Control	Visualization Characteristics	Example
2D Graphics	None	Static—one perspective	Pictures of animals
3D graphics—passive	None = (automated movement)	Multiple perspectives but controlled by format, limited inspection	3D object nested in a Web movie with rotational perspective
3D graphics—active	Rotation and zoom	Magnification	3D tour within a structure
	Pan	Inspection	Geographical flyover of terrain
3D graphics with user interface that permits quantification	Counts	Advanced inspection and measurement	3D object within a graphic user interface that includes tool features for quantification (e.g., CAD)
	Measurement		
	Volume analysis		
	Overlay of multiple objects		
	Transformation of one object into another (morphing)		
3D graphics with haptic response	Haptics	Perspective with coordinated touch	Virtual museum 3D specimens

USES OF 3D VIRTUAL LABORATORY SPECIMENS

Scientific Visualization for Learning and Research

Professional and educational success in numerous areas of science and engineering require strong spatial reasoning abilities. 3D multimedia has been shown to improve 3D spatial reasoning skills for engineering students, particularly when coupled with corresponding sketching activities (Sorby, 2009). Emersion into virtual worlds can enhance the development of science habits of the mind such as model-based reasoning and model testing and prediction (Steinkuehler & Duncan, 2008). The efficacy of virtual labs for teaching science students has been demonstrated in many studies, including their use in elementary education, where they promote student interest and increase teaching possibilities for individualization, varying learning styles, and learning repetition (Sun, Lin, & Yu, 2007).

Similarly, 3D-based tutorials appear to positively influence the development of spatial visualization skills in undergraduate students (Wang, Chang, & Li, 2007). Student enthusiasm and comprehension of complex molecules, including DNA, and their changes is improved when 3D visualization is substituted for 2D modeling (Limniou, Roberts, & Papadopoulos, 2008; Patrick, Carter, & Wiebe, 2005). Similar efforts to enhance student visualization of characteristic crystal structures and complex plate tectonic boundaries in geology have been developed with 3D interfaces and have demonstrated increased academic performance (Dong, Clapworthy, Krokos, & Yao, 2002).

Scaffolding Considerations for 3D Learning Environments

Moving from novice to expert at any age, in any field results from a reduction of cognitive load (Sweller, 1988), the ease with which a person is able to access knowledge from long-term memory for use by working memory. Miller's (1956) classic research found—and it was confirmed by later research (Bapi, Pammi, Miyapuram, & Ahmed, 2005; Gobet et al., 2001)—that the average working memory is limited to between five and nine chunks of information. Any chunk that is not secured to a knowledge structure in long-term memory is replaced by new information (i.e., forgotten). As students become more proficient at accessing long-term memory in response to working memory cues, their position on the novice to expert scale moves toward expert, which is the goal in experiential fields like science (Holtz, 2002; Sternberg, 1984).

The role of scaffolding in facilitating expertise through reduction of cognitive load is essential. Scaffolding in education refers to supportive structures, just as it does in construction. In learning science, scaffolding takes the form of learning objects that clearly illustrate or facilitate the illustration of key concepts, processes and theories (Quintana, Krajcik & Soloway, 2002).

Scaffolding is of principle concern when using 3D learning objects and virtual learning environments. These innovations do not function in isolation for teaching complex scientific concepts online, and care must be taken not to overwhelm the learner by assuming a generation-based familiarity that precludes mentoring and facilitation. For example, while 3D interactive animations and 3D animations are enthusiastically received by middle school students, these types of visualization environments may also involve a heavy cognitive load relative to static 3D images (Korakakis, 2009). Complex 3D representations may require significant scaffolding to help guide the student through conceptual understanding, as concluded by Gazit et al. (2005) for a virtual solar system geared for high school students. Likewise, appropriate levels of pedagogical content knowledge to explain the procedures should accompany online learning in 3D settings.

The application of 3D specimen-based learning objects is becoming more commonplace, but they are represented best in the medical arena, where 3D representations of human anatomy permit the learner to inspect spatial characteristics (Choi, Laver, & Gurnis, 2008). The field of medicine has long been the locus for much of the pioneering work using 3D visualization to support medical education, research, and authentic activities related to the workplace. For example, Virtual Reality Assisted Surgery (Robb & Cameron, 1995) has been around for more than a decade. Medical images are now routinely available in online-accessible formats, permitting users to interact with images and manipulate them as side-by-side functional and anatomical comparisons (Cai, Feng, & Fulton, 2001; Qi et al., 2007). Students can even go to online images of the Visible Human Project (Ackerman, 1998) and construct their own anatomical structures (Evesque, Gerlach, & Hersch, 2002).

CASE STUDY: VIRTUAL SPECIMENS IN PALEONTOLOGY

Practical use of 3D visualization and 3D learning objects is also being incorporated into archeological and paleontological studies. The software program Virtual Archaeologist (Papaioannou, Karabassi, & Theoharis, 2001) is a 3D puzzle assembler for archaeologists. Virtual Archaeologist matches complimentary pieces of 3D scans of artifact fragments for automatic reconstruction. Computer-based 3D visualization for use in specimen-based paleontological research and online exhibition is also becoming more commonplace. Rich examples of these 3D fossil objects, referred to as *virtual fossils*, include CT scans to reconstruct soft-bodied fossils from the Silurian Herefordshire (Sutton, Briggs, Siveter, & Siveter, 2001), a three-dimensional color laser scan of a juvenile *Tylosaur* species' basisphenoid-basioccipital region (Lyons, Rioux, & Patterson, 2000), and the skeleton of *Tyrannosarus rex* (Brochu, 2003).

Online virtual fossils at museums' Web sites are more common, including the inceptive work of the British Natural History Museum and its virtual fossil exhibits (www.nhm.ac.uk/nature-online/virtual-wonders/), a composite reconstruction of the Triceratops by the Smithsonian National Museum of Natural History (Moltenbrey, 2001), and cranial reconstructions of a Neanderthal child by the University of Zurick (Pasternack, 2002). Although there are a small but growing number of virtual fossil examples, the development of these learning resources has been primarily intended for research or for popularization of an online exhibit. The development of 3D fossils as a scientific visualization tool for the explicit use in instruction for online science courses has not been common.

Objective: Constructing Virtual Fossils and a Fossil Cabinet Interface

Paleontology courses traditionally are taught, as are most geology and biology courses, through a combination of conceptual and experiential learning. The experiential learning is accomplished through field trips and laboratory activities that incorporate extensive study and use of specimens. In paleontology, the 3D size, shape, and features of a fossil specimen are examined by students to determine which species or group the specimen belongs to (identification and classification) and what detailed morphological features indicate about its evolutionary relationships, functional morphology, and ecology. Paleontological instruction relies strongly on hands-on activities with fossils to foster interest as well as student observation, inquiry, and abstract conceptualization skills.

The chief instructional design issue of this case study centers on the development of learning objects for an online course in paleontology (Downing, 1999). While the Internet has a large number of static 2D pictures, it was recognized that a sole reliance on 2D representations of fossils was unacceptable for the online format of the course, as it would diminish practical work aspects of the learning experience. While an occasional 3D fossil is available online as indicated above, these are limited in kind and instructional relevance, and typically "stored" as QuickTime movies (i.e., passive 3D graphics). The challenge was to develop a representative sample of virtual fossils in an interactive 3D format to support learning objectives and exercises comparable to on-site learning experiences. The first objective was to develop a set of 3D virtual fossils approximating the character of a lab specimen. The mix of specimens needed for instruction included representatives of invertebrate, vertebrate, and plant fossil groups. In addition to individual specimens, small fossil assemblages were sought for use in paleoecological and taphonomic exercises where the death association of a group of individuals is required for analysis. A best practice in online science learning interface design is to build an interface that is as close to authentic as possible. To make the learning experience more authentic in this case, a graphic user interface (GUI) was developed that would approximate a fossil storage cabinet whose drawers would "hold" the instructional virtual fossil specimens.

Methods: Technologies and Interfaces

Images of the fossils were collected using a 3D contact sensor scanner (Roland DGA Corporation's Picza System) which has a maximum resolution of 0.02mm for the model used. Specimens were oriented and secured on the scanner stage with clay. Scan dimensions and resolution parameters were selected and original 3D data was transformed into the DXF format (the standard CAD format). 3D modeling software (e.g., Microsoft Truespace) was used for post-production enhancements, including polygon reduction, rendering in the 3D file format, adding false color, building 3D rulers and markers, and developing the 3D fossil cabinet. 3D viewing software (e.g., SolidView Lite and others with measurement capabilities) was employed to test for the inspection, comparison, and measurement characteristics of the completed virtual fossil specimens. The technological threshold described here is based on the notion and goal that such science learning objects can be developed by an instructor using a no-frills desktop 3D scanning system (including new color varieties) and 3D modeling and viewing software readily supported by colleges or available for free use on the Internet.

Results: The Virtual Collection

The initial virtual fossil collection for the Virtual Paleontology course consists of over 20 specimens comprised of vertebrate, invertebrate, plant, protist, and paleoecology specimens. Typical acquisition times for specimens using this system at high resolution is 6–10 hours, depending on size and surface characteristics and the chosen resolution (ranging from .05mm-.02mm for these fossils). A 3D depiction of a fossil cabinet is used as the GUI for the virtual fossils (Figure 14.2). When a drawer is pressed, a map view of the drawer is revealed with the prospective fossils (Figure 14.3) or fossil assemblages. Pressing a fossil initiates the 3D browser and loads the fossil for instructional use (Figure 14.4).

The resulting virtual fossil specimens can be easily panned, zoomed, measured, and rotated, much like a complex specimen being examined in a lab setting (Figure 14.5). Depending on the 3D browser used, two specimens may be loaded for side-by-side comparison and point-to-point measurements can be made. Using 3D graphics programs, an instructor can add other useful enhancements to the virtual fossil such as rulers (Figure 14.6) and scaffold in feature markers (Figure 14.7). It is also possible to develop instructional animations for online use. Limitations for virtual fos-

Figure 14.2 The Virtual Paleontology fossil cabinet. The cabinet serves as the graphic interface for students to access the fossil trays. Pressing a drawer opens that particular tray.

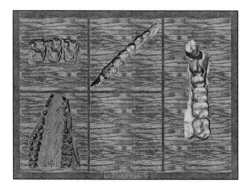

Figure 14.3 Example of a mammal tray. Pressing on a specimen loads it into a 3D viewer for observation and manipulation by the student.

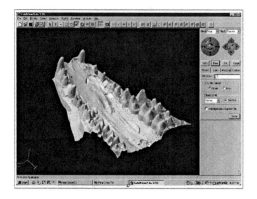

Figure 14.4 Example of highly magnified cast of *Echinosorex sp.*

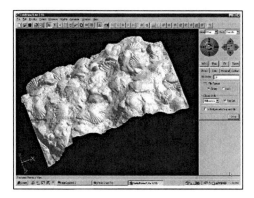

Figure 14.5 Example of rotated fossil assemblage useful for paleoecology and taphonomy exercises.

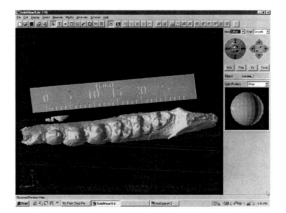

Figure 14.6 Example of *Lemuroides sp.* in the 3D viewer. Students can use any 3D viewer in conjunction with their browser to pan, zoom, rotate, and manipulate. A 3D ruler has been placed in the image for taking measurements.

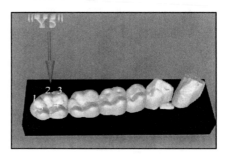

Figure 14.7 Example of modified image of *Sivapithecus sp.* Specific markers are added to focus student attention to key dental features.

sil construction revealed in this study using this type of scanner are loss of original color, image edge erosion, loss of the finest details (<.05mm), and limits on specimen size per the small stage size. We have recently upgraded our 3D scanning system to a desktop color scanner (e.g., NextEngine) and issues such as edge erosion and loss of color have largely dissipated, resulting in more informative virtual specimens as incorporated in the example exercise described later in this study.

Discussion

Generally, younger generations of students have a much higher level of facility with these types of virtual modalities, having grown up with interactive video games, multi-user virtual gaming environments, and immersive virtual world platforms like Second Life. However, virtual modalities are not a panacea for science education or an absolute replacement for actual laboratory experiences, field trips, and other forms of practical work. In a study of student perceptions of a virtual field trip on tidepool biology, Spicer and Stratford (2001) found that students view virtual field trips as a good and enjoyable way to learn, although most would prefer the actual trip. They suggested that virtual field trips might be especially useful for preparing and/or revising physical field trips, when physical trips are possible.

As an example, Hesthamme, Fossen, Sautter, Sæther, and Johansen (2002) have developed a field simulator that allows for 3D visualization of the topography of a geology field area as a pre-trip enhancement to the actual experiential learning. Students are able to navigate the field area much like a flight simulator with data imported in a 3D file format. Using virtual reality field trips as a precursor is using them as a scaffold for the actual event. However, when physical experiences are not available, as is typical in an online course, virtual experiences become the focus and must be suitably scaffolded for that purpose.

The key consideration in scaffolding for animations and simulations as online practical work is determining the learner audience. Specifically, what is the range of expertise that the target students should reasonably be expected to possess? Gazit et al. (2005) found significant visualization limitations among high school students exploring astronomy through a non-immersive virtual solar system (VSS).While the VSS was highly effective as a visual thinking tool, students experienced difficulty in making decisions based on the visual data presented, which the authors attributed to the lack of a fixed frame of reference. This lack also led to emergent perceptions and misconceptions.

While Gazit et al. (2005) refer to scaffolding in their discussion, the levels and types provided are not detailed, and they conclude by recommending "suitable scaffolding" (p. 468), without elaboration. As illustrated in Figure 14.1 and as discussed, suitable scaffolding for online practical work in learning science depends on the level of learner and the sophistication of the virtual modality. These are key examples of broader principles that apply across technology applications and content areas—wonderful illustrations of how interdisciplinary discussions could help advance understanding of best practice in instructional technology.

Case Study Summary

The virtual 3D fossils, fossil cabinet GUI, and paleontology lab interface built to enhance the online course Virtual Paleontology permit students to simulate hand specimen observations and manipulations, including rotation, panning, and magnification. The virtual fossils approximate much of the observational richness of hand specimens. In some cases, they exceed the instructional power of a hand specimen, as with the ability for a student to instantly magnify or do a side-by-side comparison and for the instructor to develop strategic markers in key morphological locations. Chief limitations were the loss of original color, edge acuity, and the limitations on the size of the specimen in proportion to the scanner stage, although newer scanning hardware and software have minimized those effects. We include an example of how 3D virtual specimens can be used to evaluate evolutionary relationships in Appendix B. The future goal of this project is to expand the variety of 3D fossils in the fossil cabinet in order to provide paleontologists and distance learning educators an extensive virtual fossil collection for course enhancement.

ACKNOWLEDGMENTS

The authors wish to acknowledge DePaul University's Quality of Instruction Council for grants supporting the purchase of hardware and software used in this project.

APPENDIX A

Online Resources for 3D Learning Objects

There are a large and growing number of 3D resources available on the Internet. An extensive review of 3D resources was completed for our 2008 publication (Downing & Holtz, 2008), far too many to include here; please refer to the publication for additional citations and links. Listed here are samples of the various types of 3D learning object types readily available for educational contexts.

3D Resources

Stereograms
  Skull:
    www.lab3d.odont.ku.dk/Gallery/gallery-docs/gallery-page4.html
  Lincoln:
    www.abrahamlincolnus.com/LOC.html
  Molecules:
    www.nature.com/emboj/journal/v26/n1/fig_tab/7601464f3.html

Autostereograms
  How to view:
    www.xaraxone.com/FeaturedArt/feb05/html/01.htm

Anaglyphs

How to develop:
video.aol.com/video-detail/photo-editing-10-create-3d-anaglyph-images-3d-glasses/1671811616

Still:
www.pulltime3d.com/04_frame.html

Still:
www.terryblackburn.us/Photography/3D/

Video Example: M.C Esher:
www.dailymotion.com/video/x8wwtc_mc-escher-relativity-in-3d-w-anagly_tech

NASA's Project 3D View (Grade School):
www.3dview.org/index.cfm

Simulations

Center for Human Simulation (Movies, 3D Polygons):
www.uchsc.edu/sm/chs/gallery/gallery.htm

Howard Hughes Medical Institute: VR Simulations:
www.hhmi.org/biointeractive/vlabs/index.html

3D Learning Object Repositories

National Science Digital Laboratory (NSDL):
www.nsdl.org/

APPENDIX B

Example Exercise: Investigating Evolutionary Patterns with 3D Specimens

Notes to the Instructor: This online science exercise requires the development of at least three 3D learning objects from a closely related group of organisms (shells, bugs, mammals, etc.). It also requires a suitable 3D browser (i.e., freeware or low-cost versions) that can be accessed and utilized by online students to investigate the 3D specimens.

Step 1. Secure three suitable subject specimens that will be illustrative for the evaluation of evolutionary relationships.

Step 2. Scan the respective objects using a 3D color scanner (e.g., NextEngine).

Step 3. Save the virtual specimens in a file format compatible with the chosen 3D browser.

Step 4. Post the virtual specimens on a server that the students can access anytime.

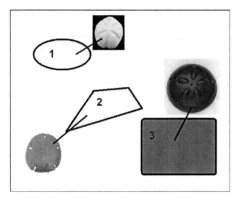

Figure 14.8 Map of three islands (1–3) where three distinct species of echinoids have been recovered by a biologist. The learning objective is to investigate possible evolutionary scenarios for the three species, applying concepts of dispersal, adaptation, and systematics. Online science students can inspect the morphology of the three species as 3D virtual specimens in a 3D browser enabled with measuring tools.

Scenario: Echinoid Dispersal and Evolution

Background. You are sailing your ship, the Fido, near the islands of Indonesia. On the three islands you visit, you recover three types of echinoderms (sea urchins) in the nearshore ocean habitat. Even though you have collected hundreds of specimens from around each island, it appears that the three types of sea urchins (1, 2, & 3) never occur together, but are found adjacent to the respective islands (Figure 14.8).

One of your geology colleagues determines that Island 1, where sea urchin type 1 occurs, is four million years old and is characterized by swiftly moving currents (from east to west) and rocky shorelines; Island 2, with urchin type 2, is two million years old and is characterized by sandy shorelines and weak currents; and Island 3, with urchin type 3, is one million years old and is characterized by dark volcanic rocky shorelines with weak currents.

Procedures

Compare and contrast the morphology of each of the three urchins by downloading the respective virtual specimen files into your 3D browser. As you investigate each urchin species, you should note their colors and details about their surface features. You should also use the measuring tool to evaluate their relative size and shape as well as the positions and sizes of key features. It is recommended that you develop a table to summarize your observations and measurements.

Questions

1. Describe the most significant anatomical features of each of three species and how these features compare among the species.

2. Based on the three-island scenario presented, what are the potential lifestyles for each of these species? For example, what would a flattened shape suggest about lifestyle? To strengthen your observation, you should search the Internet for additional information about the form and function of the urchin shape.
3. Based on your observations and information provided, develop a hypothesis as to how this arrangement of urchins arose on the three islands. You may assume that the species have a relatively close evolutionary connection to one another. You should consider possible dispersal patterns and the timing of dispersal.
4. Do your observations support your hypothesis? How so?
5. Develop and sketch an evolutionary scenario that indicates the relationships of the three species and how their respective key features may have arisen. This should be done with a branching diagram that depicts how the species shared and derived features.
6. How might you test your evolutionary hypothesis about how these urchins originated in future visits to this region?

REFERENCES

Ackerman, M. (1998). The visible human project. *Proceedings of the IEEE, 86*(3), 504–511.

Bapi, R. S., Pammi, V. S. C., Miyapuram, K. P., & Ahmed, A. (2005). Investigation of sequence learning: A cognitive and computational neuroscience perspective. *Current Science, 89,* 1690–1698.

Brochu, C.A. (2003). Osteology of Tyrannosaurus Rex: Insights from a nearly complete skeleton and high-resolution computed tomographic analysis of the skull. *Memoir of Society of Vertebrate Paleontology, 7,* 1–138.

Cai, W., Feng, D., & Fulton, R. (2001). Web-based digital medical images. *IEEE Computer Graphics and Applications, 35*(1), 44–47.

Choi, E., Laver, L., & Gurnis, M. (2008). Thermomechanics of mid-ocean ridge segmentation. *Physics of the Earth and Planetary Interiors, 171*(1–4), 374–386.

Dong, F., Clapworthy, G. J., Krokos, M. A., & Yao, J. (2002). An anatomy-based approach to human muscle modeling and deformation. *IEEE Transactions on Visualization and Computer Graphics, 8*(2), 154–170.

Dori, Y. J., & Belcher, J. W. (2005). Learning electromagnetism with visualizations and active learning. In J. K. Gilbert (Ed.). *Visualization in science education* (pp. 187–216), Dordrecht, Netherlands: Springer.

Downing, K. F. (1999). Virtual paleontology: A web-based course for undergraduates. *Geological Society of America Abstracts, 29*(7).

Downing, K. F., & Holtz, J. K. (2008). *Online science learning: Best practices and technologies.* Hershey, PA: IGI Global.

Edelson, D. (2001). Learning-for-use: A framework for the design of technology-supported inquiry activities. *Journal of Research in Science Teaching, 38*(3), 355–385.

Edelson, D., Gordon, D., & Pea, R. (1999). Addressing the challenges of inquiry-based learning through technology and curriculum design. *Journal of the Learning Sciences, 8*(3/4), 391–451.

El Saddik, A. (2001). *Interactive multimedia learning.* New York: Springer.

Evesque, F., Gerlach, S., & Hersch, R. (2002). Building 3D anatomical scenes on the web. *Journal of Visualization and Computer Animation, 13*, 43–52.

Gazit, E., Yair, Y., & Chen, D. (2005). Emerging conceptual understanding of complex astronomical phenomena by using a virtual solar system. *Journal of Science Education and Technology, 14*(5/6), 459–470.

Gilbert, J. K. (2005). Visualization: A metacognitive skill in science and science education. In J. K. Gilbert (Ed.), *Visualization in science education* (pp. 1–27). Boston: Kluwer Academic Publishers.

Gobet, F., Lane, P. C. R., Croker, S., Cheng, P. C. H., Jones, G., Oliver, I., & Pine, J. M. (2001). Chunking mechanisms in human learning. *Trends in Cognitive Sciences, 5*, 236–243.

Gould, C., & Whitford, D. (2000). Computer-aided visualization and animation of ocean wave dynamics. *Journal of Geoscience Education, 48*(3), 267–272.

Hesthammer, J., Fossen, H., Sautter, M., Sæther, B., & Johansen, S. (2002). The use of information technology to enhance learning in geological fieldtrips. *Journal of Geoscience Education, 50*(5), 528–538.

Hofstein, A., & Lunetta, V. (2003). The laboratory in science education. *Science Education, 88*(1), 28–54.

Holtz, J. K. (2009). *Creativity and research education in the clinical sciences.* Saarbrücken, Germany: VDM.

Jenkins, E. (1998). The schooling of laboratory science. In J. Wellington (Ed.), *Practical work in school science: Which way now?* (pp. 35–51). New York: Routledge Publishing.

Jenkins, E. (1999). Practical work in School Science—Some questions to be answered. In J. Leach and A. Paulsen (Eds). *Practical work in Science Education: Recent Research Studies* (pp. 19–32). Denmark: RoskildeUniversityPress.

Jenkins, E. W. (2005). The student voice in science education research and issues. *Journal of Baltic Science Education, 1*(7), 22–30.

Korakakis, G., Pavlatou, E. A., Palyvos, J. A., & Spyrellis, N. (2009). 3D visualization types in multimedia applications for science learning. *Computers & Education 52*, 390–401.

Kusnick, J. (2001). Thinking about computer-based learning. *Journal of Geoscience Education, 49*(2), 212–214.

Limniou, M., Roberts, D., & Papadopoulos, N. (2008). Full immersive virtual environment CAVE (TM) in chemistry education. *Computers in Education, 51*(2), 584–593.

Lyons,D. & Head, L. (1998). QuickTime VR: a powerful new illustrative tool for micropaleontological research. *Palaeontologia Electronica, 1*, 12. Retrieved from http://palaeo-electronica.org/1998_2/toc.htm

Lyons, D., Rioux, M., & Patterson, T. (2000). Application of a three-dimensional color laser scanner to paleontology: An interactive model of a juvenile Tylosaur sp. basisphenoid-basioccipital, *Palaeontologia Electronica, 3*(2), 16. Retrieved from http://palaeo-electronica.org/2000_2/toc.htm

McGrath, M. B., & Brown, J. R. (2005). Visual learning for science and engineering. *IEEE Computer Graphics and Applications, 25*(5), 56–63.

Millar, R. (2004, June). *The role of practical work in the teaching and learning of science.* Paper presented at the National Academy of Sciences, Washington, D.C.

Millar, R. (1998) Rhetoric and reality. In J. Wellington (Ed.), *Practical work in school science: Which way now?* (pp. 16–31). London: Routledge.

Miller, G. A. (1956). The magic number seven (plus or minus two). *Psychological Review, 63*, 81–93.

Moltenbrey, K. (2001, February). No bones about it. *Computer Graphics World.* Retrieved October 12, 2009 from http://cgw.pennwellnet.com/Articles/

Papaioannou, G., Karabassi, E. A., & Theoharis, T. (2001). Virtual archaeologist: Assembling the past. *IEEE Computer Graphics and Applications, 21*, 53–59.

Pasternack, A. (2002, September). The way we were. *Computer Graphics World.* Retrieved October 12, 2009 from http://cgw.pennwellnet.com/Articles/

Patrick, M. D., Carter, G., & Wiebe, E. N. (2005). Visual representations of DNA replication. *Journal of Science Education and Technology, 14*(3), 353–365.

Qui, W., & Hubble, T. (2002). *The advantages and disadvantages of virtual field trips in geoscience education.* Retrieved May 1, 2007 from http://science.uniserve.edu.au/pubs/china/vol1/weili.pdf

Ramamurthy, M. K. (2006). A new generation of cyberinfrastructure and data services for earth system science education and research. *Advances in Geosciences, 8*, 69–78.

Reynolds, P. A., & Mason, R. (2002). On-line video media for continuing professional development in dentistry. *Computers & Education, 39*(1), 65.

Rhyne, T. (2000). Scientific visualization in the next millennium. *IEEE Computer Graphics and Applications, 34* (1), 20–21.

Robb, R. A., & Cameron, B. (1995).Virtual reality assisted surgery program, In R. M. Satava, K. S. Morgan, H. B. Sieburg, R. Mattheus, & J. P. Christensen (Eds.), *Interactive technology and the new paradigm for healthcare* (pp. 309–321). Amsterdam: IOS Press.

Ross, S., & Scanlon, E. (1995). *Open science.* London: Paul Chapman Publishing Ltd.

Singer, S. R., Hilton, M. L., & Schwiengruber, H. A. (Eds.). (2005). *America's lab report: Investigations in school science.* Washington, D.C.: National Academies Press.

Sorby, S. (2009). Educational research in developing 3-D spatial skills for engineering students. *International Journal of Science Education, 31*(3), 459–480.

Spicer, J., & Statford, J. (2001). Student perceptions of a virtual fieldtrip to replace a real fieldtrip. *Journal of Computer Assisted Learning, 17*, 345–354.

Steinkuehler, C., & Duncan, S. (2008). Scientific habits of mind in virtual worlds. *Journal of Science Education & Technology, 17*, 530–543.

Sternberg, R. J. (1984). *Beyond IQ.* New York: University of Cambridge.

Sun, K. T., Lin, Y. C., & Yu, C. J. (2007). A study on learning effect among different learning styles in a web-based lab of science for elementary school students. *Computers & Education, 50*(4), 1411–1422.

Sutton, M. D., Briggs, D. E., Siveter, D. J., & Siveter, D. J. (2001). Methodologies for the visualization and reconstruction of three-dimensional fossils from the Silurian Herefordshire lagersättte. *Palaeontologia Electronica, 4*(1), 17.

Sweller, J. (1999). *Instructional design in technical areas.* Camberwell, Australia: Australian Council for Educational Research.

Takayama, K. (2005). Visualizing the science of genomics. In J. K. Gilbert (Ed.), *Visualization in science education* (pp. 217–252). Boston: Kluwer Academic Publishers.

Vacca, J. (1996). *VRML: Bringing virtual reality to the internet.* Boston: Academic Press.

Van Marion, P. (1999). Changing teachers' practise. In J. Leach & A. Paulsen (Eds.), *Practical work in science education: Recent research studies* (pp. 250–264). Denmark: Roskilde University Press.

Wang, H. C., Chang, C. Y., & Li, T. Y. (2007). The comparative efficacy of 2D- versus 3D-based media design for influencing spatial visualization skills. *Computers in Human Behavior, 23*(4), 1943–1957.

Wang, S. K., & Yang, C. (2005). The interface design and the usability testing of a fossilization web-based learning environment. *Journal of Science Education and Technology, 14*(3), 305–313.

Woolnough, B., & Allsop, T. (1985). *Practical work in science.* Cambridge: Cambridge University Press.

CHAPTER 15

A GUIDE TO USING TECHNOLOGY IN THE HISTORY CLASSROOM

Keith Sisson
University of Memphis

Kathleen P. King
University of South Florida

INTRODUCTION

When professors of history begin integrating digital media into their classrooms, they often discover core benefits. Consider that our goals as history professors are not only to share knowledge, but also cultivate vision and passion in our discipline. Furthermore, the development of critical thinking and research skills are the hallmarks of our field, which must be incorporated into the curriculum.

While this chapter reveals how digital technology can be used to accomplish each of these critical goals, there are additional essential benefits. In recent years, our colleges and universities have welcomed an ever-greater diversity of students (Wlodkowski & Ginsberg, 1995) with different learning

The Professor's Guide to Taming Technology, pages 239–257
Copyright © 2011 by Information Age Publishing
All rights of reproduction in any form reserved.

styles (Gardner, 1993), both "digital immigrants" and "digital natives," and more non-traditional students (adult learners) than ever before.

In a recent article, Shifflett (2007) succinctly states the advantages of using technology in the history classroom:

> Visual history has the potential to expose new interpretive relationships, provide historians with new tools to reimagine the past, and deliver the results of recent research in a timely manner and efficacious format. . . .
>
> Visual history becomes even more intriguing perhaps once historians move beyond a specific case to something broad and abstract, such as colonization, and ask the question, "What does colonization look like?" When visual history is employed to address abstract questions, the results would be delivered much more effectively electronically, because visual history, as it has come to be defined, now represents a core activity of the research and analysis. Visual history is not "history without words." Historians will always need text. Ideally, visualization will develop as a fusion technology, melding together text, artifacts, maps, and other hypermedia material with appropriate vocabularies and theoretical models. . . .
>
> Technology provides new eyes for resurrecting the past and unlocking its secrets. Images and computers, maps and historians, and special history all go together like bread and butter. In fact, it is unlikely that text alone would even elicit the questions that images sometimes raise. (Shifflett, 2007, pp. 58–59)

What Shifflet is describing includes how visual history can map population movements, demographic shifts, trade route patterns, and more. The benefit is how tools can help provide students with the foundational knowledge necessary for interpretive discussion.

Perhaps even more importantly, visual history facilitates situations where instructors can beneficially ask students abstract questions such as:

1. Why did certain population movements occur?
2. What were the causes and effects of certain demographic shifts?
3. Why did some trade route patterns flourish while others faded?

Questions such as these prompt vigorous debate and introduce students to the historical issues of cause and effect, and change and continuity over time. One of the most fundamental objectives, and one of the primary benefits of using technology in the history classroom, is to familiarize students with the nature of historical development and to teach students to think *historically*. When technology provides learning experiences like these, it is something we have to explore and master for the sake of our profession, discipline, and students.

PEDAGOGICAL/ANDRAGOGICAL FOUNDATION

The foundation for the use of technology in the history classroom emerges from the understanding that students learn in different ways (Gardner, 1993). For example, according to a Pearson Education Group study (2008), student learning styles include, but are not limited to:

- Auditory students who benefit from recordings of online lectures and from phone conversations with instructors.
- Visual students who benefit from charts, graphs, and other visual means of communicating.
- Verbal-linguistic students who enjoy writing assignments and communicating with instructors via email.

Consider how these different learning styles play out in our classrooms. Some students respond well to maps and charts, because they are visual learners. However, for another group, the maps and charts are confusing and they need to hear detailed explanations (auditory learners). A third group needs to be more active in articulating their learning in email, after-class discussion, or essays: They are called verbal-linguistic learners.

Furthering the opportunity for student retention and success, research demonstrates what we see in our classes—that more engaged students, especially in online settings, are more likely to remain in the course (thus increasing retention) and are more likely to pass the course successfully (Pearson Group, 2008). Of particular interest to this book, the adult learning literature identifies that many adult learners have similar characteristics (Cranton, 1994; Cross, 1992; Pratt & Associates, 1995; Wlodkowski, & Ginsberg, 1995):

- They are focused on practical application.
- They are usually voluntary learners.
- They are studying to improve their life conditions (i.e., social role, income, career, etc.).
- They have many competing demands and responsibilities (e.g., work, immediate family, extended family, etc.).
- They value their time in class and are more attentive than traditional-age college students might be.
- They bring a wide variety of life experiences, which they enjoy seeing used in the learning situations.
- They also often want to be actively involved in learning, more in control of their decisions because of their age, life experience, and maturity level.

So how is this information relevant to the teaching of history? History instructors need to be cognizant of what technology to use (and when and how to use it) in order to achieve the best possible outcome for the students. In the final analysis, each instructor must decide for her- or himself what works best for her or his individual courses. Whether one teaches face-to-face or online courses, recommendations such as the table in Chapter 2 (Table 2.1) can be a guide or suggestion for further exploration. And when considering our specific discipline, we must share specific resources, best practice, instructional methods, and activities in order to grow the history-related instructional technology body of innovative and best practice teaching.

INNOVATIVE HISTORY PROFESSORS: IT DOES NOT HAVE TO BE AN OXYMORON!

As experts of antiquities, some history faculty might say, "Why should we change?" There are several excellent reasons that need to be considered. Indeed, one hypothesis for the source of most of the change within the academy is technology (Tole, 2007). If this is the case, in order to keep history as a relevant and appealing subject of study, we must explore the opportunities for ourselves.

BEST PRACTICES FOR USING TECHNOLOGY IN THE HISTORY CLASSROOM

Best instructional practice for using digital media and multimedia content is to keep it as current as possible so that students are constantly being exposed to the very latest trends in historical literature and scholarship. The question then becomes: How does one use technology to teach history effectively within this recommendation? Some tools that are readily available, regularly updated, easy to use, and directed related to history include:

- Links to primary source materials
- eTexts of articles and books
  - In our experience, students prefer eTexts because they are usually cheaper, while faculty prefer them because students have full and immediate access to the required text, which allows for more focus on teaching and learning and less on bookstore issues.
- Downloadable audio lectures
- Video documentaries either embedded in the course or accessible via a link

- Digital photographs either embedded in the course or accessible via a link
- Interactive assignments such as simulations or multi-player role playing
  - After all who does not want to try their skills at being a medieval king for a day?
- Virtual explorations (Second Life is among the best known)
- Online dialogue activities: Discussion boards, blogs, wikis, and social networking sites
- And many others

Unleashing the Academic Blog

Davi, Frydenberg, and Gulati (2007) note that the use of Web logs (*blogs*) has become a popular addition to many courses in higher education as faculty attempt to integrate technology into the classroom. While blogs are a fairly recent pedagogical tool, the ability of students and faculty to update online journals promotes communication, which will enhance class discussion and create a greater sense of community outside the classroom (Davi et al., 2007).

Blogs in the classroom are sometimes used as "online diaries" in which students can write about their own experiences (especially relevant to adult learners) and also share their ideas related to course topics. The power of a blog comes when students interact with each other, thus creating a forum for discussion and conversation (Richardson, 2006; Warlick, 2005). Students are moving from being passive spectators of learning to becoming active participants. The goal of history classes is to engage students in the material so that they can develop new understanding and perspectives. And blogs provide a powerful and easy platform for this to happen 24 hours a day, 7 days a week, beyond the classroom walls and timeslots! Moreover, the rich media capability of blogs appeals to people of all ages and provides the opportunity to display and comment on different types of historical artifacts. Blog activity includes the opportunity to post not only text, but also pictures, diagrams, photos, videos, hyperlinks to other Web sites, or multimedia files.

In contrast to more traditional forums for online discussion, blogs can be made open to the world. This global visibility encourages students to share their ideas with the larger world and also gives them a sense of empowerment—a sense that their ideas are being heard and taken seriously. Blogs also encourage students to write more thoughtfully by encouraging them to make their writing more concise, which will further develop critical thinking and writing skills (Davi et al., 2007; King, 2008). A student's ability to think critically and write concisely—especially in history courses—may mean the difference between an "A" and a "B" or between securing a graduate fellowship or not.

Leveraging Primary Sources

In history education, we place heavy emphasis on teaching with primary sources because it is essential for students to learn how to weigh evidence, formulate arguments, and (as often happens) *teach us* many things about the past. So, if an instructor wants to emphasize how the English Bill of Rights influenced the American Bill of Rights (i.e., the first 10 amendments to the U.S. Constitution) or how the Declaration of Independence influenced the French Declaration of the Rights of Man and of the Citizen, the instructor could access these documents online (since they are free and in the public domain), arrange them side by side on the computer screen and then, with the aid of a digital overhead projector, show the documents to the students. And since the documents are arranged on the computer screen, the instructor can highlight certain passages in order to focus the discussion. This technique will help instructors engage the students, thus making the class more enlightening, effective, and worthwhile.

In addition, once the process is demonstrated and the findings discussed in class, the students should be well prepared to do such work on their own and come to class ready to discuss their findings. More independent outside classroom work will cultivate stronger historical analysis skills and develop more in-depth classroom discussions. This strategy is a powerful efficiency and advantage of technology; if used correctly, it can allow us to use our classroom time for more dialogue, in-depth debates, and critical analysis with the students rather than routine or repetitive tasks. Certainly this is a classroom that inspires both faculty and students!

Facilitating Online Classes

In the online setting, instructors not only need to know how to use the technology to present content, but also how to facilitate the class without their physical, and many times synchronous, presence. Depending on the particular learning management system (LMS) used by their institution (BlackBoard, eCollege, Moodle, etc.), faculty need to determine how they can best create *an engaged classroom*. Isolation, combined with poor preparation and little faculty feedback, is perhaps the main cause of online dropout (King & Griggs, 2007).

An LMS is a Web-based technology providing a "shell" or framework in which faculty may plan, deliver, and assess specific learning processes, activities, and courses. Students and instructors work within the LMS to complete the course activities, engage in discussion and feedback, and perform course administration activities such as uploading assignments into a "dropbox," posting course announcements, posting course reading schedules, et cetera. Although they may be named differently, most LMSs have a fairly standard set of features. Typical features of most LMSs and examples of application to history teaching include:

- Discussion forums: Web spaces where students participate in mediated discussions on course topics. History professors may ask students to respond to specific questions about a particular electronic photograph or to analyze a primary source document, both of which help students to think historically.
- Message boards: Usually near the front page of the course, these are where instructors can make class-wide announcements regarding assignments and deadlines. It is rather like making general course announcements at the beginning or end of class. One can also use the space to inform the class of a video documentary, history film festival, or professional conference. Other than the obvious positive effects, using the message board in this way promotes a sense of action and current community for learners.
- Lesson presentation screens: These are often what professors use as the "lectures" of the online course. In the virtual history classroom, lesson presentation screens are a particularly useful tool; they often consist of chapter readings coupled with visual images and audio playback. One might think of them as free-standing rich multimedia presentations to represent a lecture. It helps to have the different sensory materials (video, audio, photographs, images, etc.) because we are missing the live component of the classroom. Using the multimedia elements helps to engage learners, accommodate all learning styles, and reinforce the reading assignments. We like to point out that students have greater control over their individual learning needs with these tools because they can rewind and replay the difficult parts and even fast forward the familiar portions of these lectures. All of which, you have to admit, is hard to do with any live lecture!
- Interactive elements: There are scores of interactive elements that may be added to an LMS, but most will come with these onboard: chat rooms, learning games, remediation tools, email links, private feedback space, and a blog or wiki.

- Assignments: Most LMSs provide the ability for students to read the description of an assignment and then click to submit it. Alternatively, professors might design their own assignments in Microsoft Word document or PDF format and have the students complete and submit it to an LMS dropbox.
- Dropboxes and other means of submitting materials to instructors.
- Auto-graded assessments: There are several perks related to using an LMS for these items:
  - Professors can create their own questions or upload publisher-created test banks and host quizzes, mid-terms, and final exams.
  - The quiz or exam can be set to randomize the questions presented to the students.
  - The professor can impose, or not, a set time limit for the assessment and the LMS will carry it through.
  - The LMS will automatically and immediately grade the assessment so that students receive immediate feedback (a great learning benefit for assessments) and relieve work load from over-stressed professors.
- Links: The plethora of online resources and virtual libraries related to history is staggering. How much more powerful for learners to be able to access these immediately and seamlessly as part of their learning, rather than solely before or after the fact. By incorporating links to virtual libraries in the LMS, it allows students to access eTexts and electronic databases that they otherwise would not have access to, thereby promoting and enhancing historical research and analysis.

If you are unfamiliar with the LMS at your institution, we recommend finding the administrators and technical staff (Help Desk) on your campus. They will help set up your account and courses, introduce you to the basics, and show you how to access the built-in help and support. Most of these campus centers also provide ongoing training. If professors use these resources to become comfortable working within the LMS, it will ultimately make their job easier and provide additional benefits for their learners.

RESEARCH ABOUT WHAT IS HAPPENING IN OUR CLASSROOMS

As has been demonstrated in this chapter so far, technology is enabling multi-modal teaching; changing curricula; and spawning rich forms of teaching, learning, research, and collaboration across all methods and mediums of course delivery. In one case study, nearly 60% of survey respondents replied that professors will soon teach in more than one medium (The Economist Intelligence Unit [TEIU], 2008). The report also notes that despite the growing array of technology-enabled teaching tools available, nearly three-quarters of participants say that the "greatest potential benefit of technology is something far more straightforward—namely, the expanded access to educational and reference resources that it provides" (p. 6). Certainly, these findings confirm what we have seen in the field of History.

In the same survey, when asked to compare different communication technologies, 52% of survey respondents state that online collaboration tools such as discussion boards, blogs, and chat rooms would make the greatest contribution in terms of improving overall educational quality, while 48% point to the dynamic delivery of content that supports individually paced learning (TEIU, p. 6). Increasingly, the use of Web 2.0 and 3.0 capabilities in sophisticated LMSs are innovations contributing to a profound effect on higher education learning. The effective tools include those which engage students, such as enhanced video documentaries, interactive presentation tools, and others that enable them to contribute to and individually or collaboratively create content. According to the survey results, online collaboration tools, software that supports individually paced learning, and LMSs are among the communications technologies most expected to improve academics over the next five years. (Specifically, online courses, 71%, document management, 66%, text messaging/notifications, 65%, collaboration software, 59%, social networks, 56%, video podcasts, 53%, mobile broadband, 49%, blogs, 44%, wikis 41%, RFID sensor networks, 17%, others,13%, mashups, 10%.) As history professors, we need to implement these findings and design all of our courses to include the tools that have these characteristics.

In a recent article, Hannay and Newvine (2006) note that universities have long experimented with different learning environments to accommodate the needs of their students. Along with the traditional classroom, colleges and universities have utilized correspondence courses; courses on tape (telecourses); televised courses; and, most recently, Internet-based distance education (Hannay & Newvine, 2006). As both case studies indicate, technology in the classroom is the continuing wave of the future and is increasingly becoming the norm. Therefore, when history professors implement technology, they are enhancing both the teaching and the learning experience. By doing so, we not only present the "facts" in a logical and coherent manner, but also why the facts are important, which many history educators consider a primary aim for history instruction: To foster students' reasoning skills and their respect for civilized argumentation.

RESOURCES

Perhaps the best Web site concerning teaching history using technology is appropriately named The Best of History Websites (http://www.besthistorysites.net) (see Figure 15.1.) The Web site states that the site is an "award-winning portal that contains annotated links to over 1000 history web sites" and that it "has been recommended by The Chronicle of Higher Education, The National Council for the Social Studies, The British Library Net, The New York Public Library, the BBC, Princeton University—and many others" (n.d.).

The Web site The Center for Teaching History with Technology (http://thwt.org) offers many valuable resources for teaching history. Although the Center is geared towards preparatory school teachers, as a history professor, Keith has gained great insight into how to use technology for his college history classes from the material there. The Web site states that The Center for Teaching History with Technology is a "resource created to help K–12 history and social studies teachers incorporate technology effectively into their courses" (n.d.). Certainly, many of these same strategies for teaching the field of history with technology apply for the postsecondary level as well.

Another indispensable resource is the Web site HistoGrafica (http://www.histografica.com), which offers photographs of places from around the world, and all are in the public domain. Figure 15.2 provides a screen

Figure 15.1   Screenshot of http://www.besthistorysites.net

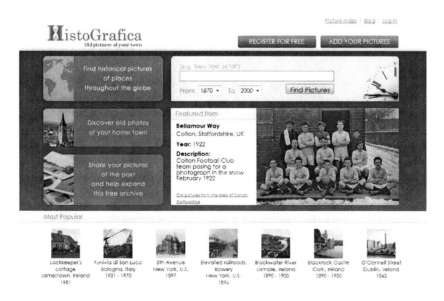

Figure 15.2 Screenshot of http://www.histografica.com/

shot of the HistoGrafica site and reveals that this site has many uses. While one might retrieve specific visual information for specific places and periods, it is also a site where people from all walks of life can contribute materials (rather like a history collection for every person) and share their perspectives of their slices of space and time.

Using this last example, HistoGrafica, we will flesh out just two examples of how it might be used in a college history class.

Up Close and Personal: Learners Discover Their Backyards

Instructions

- Visit the section of the HistoGrafica Web site that has visual materials from the region of the world you lived in during high school.
- Review any photos, drawings, and maps and the related notes from the areas closest to where you lived when you were in your first year of high school.
- Look for materials at least one century older than when you lived there.
- Using this, other online resources, and physical resources when possible, identify additional materials or comments that could be added to the HistoGrafica site.

- Upload any available materials you have found, but be sure you follow all copyright guidelines and have permission to do so.

Respond to the following questions in our class Blog or your e-journal as you complete your activity.

- What did you learn about the history of your neighborhood during this activity?
- What major changes occurred in your neighborhood between the time period that you studied and when you lived in the area?
- What contributed to those major changes? Did you notice other patterns in the changes?
- Where did you find the images you used? Share with us the story of why and how they were preserved as historical archives.
- Conduct additional online or local research to see if you can find information that supports your interpretation of the neighborhood changes.
- Arrange the images in a series, with accompanying text or audio, to present your findings. Be sure to cite sources accurately and appropriately (MLA). Prepare your final project as an online or multimedia class presentation as per your professor's instructions.
- Based on this experience, what did you learn about the issues that historians face in their work and with the materials they preserve?
- What did you learn about copyright and intellectual property of images and online materials in this assignment?

Learner Voices about Understanding Distant Communities Through Visual Aids

Instructions

- Go to the section of HistoGrafica (http://thwt.org) that has visual materials of Dublin, Ireland.
- Notice that several were submitted by "Jimmy."
- Review any descriptions and notes accompanying those photos, drawings, and maps.

Respond to the following questions in our class Blog or your e-journal.

- What do you learn about the history of this city in the early 1900s?
- What influenced change during this time?
- Do you notice patterns in the changes?
- Why do you think certain images survive in historical archives? Why would someone have kept these particular items?

- Do you see any evidence as to why the images displayed might have been chosen for inclusion in this collection?
- Based on this experience, what issues do historians have to face in their work and with the materials they preserve?

Additional Resources

Of course, there are many other valuable Web sites for teaching history beyond the ones we have mentioned. The final section of this chapter includes a longer list of some Web sites that we have found especially noteworthy in classroom application and in cultivating history scholars. These resources include not only extensive archives that have video, audio, pictures, and text (such as The Smithsonian and National Archives), but also powerful online repositories of primary sources and global history resource collections (or *source books*) across the vast variety of history specialties: Indian, Asian, Jewish, Byzantine, and medieval history, to name just a few. We hope that, as history professors, these descriptions make you eager to put down this book and start up your computer or smart phone. However, we have more beneficial resources to offer you before we finish out, so bear with us.

As instructors who are working to include technology, it is also helpful to collect recommended tools that support instructional technology integration. Therefore, we present very different Web sites in the next brief list. These sites are helpful as either online tools that are worthwhile for every subject area (Wimba and Elluminate) or discussions of higher education technology innovation (EDUCAUSE):

- WIMBA: http://www.wimba.com/
- Elluminate: http://www.elluminate.com/
- EDUCAUSE: http://www.educause.edu/home

As you explore the resources in this section, please consider how technology has allowed us to do our work more efficiently and globally as historians, teachers, scholars, researchers, and authors if we choose to use it. We are making new headway yearly with the work we do. Yet, consider how our field of history, and its many specializations, is dependent on the generations to come to continue to advance our field using all the tools, including technology, available to access knowledge, resources, and artifacts. The field is also dependent on the honed skills of analyzing and using what is retrieved. We must prepare the next scholars to fulfill these essential roles in our shared future.

SUGGESTED ACTIVITIES FOR FACULTY LEARNING AND CLASSROOMS

Reading about technology and implementing it are two entirely different things. Therefore, we provide two sample Web quests that faculty can use to explore several history-related sites and customize for use in their classrooms. These activities are not meant to be "plug 'n play" for classroom use. Instead, we encourage professors to reflect on the opportunities provided in their curriculum and use these examples as a launching point for specific developments of their own.

Over the years the Web quest instructional form has developed, better and *best* practice have emerged. Instructors have found that great Web quest activities include

- Clear framing statements or goals;
- Open-ended, but guiding questions;
- Several required resources to visit;
- Supplemental resources;
- Opportunities for students to identify findings and analyze, interpret, and discuss those findings together.

In the process, Web quests have evolved from being individual/isolated activities, to being powerful foundations for dialogue where new meanings can be explored, tested, and scaffolded (King, & Gura, 2009). Classroom instructors also realize that "switching it up" by alternating individual assignments, group work, and individual work reported in group spaces provides an energizing intellectual work space and environment for learners (King, 2003; King & Griggs, 2007). Indeed, are not these spaces of reflection, expression, and dialogue just the sort of spaces we have hoped to create in dynamic face-to-face classrooms? The benefits include using the Web quest as a foundation, discussing findings in a virtual space, and thus affording the opportunity to reach beyond the limited time we have in our classrooms. Instead of the traditional model, using these simple, well-planned technologies, the world becomes our classroom.

Web Quest 1

Introduction

In this Web quest, we use primary sources to conduct research that focuses on the development of the nation-state bureaucratic institutions and the consequences that expansion and domination had for people in the later Middle Ages.

Activity

Research the rise of the nation-state. With what two kingdoms in western Europe are nation-states most associated? Why are they important?

- http://www.the-orb.net/textbooks/muhlberger/henry_ii.html
- http://www.fordham.edu/halsall/sbook1m.html
- http://www.flowofhistory.com/units/west/11/FC79
- http://www.ucalgary.ca/applied_history/tutor/endmiddle/

Additional Resources

The following Web sites will help you complete the quest:

- http://www.fordham.edu/halsall/source/mcarta.html
- http://www.flowofhistory.com/units/west/10/FC66
- http://www.fordham.edu/halsall/sbook1l.html
- http://www.fordham.edu/halsall/sbook1w.html

Preliminary Questions to Discuss Online or in Class

- With what two kingdoms in western Europe are nation-states most associated? Why are they important?
- What indicators of the nation-state did you recognize first in your research?
- What were the steps you followed in conducting your research? Specifically, what questions were you asking yourself about the resources you were viewing and reading?
- Why did you use those particular questions?
- If you had used different questions, would you have come to a different conclusion?
- How do you know if you asked the right questions in your research?
- How does a historian know for sure what the correct questions are?

Web Quest 2

Introduction

In this Web quest, we use primary sources to conduct research that focuses on the development of early imperial China, paying particular attention to the Zhou, Qin, and Han dynasties.

Activity

Research the development of the Zhou, Qin, and Han dynasties. Why are these three dynasties so important?

- http://www.fordham.edu/halsall/eastasia/eastasiasbook.html #Imperial%20China

Additional Resources

The following Web sites will help you complete the Quest:

- Zhou: http://www.mnsu.edu/emuseum/prehistory/china/ancient_china/zhou.html
- Qin: http://www.mnsu.edu/emuseum/prehistory/china/early_imperial_china/qin.html
- Han: http://www.mnsu.edu/emuseum/prehistory/china/early_imperial_china/han.html

Preliminary Questions to Discuss Online or in Class

- Why are the Zhou, Qin, and Han dynasties so important?
- What indicators of their importance did you recognize first in your research?
- How and why did you disqualify other dynasties in your research?
- What is the possibility that other people could come to a different conclusion than you using this same data? If so, how could it happen? How would a historian handle this phenomenon?
- What barriers, if any, did you encounter in your research? What strategies did you use to overcome any barriers?

CONCLUSION

For many of us, reflecting on teaching helps us gain a broader and deeper understanding of the importance of the use of technology in the history classroom in particular and within higher education in general. These opportunities are fundamental to the higher education initiatives of the twenty-first century and will enable students to have increased participation in national and international institutions of higher learning, and ultimately in the modern global marketplace. We hope this chapter has been successful in making history faculty members feel more confident about exploring and using some of the rich technology tools and online resources in vibrant ways for teaching history and preparing our history scholars. In addition, other faculty members have gained a detailed view of how technology can be beneficially utilized in discipline-specific ways.

APPENDIX

Essential History-Related Web Resources for Instructional Use

H-net: Humanities and Social Sciences Online
 http://www.h-net.org/
Organization of American Historians (OAH):
 http://www.oah.org/index.html?hnet

Major United States Historical Archives

Each of these sites has an extensive rich media (video, audio, text, etc.) collection of original works as well as research tutorials.

The Library of Congress
 http://www.loc.gov/index.html home page
 http://www.loc.gov/index.html online catalog
Smithsonian Institution
 http://www.si.edu/
 http://www.si.edu/research/
National Archives
 http://www.archives.gov/

Primary Source Material

A plethora of free and public domain material is available at these Web sites.

Medieval Sourcebook
 http://www.fordham.edu/halsall/sbook.html
Byzantine Studies Sourcebook
 http://www.fordham.edu/halsall/byzantium/index.html
Modern History Sourcebook
 http://www.fordham.edu/halsall/mod/modsbook.html
Ancient History Sourcebook
 http://www.fordham.edu/halsall/ancient/asbook.html
African History Sourcebook
 http://www.fordham.edu/halsall/africa/africasbook.html
East Asian History Sourcebook
 http://www.fordham.edu/halsall/eastasia/eastasiasbook.html

Indian History Sourcebook
http://www.fordham.edu/halsall/india/indiasbook.html

Early Modern European History
http://www.besthistorysites.net/EarlyModernEurope.shtml

Islamic History Sourcebook
http://www.fordham.edu/halsall/islam/islamsbook.html

Jewish History Sourcebook
http://www.fordham.edu/halsall/jewish/jewishsbook.html

Women's History Sourcebook
http://www.fordham.edu/halsall/women/womensbook.html

Global History Sourcebook
http://www.fordham.edu/halsall/global/globalsbook.html

History of Science Sourcebook
http://www.fordham.edu/halsall/science/sciencesbook.html

Art History
http://www.besthistorysites.net/ArtHistory.shtml

Military History
http://www.besthistorysites.net/Military_GeneralResources.shtml

Catalogue of Illuminated Manuscripts
http://www.bl.uk/catalogues/illuminatedmanuscripts/welcome.htm

Use this website to find and view descriptions and images of medieval and Renaissance manuscripts in the British Library, one of the richest collections in the world.

Online Medieval and Classical Library
http://omacl.org/

The Online Medieval and Classical Library (OMACL) is a collection of some of the most important literary works of Classical and Medieval civilization.

Online Resources for Medievalists
http://www.marginalia.co.uk/resources.php

Patrologia Graeca
http://www.ellopos.net/elpenor/greek-texts/fathers/migne-patrologia-graeca.asp

Patrologia Latina
http://pld.chadwyck.co.uk/

The *Patrologia Latina* Database is an electronic version of the first edition of Jacques-Paul Migne's mid-19th-century *Patrologia Latina*, which comprises the works of the Latin Church Fathers from Tertullian in 200 AD to the death of Pope Innocent III in 1216.

REFERENCES

Cranton. P. (1994). *Understanding and promoting transformative learning*. San Francisco, Jossey-Bass.

Cross, P. K. (1992). *Adults as learners: Increasing participation and facilitating learning*. San Francisco: Jossey-Bass.

Davi, A., Frydenberg, M., & Gulati, G. J. (2007). Blogging across the disciplines: Integrating technology to enhance liberal learning. *Journal of Online Learning and Teaching, 3* (3), 222–233. Retrieved November 15, 2009, from http://jolt. merlot.org/vol3no3/frydenberg.htm

The Economist Intelligence Unit. (2008). *The future of higher education: How technology will shape learning*. London, New York, & Hong Kong: Author.

Gardner, H. (1993). *Frames of mind* (10th ed.). New York: Basic.

Hannay, M., & Newvine, T. (2006). Perceptions of distance learning: A comparison of online and traditional learning. *Journal of Online Learning and Teaching, 2*(1), 1–11. Retrieved November 15, 2009 from http://jolt.merlot.org/05011.htm

King, K. P. (2003). *Keeping pace with technology: Educational technology that transforms. Vol. II*. Cresskill, NJ: Hampton Press.

King, K. P. (2008). Introducing new media into teacher preparation: Transparently integrating podcasting into college classes. *ISTE SIG Handheld Computing (ISTE SIGHC) 3*(4), 4–7. Retrieved from http://www.iste.org/Content/ NavigationMenu/Membership/SIGs/SIGHC_Handheld_Computing/SIGH-Cnewsletter0508.pdf

King, K. P., & Griggs, J. K. (Eds.). (2007). *Harnessing innovative technologies in higher education: Access, equity, policy and instruction*. Madison, WI: Atwood Publishing.

King, K. P., & Gura, M. (2009). *Podcasting for Teachers: Using a new technology to revolutionize teaching and learning* (2nd ed.). Charlotte, NC: Information Age.

Pearson Education Group. (2008). *History instructor's resource guide*. Boston: Pearson.

Pratt, D. D., & Associates. (1995). *Five perspectives of teaching in adult and higher education*. Malabar, FL: Krieger.

Richardson, W. (2006). *Blogs, wikis, podcasts, and other powerful web tools for classrooms*. Thousand Oaks, CA: Corwin Press.

Shifflett, C. (2007). Seeing the past: Digital history as new model scholarship. *Journal of Online Learning and Teaching 3*(1), 58–66. Retrieved November 15, 2009, from http://jolt.merlot.org/vol3no1/shifflett.htm

Tole, M. (2007, April 5). Tech shaping history, today. *The Daily Helmsman Online*. Retrieved July 15, 2010 from http://media.www.dailyhelmsman.com/media/storage/paper875/news/2007/04/05/News/Tech-Shaping.History .Today-2824472.shtml

Warlick, D. F. (2005). *Classroom blogging*. New York: Lulu.com.

Wlodkowski, R., & Ginsberg, M. (1995). *Diversity and motivation: Culturally responsive teaching*. San Francisco: Jossey-Bass.

PART IV

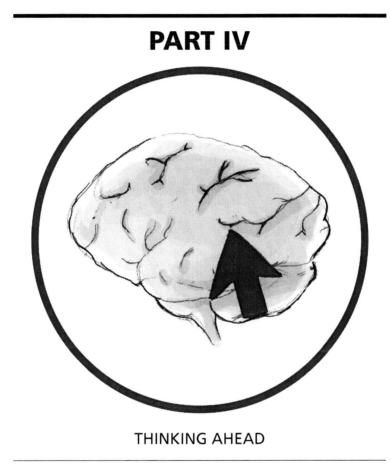

THINKING AHEAD

CHAPTER 16

ACTION STEPS FOR CONTINUED FACULTY SUCCESS IN TAMING TECHNOLOGY

Kathleen P. King
University of South Florida

Thomas D. Cox
University of Houston–Victoria

The Professor's Guide to Taming Technology has focused on explaining how to use technology, specifically digital media, in higher education best teaching practice. Technology is constantly changing at an accelerating rate; therefore, we acknowledge that any book written on the subject can sometimes be limited to its own piece of the chronological pie. Our vision has been that with this book will accomplish something broader; something that can transcend the specific technologies and make sense of the ever-expanding landscape.

The Professor's Guide to Taming Technology, pages 261–269
Copyright © 2011 by Information Age Publishing
All rights of reproduction in any form reserved.

MEETING FACULTY WHERE THEY ARE

This book is about discussing new and different approaches to teaching with technology in the higher education classroom. It is not about a specific or single technology. The book is not even about how to use podcasting, message boards, or video. The uniqueness of this book is how it provides background information, detail, and specific opportunities for readers in order for them to gain confidence and take the initiative and use technology to create a user-centered classroom. The book is about how faculty can evolve with technology and no longer be trapped in a certain method, nor cling to old patterns. It is about the continuing experience of adapting our craft.

We have found that there are many different pathways faculty follow in their teaching practice development (Brookfield, 1995; Cranton, 2001; King, 2003; Lawler & King, 2000). In other words, faculty take unique roads to get to where they are in their teaching because they have diverse prior experiences and starting points (King, 2003). This book works toward being relevant and important to faculty of all levels of technology integration expertise. As we see it, this book is for three different types of faculty readers. In many ways, these three types make up the entirety of teachers in the modern college classroom (King, 2003).

The Technology and/or Teaching Novice

The first type of teacher is new to technology teaching: the novice. They may have been teaching with literal chalk and blackboards all their lives. They might be from an older generation and have been uncomfortable with the full-tilt changes of new technologies connecting everything and everyone all the time. Alternatively, they may be brand new to the higher education teaching and have never approached technology from an educational angle before—and certainly never used the applicable technology from anything like an administrative perspective. Technology is confounding, disruptive, and a relentless reminder that they are not up to date with everyone else.

This book is certainly for our less experienced technology users, as it shares new ideas and introduces ways to explore and use them along the way. The book can be used on the first few reads as an introduction: It does, as we suggest, treat the simple things first. In teaching, as in life, complex ideas and practices develop from the basics. This book was written for the technology and teaching novice faculty.

The Technology Familiar Faculty

Some faculty who read this book will be familiar with the technology. They have used different technology tools or programs in a different context. Perhaps they have used computer programming or Web design in their recreation or previous career. Indeed, as the Net-Generation is reaching our university faculty ranks, some of our faculty might have grown up with technology their entire lives (Tapscott, 2008).

However, there is a wrinkle in the magic. This type of teacher has never had experience using technology for teaching purposes. They are proficient, but not relevantly so. They have merely watched the tide of technology rise and seep into the world of education, and they want to get into it, want to involve it in their classrooms, but they do not know where to start. They need new approaches. They need ideas. They know that technology is a powerful tool but are not sure how to harness what they need for deeper learning.

This book presents ways for technology to be integrated into the classroom seamlessly. It illustrates which skills are relevant and highlights models for success. Furthermore, this volume provides a wide selection of strategies and resources to advance the use of technology in their teaching. This book was written for the technology familiar faculty.

The Experienced Technology Innovator

The final type of reader for whom this book was written understands the technology and has used it in their classrooms. Just as our category for them (experienced technology innovator) states, these faculty may have used several of the methods and technologies we have described and demonstrated. These faculty have tried to use technology in classrooms and have probably developed effective strategies of their own.

For them, this book is a valuable resource and validator. It provides tried-and-true methods that they may not have experimented with yet. Moreover, it validates their efforts to innovate and discover better teaching methods. Innovative faculty will enjoy the open-endedness of this volume because they are not constrained. The book provides a multitude of examples of how technology can be utilized, which can be easily adapted to a wide variety of different situations.

Faculty Developers

This book is a fresh perspective for a technology faculty development guide. The fact that we address multiple technologies and teaching levels and provide details and the larger pedagogical picture are essential for higher education faculty who, by their constant research focus, question and test. We hope that faculty developers will also catch this vision and provide learning experiences wherein faculty will use the book to create their own technology-related teaching approaches.

Whether you are a novice , intermediate, or experienced user—or if you are leading faculty development for a department or college—this volume is a master source of higher education technology strategies, activities, and support.

RECOMMENDATIONS ABOUT HOW TO USE THIS BOOK

While we have provided a multitude of examples of teaching practices and instructional development in this volume, they are merely that—*examples*. These examples are intended to be models or jumping-off points, demonstrations of what can be done with technology when innovative and learner-centered approaches are used. Our vision for this book was to provide dynamic examples of how faculty can continually transform learning and technology use in postsecondary teaching and learning. We wanted this volume to reach beyond the limit of traditional lesson plans or static methods descriptions. We believe we have achieved the vision and goal with the valuable contributions of our expert authors.

Given the break-neck speed of technology change in the last 50 years, we can fully anticipate that technology will continue to change and develop with little predictability or consistency. The message of this book is that the fundamental approaches of teaching and learning need not change as recklessly. Consider the following examples.

- Being learner-centered helps teachers connect better with students, and when focused properly makes most lessons more engaging (Brookfield, 1995).
- Ten years from now, the technology for creating serial digital audio may be entirely different: They may not even be called *podcasts* anymore. But creating an audio lesson that can be accessed by students at any time from anywhere will always be a powerful self-directed learning strategy.
- Video may become replaced by something even more realistic and strangely science-fiction (to us today), but having your class collaboratively create a presentation about an assigned topic will always prove effective for learning, beneficial for work/life skills development, and engaging.

In summary, digital media, specifically, will not be the cutting edge forever: Who knows what the next generation will use to communicate and share their ideas? However, in this book, the specific technology is not the point—the opportunities for better teaching and learning through challenging ourselves to think differently, to apply best practice, and continue to innovate are.

The Antidote to Frustration

Our book is meant to be an antidote for books that make faculty feel overpowered, frustrated, or mired in the technology. Instead, the explanations and examples provided herein are living solutions, fluid applications, and mutable ideas: As technology develops, you are free to adapt and develop them alongside it. As student needs continue to shift with changing social, political, and economic conditions, faculty have opportunities to discover how to apply these responsive approaches in other areas. By taming the frustration of technology, we allow new possibilities for teaching and learning to emerge.

FACULTY AS LEADERS

Usually, we as professors walk into our classrooms (physically or virtually) and shut the door. Such is the predominant forum of higher education instruction. All too often, we as faculty forget that our teaching is not only viewed by our students, but that our fellow faculty often "watch" us as well. Just as we draw instructional or planning ideas from our conversations with our colleagues at times, they draw ideas from us. Indeed, one of the rich possibilities of the academy is such dialogue.

Instead of ignoring this powerful peer learning, we all need to recognize our role as faculty leaders in modeling how to use digital technology in our classrooms, be it video presentations, podcasts, or something as simple as fully moderated discussion boards. In fact, we find that many times what is new to one faculty member in a college/university is also new to their colleagues.

If we all continue or increase the faculty conversations about teaching practice, colleagues will learn from each other's experiences, even as you and your students do. Furthermore, if we talk with colleagues about technology and teaching experiences, we are also talking through the process, possible difficulties, and solutions. In teacher-to-teacher discourse, we come to understand situations better, clarify our thinking, and often gain new insight.

These conversations are, in essence, the beginning of an informal but powerful faculty learning community that can encourage us to continue seeking teaching innovations. The literature is replete with the power of learning communities (Palloff & Pratt, 1999, 2007; Wenger, 1999), but seldom do faculty have daily access to authentic communities of practice.

> **Imagine**: We have the opportunity to begin a simple pattern of sharing that can change that disappointing trend.

If you are in a setting where you do not have such a learning and sharing community, begin a learning and sharing *relationship* by starting conversations about innovative teaching. Another strategy is to ask questions of colleagues and share what you are doing with technology in your classrooms. Whenever we see faculty use these approaches to dialogue with colleagues, it is important that true reciprocity be evident. For example, the exchange and community will be more vibrant and long-lived if the faculty participants are open to questions *and* suggestions. The simple principle of "give and take" goes a long way in building trust, authenticity, and support.

The power of peer dialogue and collaboration is that colleagues may see something—a need, an opportunity, a problem—which we ourselves do not recognize because we are too "close" to or invested in the activity. By utilizing the power of collaboration with our faculty colleagues as well as our students, we develop a community of practice, cultivate new best practices, and help advance your university and classrooms into the next part of the 21st century.

Strategies for Successful Collaborations

Surprisingly, one of the pitfalls in such sharing can be over-enthusiasm. Consider the situation when we are so excited about the benefits of a new way of using technology in our class that we talk very quickly and use the specialized jargon related to the new technology. Of course, this delivery makes it difficult for uninitiated colleagues to understand. We should keep it simple when we introduce colleagues to our exciting and innovative applications for technology. Simplicity is golden for these situations: It allows our colleagues who are not as tech savvy to find easy entry points for understanding and questions, and it presents our more complex ideas in distilled and pristine forms.

How would we go about sharing a detailed lesson in our subject area with faculty in other departments? Where do we begin? As a simulated activity, let us take a look at one of our detailed lesson plans and consider the following points.

- Eliminate class-specific details: Our lesson plans are often cluttered with the idiosyncrasies of our individual classes. That is, there are specific solutions and details that work best with your subject matter and/or specific students. While your colleagues might be interested in such specific details, they cannot often make use them. The opposite is in fact often true: The details can cause confusion or muddy the waters.

- Provide a clear view: We suggest a "clear view." Remember the word *pristine*? Muddy waters have no place in a pristine description. Instead of copious details, share simple explanations and solutions that allow room for your colleagues to apply your discoveries to their own context and style. By illustrating and listing the critical elements only, your colleagues can gain a much clearer view of the essential structure, strategy, and impact of your approach.

- Encourage new discoveries: The next stage is the excitement of faculty discoveries for a true community of practice. When faculty share their innovations in a simple manner encouraging feedback or sharing, they may discover that their colleagues begin to extend the technology in new dimensions and applications. Consider the image of giving a gift with an open hand. In this case, you are sharing your teaching and learning ideas with an open hand of freedom (King & Gura, 2009). You are not implying that someone has to follow your steps exactly, but are clearly encouraging them to explore, modify, and expand the core concepts to the needs and purposes they recognize. The tremendous power of this approach is that one faculty member's core idea can blossom into six (a random number) more derivations as six colleagues begin using it in their classrooms, and the entire community gains six new strategies/detailed examples. The freedom to explore how all faculty can use new discoveries is an eloquent and concrete example of the richness of giving.

- Trust: To be successful in cultivating a sharing community of practice, we must also trust our colleagues to be able to read in the details when we show them the big picture of our teaching innovations. As we trust them to be able to learn the advanced steps once they are shown the simple ones, they will dig in deeper or come back with questions. Usually, the end result is that they will surprise us and many times surpass our expectations or discoveries because we did not impose unnecessary constraints.

More on Communities of Practice in Real Life

We have experienced such communities of practice with faculty colleagues within and beyond our institutions. They are spectacular reciprocal learning relationships, some of which have been captured in this volume. We hope that this volume will be both a catalyst and a support for other faculty to enjoy the academic growth we have enjoyed. Rather like a book circle, faculty might read sections of the book together or in a jigsaw fashion and use it as a starting point for sharing pedagogical conversations. Alternatively, the volume might be used as a resource in college/university information technology faculty development, or the sharing may develop more spontaneously and spread to those most ready to explore the possibilities of community.

CONCLUSION

The driving vision of this book is for all educators to no longer be trapped by tradition or technology, but instead to allow dynamic new practices to emerge; specifically, learner-centered and reflective teaching. This book encourages faculty to adapt their lessons, and that means reviewing lessons, studying how they have performed, and then revising them. Such formative change optimizes what is successful, while resolving problems encountered along the way. Even though we provide many models, examples, and methods, reflection is the essential ingredient. Without reflection, faculty gain nothing from each lesson: But with reflection, lessons improve, and both teaching and learning become fluid experiences.

If we explore the front cover image of the faculty member as "technology tamer," it is inherent in that image that faculty need to be in control. Technology is in mayhem, uncontrolled, constantly changing, and it cannot systematically drive instructional solutions, nor can it *make* decisions. Instead, faculty professional expertise within our content area, about our institutions, and regarding our students makes us the most effective agents in creating the best technology-based solutions for our classes. The critical element is reflection on these several factors, considering the opportunities, and keeping an eye on the ultimate outcome—greater understanding. What a great opportunity we have to collaborate in making this happen.

This book emphasizes learner-centeredness (Brookfield, 1995), methods that revolve around learner participation in ways that are now easier than ever before—approaches that take advantage of the Internet's possibilities for on-demand content and user collaboration. Moreover, we call for educators to accept the challenge and meet the needs of 21st-century students (Tapscott, 2008), not only using evolving technologies to make learning more interactive and efficient, but also preparing students for work within the 21st-century workplace, a workplace that demands collaboration and technological savvy.

We hope that the broad reach of this volume for a variety of faculty and readers will stimulate further transformations in an already innovative world. We stand at a prime time for faculty to take back control of their classrooms and move ahead in their understanding, utilizing the new opportunities of the 21st century in their classrooms. This book is dedicated to providing the support and resources you need to take the next steps in your journey of development, taming the technology for your purposes.

REFERENCES

Brookfield, S. (1995). *Becoming a critically reflective teacher.* San Francisco: Jossey-Bass.

Cranton, P. (2001). *Becoming an authentic teacher in higher education.* Malabar, FL: Kreiger Publishing.

King, K. P. (2003). *Keeping pace with technology: Educational technology that transforms. Vol. II.* Cresskill, NJ: Hampton Press.

King, K. P. & Gura, M. (2009). *Podcasting for teachers: Using a new technology to revolutionize teaching and learning* (2nd ed.). Charlotte, NC: Information Age Publishing.

Lawler, P., & King, K. P. (2000). *Effective faculty development: Using adult learning principles.* Malabar, FL: Krieger.

Palloff, R. M., & Pratt, K. (2007). *Building online learning communities: Effective strategies for the virtual classroom.* San Francisco: Jossey-Bass.

Palloff, R. M., & Pratt, K. (1999). *Building learning communities in cyberspace.* San Francisco: Jossey-Bass.

Tapscott, D. (2008). *Grown up digital.* Chicago, IL: McGraw-Hill.

Wenger, E. (1999). *Communities of practice.* Cambridge: Cambridge University Press.

THE AUTHORS
AND CONTRIBUTORS

EDITORS

Kathleen P. King, Co-editor and Author

Kathleen P. King, Ed.D., is a professor of higher education at the University of South Florida (Tampa) in the Department of Adult, Career, and Higher Education. While serving as a senior professor in the doctoral programs in higher education, she continues her leadership as president of the professional development and educational technology consulting firm, Transformation Education, LLC. From 1997–2010, Dr. King was a professor of education at Fordham University's Graduate School of Education in NYC and director of the university's RETC, Center for Professional Development. In 1990–1997, King was an instructor of engineering, computer technology, and medical science at Pennsylvania Institute of Technology (PIT), Media, PA.

King's major areas of research include faculty development, distance learning, transformative learning, new media, diversity issues, and career and technical education. She is an award-winning author (18 books), popular keynote and conference speaker, editor, mentor, and consultant. She has been recognized for her research, service, and contribution to the fields of research and publication and technology innovations in learning. Her books include *Podcasting for Teaching* (2nd ed.) (2009) (with Gura), *Handbook of Evolving Research in Transformative Learning* (10th anniv. ed.) (2009), and *Empowering Women Through Literacy* (2009) (with Miller). Examples of the awards she has received for her books and research include those from AERA, ACHE, POD Network, and NYACCE. Through distance technologies, Dr. King and her collaborators have reached over 6.5 million learners. Dr. King earned her Ed.D. from Widener University, Chester, PA. She also

The Professor's Guide to Taming Technology, pages 271–277
Copyright © 2011 by Information Age Publishing

has an M.Ed. in Adult Education from Widener; an M.A. from Columbia International, Columbia, SC; and a B.A. from Brown University, Providence, RI. Visit her Web sites for more information: www.TransformationEd.com and www.kpking.com

Thomas D. Cox, Co-editor and Author

Thomas D. Cox, Ed.D., is program coordinator and an assistant professor of adult and higher education at the University of Houston–Victoria's School of Education and Human Development in Victoria, TX.

Dr. Cox's major areas of research include adult learning, distance learning, liberal studies, adult development, and issues of diversity. He has been nominated for several national awards and was named Distance Education Advisor in 2008 at the University of Memphis–University College. He has published numerous articles of research and practice in peer-reviewed journals nationwide. His leadership in the field is evident in his service as secretary-treasurer of the Commission of Professors of Adult Education (CPAE) (2009–2011). Dr. Cox earned his Ed.D. in Higher and Adult Education from the University of Memphis; an M.A. in Liberal Studies from the University of Memphis; and a B.S. from Blue Mountain College, Blue Mountain, MS.

CONTRIBUTORS

Alice Anderson

Ms. Anderson is the technology accessibility program coordinator at the University of Wisconsin–Madison, Division of Information Technology. She plays a significant role in strategic planning, policy, and resource development in the area of technology accessibility for the campus. Alice coordinates or serves on several advisory committees that address accessibility and usability, including the UW–Madison Accessibility and Usability Committee, the UW System Accessibility Committee, and the CIC (Committee on Institutional Cooperation, consortium of the Big Ten universities plus the University of Chicago) Accessibility and Usability Committee.

Mary Bold, Ph.D., CFLE

Dr. Mary Bold is Chair of the Department of Digital Learning & Teaching at the American College of Education. She is a Certified Family Life Educator (CFLE) as well as a consultant in the field of higher education assessment and distance learning. Publications and presentations include

JALN, Sloan-C Emerging Technology, EDUCAUSE, SACS Annual Meeting, IUPUI Assessment Institute, and Texas A&M Assessment Conference. Bold is the co-author of an undergraduate textbook on internships. She blogs on assessment topics at http://higheredassessment.blogspot.com and can be reached at bold@marybold.com.

Sheryl Burgstahler, Ph.D.

Dr. Burgstahler founded and directs the Assistive Technology division of UW Technology Services and the DO-IT (Disabilities, Opportunities, Internetworking, and Technology) Center at the University of Washington in Seattle. DO-IT promotes the success of individuals with disabilities in college and careers, particularly in high-tech fields, and uses technology as an empowering tool. DO-IT includes the Center on Universal Design in Education. Most of Dr. Burgstahler's work is funded by the National Science Foundation, the U.S. Department of Education, and State of Washington. She has published books, curricula, and hundreds of journal articles and is a regular speaker at national conferences related to technology, disability, and education.

Teresa (Terry) J. Carter, Ed.D.

Dr. Carter is an Assistant Professor in the School of Education at Virginia Commonwealth University in Richmond, VA. She holds an M.A. in Human Resource Development and an Ed. D. in Executive Leadership in Human Resource Development from The George Washington University. Since entering academia in 2005 from the corporate sector, she has been the coordinator of the graduate program in Adult Learning and director of the M.Ed. program for medical educators at VCU. Dr. Carter's research interests include transformative learning among professionals in the workplace, the scholarship of teaching and learning with technology, and organization development.

Brian W. Donavant, Ph.D.

Dr. Donavant is an Assistant Professor of Criminal Justice at The University of Tennessee at Martin. Previously serving in a variety of capacities during his 21-year law enforcement career, he most recently was a lieutenant and the Training Director for the Gulfport, Mississippi, Police Department, and programs under his direction have been recognized nationally as models for providing multi-agency, collaborative training. Brian received his Ph.D. in Adult Education from The University of Southern Mississippi, his B.A. from Memphis State University, and his M.Ed. from William Carey

College. A frequent presenter at regional and national conferences, he has published numerous articles and professional papers and is engaged in research in the areas of curriculum development, experiential learning, and the use of educational technology.

Kevin F. Downing, Ph.D.

Dr. Downing is a Professor at DePaul University's college for adult learners, the School for New Learning. His research interests include the investigation of Miocene fossil mammals, the record of stratigraphic and paleogeographic change during the Himalayan Orogeny, and online science learning practices. He teaches geosciences and biology courses both on-site and online and is the co-author of the recent *Online Science Learning: Best Practices and Technologies.*

Rebecca English

Rebecca English is a Lecturer in Teacher Education in the Faculty of Education at the Queensland University of Technology. Her research focuses on online education, online communities, secondary schools, internationalization of education, sociology of education and Critical Discourse Analysis. During her 10-year career as an educator in Australia, she has worked in a number of disciplines and across various levels of education. She maintains a regular blog at rebeccaenglish.tumblr.com. Email: r.english@qut.edu.au

Tara Gallien, Ph.D., CHES

Dr. Tara Gallien is a Certified Health Education Specialist (CHES) and an Assistant Professor of Health Education in the Department of Health and Human Performance at Northwestern State University in Natchitoches, LA. She is currently serving as the Chair of the E-learning Advisory Council, a committee responsible for ensuring quality E-learning practices at her institution. She has published and presented internationally and nationally on effective online learning strategies, most of which have been related to improving instructor feedback. Dr. Gallien is committed to the advancement of E-learning practices that engage students and enhance learning. She can be reached at Tarag@nsula.edu.

Jennifer K. Holtz, Ph.D.

Dr. Holtz is an Assistant Professor at DePaul University, where she has authored multiple distance course guides in the sciences and teaches almost exclusively online, including the mentoring of distance students. Dr. Holtz has published widely in clinical sciences, clinical education, and in distance learning and assessment in the sciences. Her Ph.D. is in Adult and Continuing Education with emphasis in research education, from Kansas State University; her Masters is in Gerontology with clinical emphasis, from Wichita State University; and her Bachelors is in Biology with emphasis in human biology, from Kansas Newman College (now Newman University).

Jennifer Howell, Ph.D.

Dr. Jennifer Howell is a Senior Lecturer in teaching Education Studies at Australian Catholic University. Her research focuses on online communities, continuing teacher professional development, E-learning, mLearning, Web 2.0 technologies, building teacher capacity, STEM (Science, Technology, Engineering, and Mathematics) Education, and electronic research methodology. During her 15-year career as an educator, she has worked in Australia, the United Kingdom, Hong Kong, the Philippines, and India. She has developed several online initiatives, including The eMerge Community, for pre-service teachers, and The Teachers Capacity Network (TCN), an online professional development initiative. Email: Jennifer.Howell@acu.edu.au

Pooneh Lari, Ed.D.

Dr. Pooneh Lari is an Assistant Professor of Adult Education at North Carolina State University. She is the Coordinator of Distance Education Development in College of Education. Her research interests include online learning and teaching, adults in higher education, online presence, online learning communities/communities of practice, transformative learning, and leadership in online environment.

Mike Litzkow

Mr. Litzkow is a professional software developer participating in a wide variety of research projects at the University of Wisconsin–Madison. He has worked on projects ranging from Grid computing systems and parallel architecture simulators to delivery of course lectures and instructional content over the World Wide Web. His current interests include making multimedia interactive Web applications accessible to screen reader users and developing innovative games for higher education.

Ellen Manning, Ph.D.

Dr. Ellen Manning is a full-time professor at Kaplan University and has been either teaching or in educational administration for over 30 years. She earned a master's degree in English from Brooklyn College and a doctorate in English from the University of Miami and the University of South Africa. She has taught at the University of Miami; in various community colleges; and Nova Southeastern University, Graduate Teacher Education Program (GTEP). She has had extensive administration experience, serving as the Director of Cultural Affairs for Broward Community College and subsequently the City of Hollywood. She has developed several training modules and workshops on learning styles, wellness, and managing stress in the online community and on using Skype and other synchronous tools in the online classroom.

Jody Oomen-Early, Ph.D., CHES

Dr. Jody Oomen-Early is currently the Director of Undergraduate Programs in the School of Health Sciences at Walden University. Jody has worked in higher education for over 16 years, and has a passion for connecting the global community to the online classroom. She has spent the last decade developing and directing quality online programs in the health sciences, and much of her research explores the use of technology in the field of health education. In March 2010, Jody was awarded the 2010 HEDIR Technology Award from the American Association of Health Education (AAHE) for her pioneering contributions relating to E-learning within the field. Her primary research is focused on E-learning, global and community health, and women's health, and she is a co-author of a community health textbook for undergraduates. She can be reached at Jody.Early@Waldenu.edu.

Keith Sisson, Ph.D.

Dr. Sisson holds a Ph.D. in medieval history from the University of Memphis. He also studied at the Center for Medieval Studies at Fordham University in New York. He is currently an instructor of Interdisciplinary Studies, University College, at the University of Memphis. Dr. Sisson serves as a faculty mentor for the Tennessee Board of Regents Online Degree program, where he is involved promoting teaching excellence in online programs. He can be reached at ksisson@memphis.edu.

April V. Williams, RDH, BHSA, MDH

Ms. Williams is a full-time assistant professor at The University of Tennessee Health Science Center College of Allied Health, Department of Dental Hygiene. She received her Associates of Applied Science degree in Dental Hygiene from Macon State College in Macon, GA; her Baccalaureate online degree in Health Services Administration from Baker College in Flint, MI; and her Master's online degree in Dental Hygiene from The University of Tennessee Health Science Center in Memphis, TN. She is currently pursuing her Ph.D. from The University of Memphis in Educational Research with an emphasis in Public Health.

COPYEDITOR AND PROOFREADER

Seamus King

Mr. King is a technical assistant and freelance editor who has an ongoing relationship with Transformation Education, LLC. He has studied Political Science at Middle Georgia College and History at the University of Georgia, and is currently working on perfecting his editing skills. While working across sectors—business, academic, fiction, nonfiction—the bulk of his recent editing work has been academic copyediting, proofreading, and research support. Mr. King resides in Athens, GA. He may be reached at Bardagh@gmail.com.

ILLUSTRATION | GRAPHIC DESIGN

DaKoda Davis

Dakoda Davis is from Bauxite, AR. From a young age, he found the greatest satisfaction by drawing the drab real world around him, and the happier imagined one. This evolved into a strong interest in painting and diversified into design, computer arts, and graphic design. Mentors and professors at OTIS College of Art and Design in Los Angeles, CA provided guidance and encouragement. Dakoda earned his B.F.A. in illustration from the Memphis College of Arts in May of 2009. He has continued work in design and illustration, also doing freelance work for galleries and various clients. He anticipates working on books for children, educational publishing, adult cartoons, political satire, and concept designs for businesses. Web site: www.dakodadavis.com.

CPSIA information can be obtained at www.ICGtesting.com
Printed in the USA
242335LV00001B/5/P